Farm
AND
Food Policies
AND
Their Consequences

Kenneth L. Robinson

Cornell University

PRENTICE HALL, Englewood Cliffs, New Jersey 07632

Library of Congress Cataloging-in-Publication Data

ROBINSON, KENNETH LEON
  Farm and food policies and their consequences / Kenneth L.
Robinson.

  Bibliography.
  Includes index.
  ISBN 0-13-304999-X
    1. Agriculture and state—United States. 2. Agricultural
subsidies—United States. 3. Produce trade—Government policy—
United States. 4. Food supply—Government policy—United States.
5. Agriculture and state. 6. Agricultural subsidies. 7. Produce
trade—Government policy. 8. Food supply—Government policy.
  I. Title.
HD1761.R57 1989   88-22674
338.1'873—dc19   CIP

Editorial/production supervision and
  interior design: Ed Jones
Cover design: Joel Mitnick Design, Inc.
Cover drawing courtesy of *Choices,*
  the magazine of food, farm, and resource issues.
  Artist: Bruce Welnack, of Dunnington,
  Klasse & Feather Marketing, Inc.
Manufacturing Buyer: Robert Anderson
Page layout: John Fleming

 ©1989 by Prentice-Hall, Inc.
A Division of Simon & Schuster
Englewood Cliffs, New Jersey 07632

Printed in the United States of America
10 9 8 7 6 5 4 3 2 1

ISBN   0-13-304999-X

Prentice Hall International (UK) Limited, London
Prentice Hall of Australiz Pty. Limited, Sydney
Prentice Hall Canada Inc., Toronto
Prentice Hall Hispanoamericana, S.A., Mexico
Prentice Hall of India Private Limited, New Delhi
Prentice Hall of Japan, Inc., Tokyo
Simon & Schuster Asia Pte. Ltd., Singapore
Editora Prentice Hall do Brazil, Ltda., Rio de Janeiro

Contents

Preface

This textbook is designed for an undergraduate course in farm and food policies. While it would be helpful for readers to have had a course in economics, I have tried to present the material in such a way that students from many disciplines other than economics can understand the concepts. With a modest amount of supplementary instruction in the tools of economics, students who major in such diverse fields as animal science, nutrition, agronomy, sociology, and agricultural education should have no difficulty in coping with the text.

My objective in writing the book has been to provide students with a guide to thinking about policy issues. The emphasis is on policy analysis rather than prescription. The policy issues addressed are those that have dominated farm and food policy debates in Congress over the past fifty years. For each major issue or public problem, the principal alternative courses of action are first outlined. This is followed by an assessment of the consequences of pursuing each alternative.

Any textbook will rapidly become dated if the details of current programs are incorporated in the text. Consequently, I have elected to omit detailed descriptions of existing programs. In my own teaching, I find it essential to provide this kind of information, but I do so by supplementing the textbook with excerpts from newspaper articles, farm publications, U.S. Department of Agriculture reports, and extension leaflets.

I am indebted to many individuals, including former professors and students, for their ideas and indoctrination on how to approach policy issues. I owe much to F.F. Hill, who taught the course I inherited in 1952. His enthusiasm for the subject and many of his ideas have remained a part of me for thirty-five years. J. Carroll Bottum and J.B. Kohlmeyer, both associated with Purdue University, at an early stage in my professional career impressed on me the virtue of outlining the alternatives and assessing the consequences in educating the public about policy issues.

I also am greatly indebted to a number of individuals who reviewed all or part of the manuscript. My greatest debt is to my wife, Jean Robinson, for her patience in making detailed comments on all chapters. Among my colleagues, I especially want to thank Nelson Bills, Keith Bryant, Frederick Buttel, Olan Forker, Christine Ranney, and Bernard Stanton for their useful comments on specific chapters.

Mary Margaret Fischer provided excellent guidance in editing the manuscript and taught me something about writing. The assistance of Judy Watkins proved to be invaluable in typing the manuscript and cheerfully incorporating the many changes that subsequent revisions required. I'm grateful for the assistance of two other individuals for their care in preparing the final manuscript. Patricia Baker came to my rescue in making last-minute corrections and in expertly instructing the computer in what needed to be done. Joseph K. Baldwin once again demonstrated his skill in drawing clear and accurate figures and graphs.

I would also like to express my appreciation to the Rockefeller Foundation for providing me with the opportunity to begin writing under ideal conditions at the Bellagio Conference center in Italy.

Kenneth L. Robinson
Cornell University

1

Government Intervention in Food and Agriculture

Since the 1930s, government intervention in food and agriculture has become the rule rather than the exception. Few nations are now willing to rely solely on market forces to dictate returns to farmers or to determine how much food will be produced and sold or stored for future use. Most industrialized countries seek to enhance the income of farmers by supporting farm prices and controlling imports.

The combined treasury and consumer costs of supporting agriculture have risen enormously since 1979. According to a report prepared for the Organization for Economic Cooperation and Development, agricultural support programs cost the leading industrial nations over $100 billion per year in the early 1980s (OECD, Annex III, p. 8). While such programs are widely criticized, attempts to curtail government expenditures and reduce support prices have met with little success in recent years.

Government intervention in food and agriculture, of course, is not confined to price-support programs. In addition to attempting to enhance farm prices and incomes, the U.S. and other governments seek to influence the cost and availability of farm inputs, especially credit, and the rate at which land and water resources are being depleted. Government intervention may also take the form of subsidizing domestic food consumption, exports, and rural development programs. Trade restrictions are another common form of government intervention.

THE SCOPE OF GOVERNMENT INTERVENTION IN FOOD AND AGRICULTURE

The scope of government intervention varies greatly among countries and even among commodities within countries. Almost every nation contributes to agricultural research and provides indirect assistance to farmers in the form of special credit facilities and support for farm supply and marketing cooperatives. The principal differences among nations are found in the degree to which they intervene in pricing farm and food products and in subsidizing food consumption and exports. Japan stands at one extreme among noncommunist industrial nations. Nearly all farm and food prices in Japan are strongly influenced by government decisions. Farmers are almost completely insulated from world market forces. New Zealand lies close to the other extreme. Farm prices in that country are influenced relatively little by government intervention; they are dictated mainly by world supply-and-demand conditions. The United States falls somewhere between these two extremes. Government action strongly influences the prices of some commodities but not others. Those that are supported account for roughly half the gross income of U.S. farmers. Market forces largely dictate the prices for the remaining half.

REASONS FOR GOVERNMENT INTERVENTION

The universal (or nearly so) acceptance of government intervention in pricing farm products requires some explanation. Among the reasons most frequently cited for intervention are to insure adequate food supplies, protect and preserve small-scale farms, reduce price instability, and minimize dependence on imports. More generally, one can view government intervention as a response to either a "food problem" or a "farm problem." A food problem arises whenever the rate of growth of output fails to match the rate of growth of demand, thus exerting upward pressure on food prices. A farm problem arises whenever the opposite conditions prevail; that is, whenever the rate of growth of output exceeds the rate of growth of demand, thus depressing farm prices. In practice, it has proved to be extremely difficult to match the rate of growth of agricultural output with demand. Consequently, most countries have had to contend with either a food problem or a farm problem.   In response to an existing or anticipated food problem, countries generally have sought to encourage production by investing in research and funding projects designed to raise yields, bring additional land under cultivation, or augment water supplies. In addition, they frequently subsidize input use, especially fertilizer and credit, and may guarantee minimum prices to producers. In response to a farm problem, governments have sought to assist farmers by offering credit on more liberal terms, restricting imports, and purchasing or storing surplus commodities. This often leads to subsidizing internal consumption or exports or to restricting production. Not all governments have responded in the same way, but most have felt compelled to take action whenever food prices have risen dramatically or farm prices have collapsed.

Since 1920, except for a brief period following World War II and again in the mid-1970s, the United States has been confronted with the problem of excess capacity (a farm problem rather than a food problem). Thus, there has been far greater emphasis on policies designed to support prices and to curb production than on policies aimed at protecting consumers.   Proponents of government intervention in commodity markets argue that such intervention is necessary to give farmers a fair return for their labor and to maintain purchasing power in rural areas. Merchants and bankers on Main Sreet are as interested in preventing the collapse of prices as farmers themselves.   Agribusiness firms were among the early supporters of government aid for farmers in the 1920s (Benedict, p. 208). Since the 1930s, farm programs have been continued, partly because elected officials are apprehensive about what might happen to the local economy if agricultural support programs were withdrawn.

One of the consequences of rapid technological developments in agriculture has been a persistent tendency for average farm incomes to lag behind average nonfarm incomes.   Historically, average labor returns to those employed in agriculture have been relatively low. Thus, government intervention has been justified on the grounds that such intervention is necessary to achieve income equality for farmers. Similar arguments have been advanced for maintaining income enhancement policies in Europe (Ritson, p. 349).

Another argument for government involvement in commodity markets has been to stabilize prices. Widely fluctuating prices can lead to cycles in production and to inefficient use of resources (Schultz, 1949, pp. 170–71). In periods of high prices farmers overexpand. This leads to the collapse of prices and to idling resources. Consumers and processing firms would much prefer more stable supplies.   Public interest in programs designed to stabilize prices tends to increase whenever farm prices rise dramatically as they did during the mid-1970s, while producer interest in such programs is usually greatest when prices are falling.

The threat of food shortages has been an even more compelling argument for government intervention in food deficit nations. Self-sufficiency is a popular objective, especially in countries that have experienced deprivation. Even urban residents in countries like Japan and the United Kingdom support policies which, in effect, raise the cost of food. Their support is partly a legacy of having endured food shortages during and immediately after World War II.

Countries which must import food justify protecting domestic agriculture as a way of saving foreign exchange. By cutting back on imports, a food deficit country also may be able to buy what it needs at a lower price.[1] This argument for supporting agriculture obviously has great appeal to a country suffering from a severe balance of payments problem.

Still another argument frequently cited for supporting agriculture is to save small farms and preserve rural communities. Switzerland and Norway are among the countries where public support for government intervention to protect small-scale producers has been strongest. Somewhat less emphasis has been given to this argument in the United States than in Europe and Japan, where small farms are more common. But even in the U.S., lobbying groups and members of Congress frequently express concern about the effect of a declining farm population on rural communities. Saving the "family farm" is a popular idea. Proponents often cite the need to preserve farms as justification for maintaining support programs, particularly for such commodities as milk, peanuts, and tobacco.

Social concerns have played a prominent role in building support for domestic food-subsidy programs, another form of government intervention that has grown in the United States over the past two decades. Food subsidies make it possible to maintain or raise prices to farmers without adversely affecting consumers but, of course, at the expense of the treasury. Government intervention in the form of subsidies or food stamps is also justified on the grounds that assistance is needed to reduce or eliminate hunger and malnutrition.

Groups outside of agriculture, especially those concerned with protecting the environment, safety, and health, have succeeded in broadening the food and agriculture policy agenda in recent years. This

---

[1]For a more complete discussion of the potential price or "terms of trade" effect of expanding home production and reducing imports, see McCrone, pp. 88–100, and Ritson, pp. 334–36.

has led to more government intervention, particularly in areas related to pesticide use, food and feed additives, and farm labor.

GOVERNMENT INTERVENTION IN THE UNITED STATES

Programs and policies related to food and agriculture in the United States are complex and often inconsistent. Subsidies for research, irrigation, and credit, for example, tend to raise output while efforts are made to curtail production. The existing array of activities is not the result of an overall plan or a comprehensive policy, but of adding programs or activities in response to a particular crisis or sequence of events. This incremental process has left the Department of Agriculture with a long list of programs that it must implement.[2] The major activities related to food and agriculture which the U.S. Government now supports are as follows:

- agricultural research
- crop and livestock production estimates
- marketing services, including grading and inspection and information on markets and prices, both at home and abroad
- credit programs
- administrative and technical support for farm supply and marketing cooperatives
- cooperative federal-state extension programs
- soil conservation activities
- price-support loans, purchases, and deficiency payments to farmers
- acreage diversion, set-aside, and land retirement programs
- marketing orders
- producer assessments for product promotion and research
- domestic food subsidy programs
- international food aid

[2]Government intervention in food and agriculture is not confined to programs or activities administered by the U.S. Department of Agriculture. Irrigation projects in the West and grazing on public lands, for example, are administered through the U.S. Department of Interior. Federal support for teaching agriculture in high schools is channeled through the Department of Education. Regulations which apply to farm labor are enforced by the Department of Labor. There also are some activities administered through the Department of Agriculture that are not closely linked to food and agriculture; for example, activities of the Forest Service.

• export subsidies and special credit programs to encourage farm exports.

The range of activities has widened, and the total cost of farm- and food-subsidy programs has increased enormously over the past fifty years. Most of the increase in cost has been associated with efforts to support or enhance farm incomes and to subsidize food consumption. In the mid 1980s, farm price-support and domestic food-subsidy programs accounted for 80 to 90 percent of the $40 to $50 billion spent each year by the U.S. Department of Agriculture. Traditional activities such as agricultural research, extension, crop reporting, and marketing services account for a relatively small proportion of the total USDA budget. While everyone complains about the bureaucracy in Washington, salary costs are much less than the cost of making payments to farmers, purchasing and storing commodities, paying for food stamps, and subsidizing exports. The bureaucracy required to administer food and agricultural programs is indeed very large, but salary and overhead costs probably added no more than 10 percent to the 1986 budget of the U.S. Department of Agriculture.

FOOD AND AGRICULTURAL POLICIES ABROAD

The United States, of course, is not unique in supporting agriculture. Those countries that must import food, such as Japan, find it relatively easy to maintain high internal prices simply by restricting or taxing imports. Under these conditions, the cost of supporting agriculture is borne by consumers, not by the government. Once total supply exceeds domestic demand, the government cost of supporting agriculture inevitably rises. This has been demonstrated recently in the European Community where agricultural support costs have risen dramatically since the late 1970s because of excess production of such commodities as wheat, beef, and butter. The Community has been forced to pay large export subsidies to get rid of their surpluses.

While most industrialized countries attempt to support or stabilize farm prices and incomes, few of them subsidize domestic consumption or conservation activities to the same degree as the United States. Many countries, however, intervene much more directly in the land market and seek to limit who can purchase farms. Land use and land-tenure arrangements also are more likely to be regulated or controlled in European countries than in the United States.

Government intervention in food and agriculture is common in less-developed countries (LDCs) as well as industrialized nations, but the objective of government intervention in LDCs is often quite different. In many cases, governments seek to hold down farm and food prices to satisfy civil servants and minimize urban unrest. Underpricing of farm products (in relation to prices that might be expected to prevail in the absence of government intervention) occurs in many developing countries, in contrast to the overpricing that commonly prevails among industrialized countries (Schultz, 1978; Bale and Lutz). Governments can effectively hold down internal prices by compelling farmers to sell to monopoly marketing boards at fixed prices, by increasing imports (and selling imported commodities at lower prices if necessary), and by maintaining an overvalued exchange rate. The effect of an overvalued currency (common among LDCs) is to make imports relatively cheap and to depress the real value of exports.

Self-sufficiency in basic foods is a major goal of most developing countries, but governments are reluctant to raise farm prices because they fear the political consequences of higher food costs. Instead of offering farmers more favorable prices, governments in many developing countries subsidize fertilizer, credit, and farm mechanization or may undertake expensive land development schemes.

Popular support for cheap food policies has led a number of LDCs to introduce large-scale food-subsidy programs, not unlike those adopted in the United States. Such programs, for example, have been adopted in Egypt, Sri Lanka, and India. In some instances, basic food grains such as wheat and rice are sold at subsidized prices through selected outlets or are made available to low-income families in exchange for ration coupons. In other instances, free food is distributed through health centers or schools to segments of the population that are considered to be nutritionally vulnerable, such as pregnant and nursing mothers, infants, and children.

ASSESSING THE IMPACT OF GOVERNMENT PROGRAMS

In the following chapters, the impact of government intervention in food and agriculture is assessed. The objective is neither to condemn nor to endorse a particular program or activity, but to provide a guide to those responsible for making policy decisions. The focus is on policy analysis, not prescription.

Few, if any, policies are wholly good or wholly bad. Government intervention inevitably leads to gains for some and losses for others. The task of the policy analyst is to identify winners and losers, that is, to ascertain just who will benefit and by how much, and who or what groups will bear the cost. Information of this kind is useful to organizations and legislators confronted with the task of choosing between alternative courses of action. Objective analysis can help to minimize arguments over what is likely to happen if a particular course of action is followed, but it will not eliminate conflicts over farm and food policies. The consequences will be viewed as favorable for some groups but not for others. Ultimately, the choice among policy alternatives depends on which group one wants to favor and the weights one attaches to each of the benefits or costs.

One of the alternative courses of action is to retain the existing set of policies or programs. Politically, the status quo has an advantage; consequently proposed policies must be examined in relation to what is likely to happen if the current set of policies is retained. Policy analysts must recognize that no government starts with a clean slate. Each inherits policies which are a reflection of past crises and political compromises. One cannot deal realistically with farm and food policies without knowing something about their historical antecedents. For this reason, the next chapter is devoted to a brief review of when and why particular policies or programs were adopted in the United States.

To be useful to policymakers, a policy analyst needs to understand the problems that give rise to demands for public action. Chapter 3 is designed to provide this kind of information. The major public problems that have led to government intervention in agriculture are described and the causes identified. In subsequent chapters, the principal policy instruments or alternative courses of action that attempt to cope with the problems outlined in Chapter 3 are described, and the consequences are assessed.

The topics covered are those that have ranked high on the U.S. farm and food-policy agenda over the past fifty years. Congressional debates have focused on proposals to stabilize or raise farm prices and incomes, protect and preserve family farms, alleviate rural poverty, reduce soil erosion, and minimize hunger and malnutrition. While the agricultural committees of Congress still devote most of their time to farm price support programs and related issues, they have given more attention in recent years to policies that bear on export markets. Some of these issues are dealt with in the chapters on trade policies, international commodity agreements, and international food aid.[3]

---

[3]It is not possible in one course to cover all the important policy issues that influence farm exports. Anyone concerned with American agriculture must consider macroeconomic policies as well as those that directly affect farm production and prices. Exports are likely to be influenced as much by policies which affect exchange rates and the ability of other countries to purchase U.S. farm products as they are by changes in support prices or export subsidies. Limited space precludes dealing with the complex consequences of alternative macroeconomic policies.

The final chapter is devoted to the politics of food and agriculture. A knowledge of how the U.S. political system operates is essential to avoid frustration and to forecast what changes in existing policies are likely to be adopted. Critical steps in the legislative process are identified as a guide to those seeking to influence policy decisions.

DISCUSSION QUESTIONS

1.1. Why do industrial countries commonly support or raise farm product prices, while many low-income countries seek to hold down farm prices despite food shortages?

1.2. What are the most common forms of government intervention in agriculture, and which activities are likely to be most costly to the taxpayer?

1.3. Why is it unrealistic to expect Congress to agree on a set of farm and food policies even if they can reach agreement on the consequences of alternative policies?

REFERENCES

BALE, MALCOLM D., and ERNST LUTZ, "Price Distortions in Agriculture and Their Effects: An International Comparison," American Journal of Agricultural Economics 63 (1981), 8-22.

BENEDICT, MURRAY R., *Farm Policies of the United States, 1790-1950.* New York: The Twentieth Century Fund, 1953.

MCCRONE, GAVIN, *The Economics of Subsidising Agriculture: A Study of British Policy.* London: George Allen and Unwin, 1962.

OECD, *National Policies and Agricultural Trade.* Paris: Organization for Economic Cooperation and Development, 1987.

RITSON, CHRISTOPHER, *Agricultural Economics: Principles and Policy.* Boulder: Westview, 1982.

SCHULTZ, THEODORE W., *Production and Welfare of Agriculture.* New York: MacMillan, 1949.

SCHULTZ, THEODORE W., "On Economics and Politics of Agriculture," *Distortions of Agricultural Incentives,* edited by Theodore W. Schultz. Bloomington: Indiana University Press, 1978.

2

The Evolution of Farm and Food Policies in the United States

The history of farm and food policies in the United States illustrates two important principles: First, significant policy changes occur infrequently and mainly in response to a real or perceived "crisis" or a major realignment of political forces; and second, new policies or programs, once adopted, tend to persist. Many of the activities undertaken during the 1930s still survive, although in a somewhat modified form. Farm programs have not disappeared, despite a marked decline in the farm population and the attempts of conservative presidents and their secretaries of agriculture to eliminate or curtail such programs.

Innovations in agricultural policy have not been smooth or continuous. Major breakthroughs in policy in most cases have been the result of a unique event, such as the depression of the 1930s. Increased government intervention in food and agriculture over the past fifty years is also the result of greater public acceptance of programs to assist those thought to be disadvantaged and, equally important, the capacity to pay for relatively expensive programs. Growing tax revenue has made it possible to live with programs that would have been rejected as far too expensive a generation or two ago. Once programs have been introduced and accepted, inertia tends to rule. It is much easier to retain what has been accepted than to kill the existing program or try to reach agreement on a new program.

The conditions which have led to major innovations in policies are emphasized. The objective is not to justify the existing combination of programs and activities, but to explain why they were initially adopted.

FACTORS ASSOCIATED WITH CHANGES IN POLICIES

Among the lessons one learns from a review of U.S. history is that policies or programs are unlikely to change in the absence of a crisis. Pressure for government intervention or a change in existing programs or policies usually is associated with growing distress or disenchantment. In the United States, innovations or changes in farm and food policies have usually been associated with one of the following events:

- declining farm prices, depressed incomes, and rising foreclosures or debt repayment problems for farmers
- food shortages or the threat of shortages
- slumping export markets and the accumulation of surplus stocks
- excessive government costs
- natural disasters such as a severe drought
- publicity given to hunger and malnutrition.

Falling farm prices, whether in the period following the Civil War, the 1920s and early 1930s, or the 1980s, have generally led to pressure on Congress to do something to assist farmers. Congress has not always responded with new programs, but the economic environment has set the stage for the acceptance of such programs. There have been fewer occasions in the United States when the public was concerned about lagging production and the threat of shortages; however, on the few occasions when this did occur, Congress responded with new programs. Slumping export markets and rising carryover stocks were in part responsible for the introduction of land-retirement schemes, more generous food aid, and export promotion programs in the 1950s and again in the 1980s. The "dust bowl" of the 1930s created an environment favorable to the adoption of conservation programs. Media coverage of "hunger in America" added to demands for liberalizing domestic food subsidy programs in the 1960s.

Even a crisis atmosphere, however, may not lead to changes in policies. The political environment must also be conducive to change. Conflicts between the Senate and House of Representatives or between Congress and the President may make it difficult to get any new legislation adopted, even when there is general agreement that existing policies are unsatisfactory. It is much easier to attack existing policies than to reach agreement on specific changes. Budgetary constraints or the inability of agriculture to form coalitions with other disenchanted groups may also thwart the efforts of activists to modify existing policies. Politically, the status quo enjoys an enormous advantage because of the checks and balances built into the U.S. political system.

LEGACIES OF THE 19TH CENTURY

There was little direct government involvement in food and agriculture during the 19th century. Prior to 1862, about the only services provided by the government to farmers were free seeds. Land policies, however, were of critical importance. The decisions ultimately made with respect to the pricing and distribution of public land insured that most of the land would be farmed by families rather than large landholders and tenants. Policies adopted in the last half of the 19th century not only established the pattern of land ownership, but also provided the framework for the support of agricultural research and higher education.

Congress voted to distribute public land in such a way as to favor family farms rather than large estates, except in a few areas of the Southwest where Spanish landholding traditions prevailed. In many cases, families who moved westward and settled illegally on government land were granted ownership rights retroactively under so-called preemption acts. Settlers or "squatters" were permitted to purchase a minimum acreage at modest prices. During the first half of the 19th century, the terms and conditions of public land sales were gradually modified to enable an individual with limited capital to purchase a farm. Under the Homestead Act of 1862, settlers were given the opportunity to obtain free land, provided they lived on the land and farmed it for five years. Originally, homestead units consisted of 160 acres. Later, the maximum acreage was raised in an attempt to create more viable economic units in areas where rainfall was lower and more uncertain. While railroads and land speculators were able to acquire substantial areas of land (sometimes through fraudulent practices), there is no doubt that 19th century land disposal policies succeeded in dividing up most of the public domain into family-sized farms (Gates, p. 12).

Under the Land Grant College Act of 1862, rights to government land were given to designated colleges in each state. The land acquired by the colleges was sold to settlers or, in some cases, to mining, lumber, or grazing companies. This produced revenue for the construction, operation, and maintenance of the chosen colleges. In return, these institutions were required to offer instruction in "agriculture and the mechanic arts."[1] Later (in 1887) the federal government began granting funds for carrying out agricultural research at state experiment stations. Until well after the turn of the century, about the only activities related to agriculture which the federal government subsidized were agricultural research and the collection of information on crops and livestock.

Attempts to regulate middlemen and to create economic conditions more favorable to debtors, including farmers, are also a legacy of the 19th century. Generally declining prices during the thirty-year period following the end of the Civil War led to widespread distress, especially among farmers living on the frontier. Newly formed farm organizations and political parties such as the Populists and the Greenback Party pressed for measures designed to ease the plight of farmers. Among these were proposals to print more money or to monetize silver in order to reverse the deflationary environment. Many farmers were in debt, and with falling prices found it difficult to meet repayment obligations. In addition, drought and grasshopper damage caused a series of disastrous harvests for farmers in Kansas and other newly settled areas of the Great Plains. Farm prices also were depressed by high transportation and marketing costs.

Railroads and middlemen became favorite targets of criticism. Protest movements flourished under these conditions. Organizations representing farmers sought legislation to regulate railroads and grain elevators (storage facilities), curb monopolies, and provide additional credit for farmers. The Populist party proposed that the government make low-interest loans on stored commodities, a forerunner of the price-support loan program adopted in the 1930s (Shannon, p. 146).

Modest success was achieved in regulating railroads and monopolies under the Interstate Commerce Act (1887) and the Sherman Anti-Trust Act (1890). The government, however, did little else to assist farmers, partly because the political environment was not favorable to intervention. Most of the presidents elected during that period, even the Democrats such as Grover Cleveland, objected to much of the proposed legislation. Agricultural interests were divided in Congress between the Southern Democrats and the Midwestern Republicans, a legacy of the Civil War. This division enabled the conservative Republicans from the Northeast to hold the balance of power. They represented mainly busi-

---

[1]In 1890, Senator Morrill introduced a bill providing for additional support for land grant colleges. The bill stated that no distinction of race or color was to be made in the admission of students; however this requirement was deemed to be fulfilled if separate colleges were maintained for white and black students (Cochrane, p. 444). This led to the creation of so-called 1890 Land Grant Colleges in the South. For many years, these colleges provided the only opportunity for black students in southern states to pursue studies in agriculture.

ness interests and, consequently, were unwilling to accept the kinds of government intervention proposed by the "radical" farm organizations and populists. This was in sharp contrast to the 1930s, when farmers from the Midwest and South were able to form an alliance with representatives of urban areas in passing relief legislation.

THE RESPONSE TO RISING PRICES AND THE THREAT OF FOOD SHORTAGES (1900-1920)

The policy environment changed radically between the last quarter of the 19th century and the first two decades of the 20th century. Farm prices reversed direction and began rising, slowly at first, and then rapidly during World War I. The disappearance of free land, in addition to lagging productivity, led to a much slower rate of growth in farm production. This occurred at a time when urban demand for food was growing rapidly, partly due to large-scale immigration. Export demand was growing as well. Fears of food shortages became widespread. Thus, the focus of attention shifted to policies designed to maintain or increase production and to help farmers cope with the rapidly rising cost of farmland.

The policies or programs adopted during this period were precisely those now recommended for developing countries seeking to become self-sufficient in food production. In an attempt to increase output, Congress took action to provide additional credit for farmers, technical information on how to raise yields, subsidies for agricultural education, and support for irrigation projects in the West. A major objective of the Smith-Lever Act of 1914 was to extend to farmers and homemakers the results of research conducted by the U.S. Department of Agriculture and Land Grant Colleges. County agricultural agents were expected to help farmers "make two blades of grass grow where one grew before." Federal support for agricultural education was extended to high schools under the Smith-Hughes Act (1917). The Reclamation Act of 1902 established the policies which have governed federal reclamation projects in the eleven western states for the past eighty-five years.

Congress responded to the demand for improved credit facilities for farmers by sending a commission to Europe to review the experience of Danish and German cooperative credit societies. The report of the commission ultimately led (in 1916) to a government-sponsored cooperative farm credit system. Under this system, funds are borrowed from the central money market for re-lending to local cooperative associations who, in turn, lend to farmers.

LEGACIES OF THE 1920s AND 1930s

The 1920s brought a new set of demands for government intervention. Farm prices collapsed in 1921, following the bonanza years which accompanied the first World War. As typically happens in periods of deflation, farm prices fell earlier and further than the prices of nonfarm goods, thus creating unfavorable terms of trade for farmers. As in the 1870s and 1880s, unrest among farmers became widespread, especially in areas producing wheat, corn, cotton, and tobacco, the principal export crops. In contrast to the earlier period, members of Congress from rural areas united to form what became known as the "Farm Bloc." They shared a common interest in seeking relief for farmers. Initially, this took the form of providing additional credit for farmers and strengthening the legal status of farm cooperatives. By forming cooperatives, Congress hoped farmers would be able to cut the cost of inputs and reduce the spread between farm and retail prices. The Capper-Volstead Act (1922) exempted farm cooperatives from some provisions of the antitrust laws. The purpose of this exemption was to enable farmers to enter into agreements to control sales and thereby attempt to raise prices.

Many in Congress were convinced that more direct action was needed to boost farm prices. A number of bills were introduced in the 1920s with this objective in mind, but none became law. The principal proposal was a plan introduced in Congress by Senator McNary of Oregon and Representative Haugen of Iowa. The McNary-Haugen plan would have maintained what amounted to a two-price system for export crops such as wheat, corn, and cotton—a high price protected by tariffs for that part sold for domestic use, and whatever price prevailed on world markets for the remainder, which was to be exported. Congress considered several versions of the plan and eventually two of these were approved by both the House and the Senate. Each time, however, the bill was vetoed by President Coolidge (Benedict 1953, pp. 227-29). The Senate was unable to obtain the necessary two-thirds vote to override the veto. Thus, in the 1920s, just as in the 1870s and 1880s, farmers were thwarted in their efforts to obtain higher prices through government intervention.

President Hoover proved to be somewhat more willing than his predecessor to assist farmers. He approved legislation creating the Federal Farm Board, a new institution authorized to purchase and store farm products or lend money to cooperatives to perform this function. The Farm Board began making loans in 1929, just as prices started downward. Within two years, it had exhausted the initial capital ($500 million) provided by Congress. Prices continued to decline despite their efforts. In an attempt to support prices, the Board had accumulated millions of dollars worth of farm products which it could not sell.

By 1932, nearly everyone was ready for a change. President Roosevelt was swept into office at a time when the public (and even Congress) was in a mood to try almost anything to bring the country out of the Depression. Normal barriers to government intervention broke down as Congress rushed through proposal after proposal to provide relief for various groups, including farmers, and to stimulate employment.

Leaders of the major farm organizations worked closely with officials of the Department of Agriculture in drafting an omnibus farm bill that would enable the government to engage in a wide array of price-raising activities. The Agricultural Adjustment Act of 1933 incorporated most of their suggestions. It authorized the government to make price-support loans to farmers and to control production. In an attempt to raise prices immediately, cotton (already planted when the Act was passed) was plowed under, and young pigs were slaughtered. As one might expect, these attempts to limit production were widely criticized, especially since they were introduced at a time when many people were hungry. In 1936 the Supreme Court declared some of the provisions of the 1933 act unconstitutional. The court's objections were circumvented later by eliminating the processing taxes used to finance the program and by linking production control to soil conservation objectives. The 1938 replacement for the original Agricultural Adjustment Act (although much amended since then) still provides the legal authority for price-support and acreage-control programs for wheat, corn, cotton, rice, and tobacco.

The Agricultural Adjustment Acts of 1933 and 1938 dealt mainly with storable commodities. Two additional programs were adopted in an attempt to aid producers of perishable farm products. First, Congress passed enabling legislation which made it possible, but not mandatory, for producers of certain commodities (chiefly milk, fruits, and vegetables) to adopt marketing agreements (voluntary) or marketing orders (compulsory if approved by a two-thirds vote of producers). Second, Congress created a special fund derived from customs receipts (now known as Section 32 funds) which could be used at the discretion of the Secretary of Agriculture to purchase surplus commodities for distribution to schools, welfare institutions, or families on relief. The marketing order enabling legislation was designed to help producers stabilize prices and increase returns by legalizing classified pricing schemes for milk. Cooperatives wanted legal support for their attempts to raise returns to producers, which involved charging buyers higher prices for milk which was bottled and sold for fresh use than for milk which was converted into butter, cheese, or other dairy products. The legislation also permitted producers of fruits and vegetables to limit sales of low-quality produce and/or to restrict shipments during certain periods.

In addition, the Roosevelt administration initiated programs to dispose of surpluses and to improve diets. Surplus commodities were donated to schools and, later, additional money was appropriated to assist schools in serving free or low-cost lunches. An experimental food stamp program was introduced in the late 1930s. Under this program, participating low-income families were given free stamps which they could use to purchase certain designated surplus commodities in food stores. The program was dropped during World War II but revived in a somewhat different form in the 1960s.

Congress authorized new credit programs for farmers in an attempt to limit foreclosures and to enable tenants and beginning farmers to obtain loans on favorable terms. Congress augmented the capital of the Federal Land Banks so that these banks could borrow money at lower rates of interest to help refinance farmers threatened with foreclosure. This also provided an indirect form of relief for rural banks by making it possible for farmers to repay their bank loans. Another new credit agency (the Rural Electrification Administration) was created to encourage farm electrification.

Most of the legislation adopted during the 1930s was aimed at raising farm prices and avoiding foreclosures. Some of the more socially-minded individuals within the Roosevelt administration argued that more should be done to help low-income farmers, especially sharecroppers. The President was persuaded to create a new agency called the "Resettlement Administration" to assist poor rural households. Many of the activities undertaken were controversial. The Resettlement Administration funded subsistence homesteads for the unemployed, created cooperatives to produce and market such items as furniture and women's hosiery, and established a number of cooperative farming projects patterned after those in Israel (Benedict 1955, p. 190 and Conkin, pp. 208 and 210-13). Because many of the projects were extravagant and/or unsuccessful, Congress forced the agency to abandon some of the more controversial activities, such as the resettlement schemes and cooperative farming projects.

In 1937, the remaining activities of the Resettlement Administration were incorporated in a new agency within the Department of Agriculture, called the Farm Security Administration. A principal activity of the new agency was to provide credit to enable tenants and sharecroppers to become farm owners. This agency was subsequently reorganized and, in 1946, became the Farmers Home Administration. Its principal function since then has been to provide farm ownership, production, and subsistence loans to farmers who could not obtain credit elsewhere (Rasmussen, p. 1159). More recently, however, the agency has funded rural housing and rural development projects and also has provided substantial amounts of emergency credit to farmers.

A number of individuals in the Department of Agriculture had been arguing for some time that more ought to be done to prevent soil erosion and to control land use. Their lobbying efforts with Congress were aided by the massive dust storms that resulted from the prolonged drought of the mid-1930s. Dust clouds spread as far as Washington, D.C. Papers were full of pictures of "blown-out" farmers. This created an environment favorable to the adoption of soil conservation programs. Congress responded to the emergency by creating still another new agency, the Soil Conservation Service. Its mission was to provide farmers with conservation plans and to assist them in carrying out these plans. For a brief period, the Department of Agriculture undertook to promote land-use planning at the local level, but this activity encountered much opposition and was eventually dropped.

POLICY ISSUES DURING THE 1940s

Despite all the efforts that were made during the 1930s to help farmers, agricultural incomes never fully recovered. It was World War II that brought an end to the Depression and a dramatic recovery in farm prices. Surpluses gradually disappeared. Thousands of farmers, farm workers, and sharecroppers left agriculture, due to the military draft and the availability of off-farm job opportunities. Congress wanted to encourage production and to protect farmers against a price decline similar to that experienced in 1920 following the first World War. With this objective in mind, Congress added several commodities to the compulsory support list, raised minimum support prices, and mandated that they be held at this higher level for two years after the cessation of hostilities (Benedict, 1953, pp. 415-16). These provisions created few problems during the 1940s (except for eggs and potatoes). Surpluses of grains and cotton began to build up in 1948, but the surge in world demand which accompanied the Korean War enabled the government to dispose of what it had accumulated.

By 1948, it had become clear to many members of Congress that prices of grains, cotton, and milk could not be maintained indefinitely at the mandated level of support (90 percent of so-called "parity prices")[2] without incurring high government costs. Support prices, it was argued,

---

[2] The concept of parity was introduced in the 1930s to provide a basis for establishing "fair" prices for farm products. Parity prices were defined by law as those prices that would give farm commodities the same purchasing power with respect to articles farmers buy as they had in the period from 1910 to 1914. Prices were never supported at 100 percent of parity during the 1930s. It was only later that support prices

should be flexible rather than rigidly tied to a high percentage of parity. A formula was proposed to link support prices to the level of surplus stocks. Under the proposed formula, support prices would be reduced as the level of carryover stocks rose. After an extended and bitter debate, Congress agreed to incorporate the flexible pricing formula in the Agricultural Act of 1948, but delayed the time when it would go into effect.

Two policy failures from the decade of the 1940s are significant because they influenced subsequent decisions. The first was the experiment with price supports for eggs and potatoes; the second was the defeat of a proposal to move away from reliance on price-support loans and storage programs to deficiency payments as the principal means of supporting farm incomes. The latter is frequently referred to as the "Brannan Plan," named for the Secretary of Agriculture who proposed it.

Congress added eggs and potatoes to the mandatory support list during the war to encourage production. Because of rapid improvements in technology, the support level established for each of these commodities turned out to be too high. Production rose much more than demand, thereby compelling the government to purchase and store large quantities of eggs and potatoes. Eggs were converted into powdered form, but even in this form, large losses occurred in storage. Even greater losses occurred with potatoes. Pictures of bulldozers pushing surplus potatoes into pits for burial gave the program a poor public image. Eventually, Congress eliminated supports for these two commodities. This experience has made Congress reluctant to add new commodities to the support list, especially perishable commodities.

Secretary Brannan argued that it made more sense to support the prices of livestock products, for which demand was rising, than grains and cotton. To encourage use, he suggested that prices be permitted to fall to market-clearing levels and that losses to farmers be made up by direct payments from the treasury. He also proposed that the volume of production eligible for support be limited so as to avoid making large payments to those at the upper end of the size distribution (Cochrane, pp. 144-45). The plan proposed by Secretary Brannan proved to be extremely controversial and failed to win wide support in Congress. Most southern Democrats opposed Secretary Brannan's plan, because they feared shifting supports to livestock products would jeopardize existing programs for crops like tobacco, peanuts, and cotton. While the plan attracted limited support, it set the stage for later policy modifications. Eventually, the concept of deficiency payments to compensate for low

were linked to a fixed percentage of parity. Parity prices and the limitations of the parity formula as a basis for pricing farm products are discussed in greater detail in Chapter 4.

support prices was incorporated in legislation. Payments were first made to producers of wool and later to producers of wheat, corn, cotton, and rice. Payment limitations have also become an integral part of every major farm bill enacted since 1973.

COPING WITH SURPLUSES—POLICY MODIFICATIONS IN THE 1950s AND 1960s

Rapid technological improvements, combined with cheap fertilizer and declining exports, led to the reemergence of surpluses in the 1950s. To cope with the surplus problem, farmers were paid to keep land idle and new programs aimed at expanding exports were authorized. The "Soil Bank" program was introduced during the early years of the Eisenhower Administration as an alternative to compulsory acreage controls. It was a voluntary program under which farmers were paid to idle all or part of their farm. Participants were allowed to plant the idle land to grass or trees or could even convert it to a nonfarm use such as a golf course. The original program ended in the late 1950s, but was revived in modified form during the 1960s. The program had strong bipartisan support and, therefore, became an important component of farm policy in both the Eisenhower and Kennedy administrations. Sufficient land was idled under these programs in the late 1960s to hold surpluses to manageable levels.

Overseas surplus disposal programs were expanded under provisions of Public Law 480, now commonly referred to as P.L. 480 or the "Food for Peace" Act. P.L. 480 has been extended and amended every four or five years since it was adopted in 1954. The Act authorizes the sale of surplus commodities (for foreign currency or for credit with generous repayment provisions) and donations of food to foreign governments, international relief organizations, and private groups that distribute food abroad.

Hunger in America became an issue in the late 1960s, in part because of a television documentary emphasizing the magnitude of the problem. Earlier, President Kennedy had liberalized food distribution programs to make participation easier and more attractive (Kotz, p. 49). But these reforms were widely viewed by social activists as inadequate. The Senate responded to these concerns by appointing a Select Committee on Nutrition and Human Needs (Kotz, p. 144). The so-called hunger lobby (consisting of church groups, doctors, nutritionists, and social activists) used this committee as a forum to express their views. While the committee had no authority to introduce legislation (only to hold hearings), it kept the hunger issue before the public and indirectly contributed to pressure for revival of the Food Stamp Program. The program was reintroduced on an experimental basis in the 1960s and over the next decade expanded rapidly.

Antipoverty programs flourished during the 1960s, but few of these programs were targeted to the specific needs of the rural poor. Having grown up on a poor Texas farm in the 1930s, President Johnson was personally familiar with rural poverty and wanted to do something to alleviate the problem. With this in mind, he appointed a commission in 1966 to look into the causes of rural poverty and to make recommendations. The commission issued its report in late 1967, but by then the President had decided not to seek reelection. His successor, President Nixon, was uninterested in initiating legislation based on the commission's report. Rural poverty, unlike the hunger issue, failed to arouse the public and, consequently, generated little interest in Congress.

CHANGES IN FARM AND FOOD PROGRAMS DURING THE 1970s

The sudden surge in export demand in the mid-1970s radically changed the economic environment for agriculture. Grain surpluses disappeared and prices rose dramatically. General inflation reinforced the upward trend in commodity prices. Producers of wheat, corn, and soybeans were the major beneficiaries of the export boom. The livestock subsector did not share in the gains and, in fact, suffered losses because of the rise in feed ingredient costs. One of the effects of the export boom was to bring about a significant redistribution of income within agriculture from the livestock sector to the crop sector. Optimistic expectations reinforced by projections of a continuing upward trend in exports of grains and soybeans (and products derived from soybeans) led successful farmers to bid against each other for land that appeared on the market. Non-farmers seeking a hedge against inflation added to the upward pressure on land prices, especially in grain-producing areas of the Midwest. Within a period of six years, land in some counties tripled in value.

The "internationalization" of U.S. agriculture was confined to a relatively small group of commodities, but it made both producers and users of grain much more vulnerable to changes in export demand and to monetary and fiscal policies that influence the value of the dollar. The surge in export demand coincided with the decision to "float the dollar," that is, to permit its value to rise and fall rather than to remain fixed in relation to other major currencies. At first, the dollar fell in value, which helped make U.S. farm products cheaper on world markets. Rising exports and a cheaper dollar also added upward pressure on domestic prices. Later, the trend was reversed, and the value of the dollar rose rapidly. This contributed to the loss in export sales which occurred between 1981 and 1986.

Changes in the economic environment in the mid-1970s produced equally dramatic shifts in policy. Land previously retired under government programs was brought back into production. Support prices were increased and farmers were offered generous disaster payments to encourage planting. Farmers responded to the secretary of agriculture's plea to plant from "fence row to fence row," and even planted beyond the traditional boundaries in some areas by plowing up marginal land.

The threat of shortages (which quickly disappeared) brought a revival of interest in storage programs. Food security became an issue. Importing countries feared they would be unable to obtain the grain they needed (or could not afford to buy it because of high prices) if larger reserves were not maintained. There was also considerable dissatisfaction with the way U.S. government grain stocks had been handled when the Soviet Union and other buyers entered the world market. Many thought the stocks had been sold too quickly. In any event, the government, not farmers, gained from selling the accumulated stocks. Dissatisfaction with the government's performance led to formulating new rules for the release of government-held stocks and greater incentives for farm storage of grain. The program initiated was known as the Farmer-Owned Reserve. In practice, the program turned out to be a device to hold up prices. Farmers were paid to hold grain off the market when surpluses reemerged in the late 1970s.

To encourage production and to protect the incomes of farmers, guaranteed or target prices were introduced for grains and cotton. If actual market prices fell below these guaranteed levels, farmers were eligible for cash payments, which made up the difference between the average market price (or the price-support loan rate if above the market price) and the target or guaranteed price. Support prices were raised based on inflationary trends prevailing at the time. In retrospect, these support prices turned out to be too high. By 1977, production had more than caught up with demand. Falling prices for grains, combined with high interest rates and much larger debts, left many farmers in a precarious financial position. Protest movements flourished, and farmers drove their tractors to Washington. Congress reacted by rescinding or delaying downward adjustments in support prices. The Administration also made available more emergency credit for farmers.

Domestic food-subsidy programs expanded under both Republican and Democratic presidents during the 1970s. In addition, Congress was under pressure from the hunger lobby to do more to improve diets. The Senate Select Committee on Nutrition and Human Needs, partly in response to these demands, proposed dietary guidelines for consumers that, if implemented, would have resulted in a decline in the consumption of meat, animal fats, eggs, dairy products, and sugar. An assistant secretary of agriculture in the Carter Administration incurred the wrath of poultry farmers by issuing guidelines for school lunch programs that would have resulted in reduced consumption of eggs. Proposals were also made to restrict advertising of nonnutritious foods on children's TV programs and to compel food manufacturers to include more nutrition information on product labels. Congressional hearings were held on a broad range of topics related to food and nutrition, but no significant legislation emerged from these hearings. The election of a conservative president in 1980 ended efforts to improve nutrition through regulation or other forms of government intervention.

Environmentalists and proponents of the "small is beautiful" concept also began taking a more active interest in farm policy during the 1970s.[3] They wanted to reduce the use of pesticides, preserve more land for agriculture, restrain the growth of large farms, and alter the research agenda to give higher priority to organic agriculture. Secretary of Agriculture Bergland's call for a national dialogue on structural issues was partly a response to the concerns of this group. He, too, was apprehensive about the concentration of production on larger units and the disappearance of small- and medium-sized family farms. The critics of modern agriculture succeeded in broadening the policy agenda but had little influence on the comprehensive farm bills that were enacted in 1977 and 1981.

ATTEMPTS TO REFORM AGRICULTURAL POLICIES IN THE 1980s

The Reagan Administration came into office in 1981, intending to limit government involvement in agriculture and to reduce the cost of support programs. For the most part, their efforts to reform agricultural policy ended in failure. Congress refused to accept many of their recommendations to eliminate or reduce support prices. The Administration was forced to contend with a weak export market, rising surplus stocks of

---

[3]From the 1920s through the 1970s, farm and food policies were determined mainly by a group often referred to as the "agricultural establishment." It consisted of the general farm organizations, commodity interest groups, the Department of Agriculture, the Land Grant Colleges, and the agricultural committees of Congress. Don Paarlberg, an Assistant Secretary of Agriculture in the Eisenhower, Nixon, and Ford administrations, argued in the 1970s that these organizations could no longer control the agricultural agenda (Paarlberg, pp. 60-61). Consumer activists, environmentalists, and church groups have succeeded in broadening the food and agriculture policy agenda in recent years, but their influence on farm policies has been negligible.

wheat and corn, and record-high government costs. Farmers became more dependent on government payments.

The 1980s turned out to be an unpropitious time to get the government out of agriculture. Rising production abroad, a slower rate of economic growth in developing countries, severe balance of payment problems of potential buyers, and a strong dollar in the early 1980s all contributed to a drop in U.S. agricultural exports. In an attempt to restore the competitiveness of U.S. exports, price-support loan rates were reduced in the Food Security Act of 1985. But Congress refused to lower the incomes of farmers by cutting target prices. This meant that the gap between target prices and loan rates widened. Payments from the treasury were used to bridge the gap. To qualify for such payments, farmers had to reduce the acreage planted to wheat, corn, cotton, and rice. Agribusiness firms supplying inputs such as fertilizer were unhappy with the voluntary acreage set-aside programs that were offered to farmers, but the Administration could find no acceptable alternative to idling acreage.

Payment-in-kind or PIK certificates were introduced to avoid large cash outlays from the treasury and to put more commodities on the market, thereby helping to hold down market prices. Farmers were offered PIK certificates in return for idling a certain proportion of their cropland, and also to make up part of the difference between target prices and loan rates or market prices (whichever were higher). The certificates were negotiable and convertible into commodities. This meant that farmers participating in set-aside programs were paid partly in grain rather than in cash. The additional grain released from government stocks helped to reduce surpluses and prevented prices from rising as much as they might have done in response to the cuts in acreage. By holding down prices, the Administration hoped to stimulate exports (or at least prevent other exporters from capturing a larger share of the world market) and also to reduce incentives for farmers to ignore the voluntary set-aside program and plant additional acreage.

In addition to lowering price-support loan rates, Congress made available additional funds for subsidizing exports, either directly or indirectly in the form of low-cost credit. Trade restrictions were blamed in part for the loss in U.S. farm exports. The Administration pushed negotiations with the European Community in an attempt to curb subsidized exports. The protectionist policies of Japan also came under attack. Threats of retaliation were used in an attempt to get Japan to liberalize imports of beef and citrus fruit.

Old supply control measures, such as long-term land retirement schemes, were revived, and new programs were added in an attempt to reduce dairy surpluses. In 1984, dairy farmers were offered payments in return for reducing milk production. Two years later, a whole-herd buy-out plan was introduced. Farmers were offered the option of selling their cows for slaughter (or export) in return for substantial payments. Participants in the program had to agree not to produce milk on the farm for a period of five years, and not to permit others to do so.

Farm credit reemerged as a major policy issue in the mid-1980s because of the large losses incurred by rural banks and the farmer-owned Cooperative Farm Credit Service. Many farmers, particularly those who had expanded in response to optimistic forecasts and higher farm prices in the mid-1970s, found they could not meet their debt repayment obligations when farm prices fell in the late 1970s and again in the mid-1980s. The squeeze on farm incomes was accompanied by a drop in land values, which meant that the value of the assets was less than the total debt on many farms. The Cooperative Farm Credit Service was particularly affected because it had been an aggressive lender during the boom years of the 1970s. Losses on farm loans severely depleted its capital and forced the more financially secure regional banks to help support the weaker banks. Congress ultimately agreed to help "bail out" the Cooperative Farm Credit Service by offering the banks a line of credit with generous repayment terms. Local banks also were offered the opportunity to package and sell farm loans to a government-sponsored corporation, thus providing a secondary market for farm mortgages similar to that already available for home mortgages.

The high cost of support activities in the 1980s might have been reduced by cutting target prices or by introducing compulsory supply management programs, but neither alternative was acceptable to Congress. The Administration also was philosophically opposed to compulsory sales quotas. Congress and the Administration were forced to live with high-cost programs because they could not agree on reform measures. Cutting off government payments was not considered a viable alternative because this would have had a devastating effect on farm incomes in the Midwest and parts of the South. In the absence of government payments, land prices would have declined even further, resulting in still greater losses for banks and other creditors. The experience of the 1980s illustrates how difficult it is to retreat from subsidies once a significant segment of society becomes dependent on government largess.

CONCLUSIONS

History demonstrates the critical importance of external events in shaping U.S. farm and food policies. Surviving programs or activities reflect the response of Congress to a series of crises—the depression of the 1930s, drought in the mid-1930s, the buildup of surpluses in the 1950s, the loss of export markets in the mid-1980s, etc. A different sequence of events probably would have left a quite different legacy of farm and food policies. For example, if export demands had continued to grow in the 1980s as they had in the 1970s, and/or yields had not increased, it might have been possible for the Reagan Administration to reduce the degree of government intervention in agriculture.

The foregoing review also illustrates the principle of inertia in government. Measures adopted in the 1930s in response to what was thought to be a temporary emergency have survived for more than fifty years. This has occurred despite a decline in the farm population, from 20 percent of the total population at the time of the Great Depression to less than 3 percent in the mid-1980s. Congress has consistently voted to retain support programs for a key group of commodities because of recurring oversupply problems and the fear of what might happen to farm incomes, land values in the South and Midwest, and small town merchants and banks if such programs were abandoned.

Most of the programs or activities relating to food and agriculture that were introduced in the 19th and early 20th centuries have survived because there is a broad basis of support for such activities. Agricultural research, education and extension programs, assistance for farm cooperatives, special credit facilities for farmers, and conservation programs fall in this category. International food aid and domestic food subsidy programs also enjoy widespread support from both parties in Congress. Few senators or representatives oppose these activities, although conflicts arise over the level of funding and eligibility requirements for aid recipients.

Among the items which have moved up or down on the policy agenda, depending on the political environment, are programs aimed at improving nutrition, conserving soil and water, alleviating rural poverty, and protecting farm labor. Land tenure policies have not had the priority in the United States that they have had in many countries in Europe and Latin America.

Farm price and income support programs clearly are the most controversial of all government activities relating to food and agriculture, and have dominated farm policy debates over the past fifty years. Congress has opted for four- or five-year commodity programs rather than permanent legislation. This has made it necessary to consider comprehensive farm bills at least once during every president's term. A high proportion of the time spent by the agricultural committees of Congress has been devoted to working out acceptable compromises regarding support levels and supply adjustment programs for a small group of commodities, mainly wheat, corn, cotton, rice, tobacco, sugar, and milk. Recent farm bills, however, have included authorization for a number of other activities as well as support programs. By incorporating authorization for such continuing activities as domestic food subsidy programs in comprehensive farm bills, the agricultural committees have sought to broaden the basis of support for farm programs, but in doing so they have lengthened the decision-making process because so many more interests are involved. Enacting a comprehensive farm bill has become an exceedingly complex and difficult task.

Finally, a review of history illustrates the incremental nature of U.S. farm and food policies. The tendency has been to make marginal changes in existing policies in the absence of a crisis and to add programs in times of stress.

DISCUSSION QUESTIONS

2.1. Why were farmers more successful in obtaining government assistance in the 1930s than in the 1880s and 1890s, despite a marked decline over the intervening period in the proportion of the population engaged in agriculture?

2.2 What farm policy changes were made in the United States in response to: (1) rising farm prices and the fear of food shortages between 1900 and 1920 and (2) weak or falling farm prices and the build up of surpluses in the 1950s?

2.3. Why did the cost of price-support programs rise so dramatically in the 1980s despite the election of a conservative president committed to the goal of reducing government expenditures and freeing agriculture from government intervention?

2.4 Based on past U.S. experience, under what conditions would you expect farm and food policies to change significantly?

REFERENCES

BENEDICT, MURRAY R., *Farm Policies of the United States, 1790-1950*. New York: The Twentieth Century Fund, 1953.

BENEDICT, MURRAY R., *Can We Solve the Farm Problem?* New York: The Twentieth Century Fund, 1955.

COCHRANE, WILLARD W., *The Development of American Agriculture—A Historical Analysis*. Minneapolis: University of Minnesota Press, 1979.

CONKIN, PAUL K., *Tomorrow a New World: The New Deal Community Program*. New York: Da Capo Press, 1976.

GATES, PAUL W., *Landlords and Tenants on the Prairie Frontier: Studies in American Land Policy*. Ithaca: Cornell University Press, 1973.

KOTZ, NICK, *Let Them Eat Promises--The Politics of Hunger in America*. Garden City, N.Y.: Doubleday & Co. (Anchor Edition), 1971.

PAARLBERG, DON, *Farm and Food Policy--Issues of the 1980s.* Lincoln: University of Nebraska Press, 1980.

RASMUSSEN, WAYNE D., "The New Deal Farm Programs: What They Were and Why They Survived," *American Journal Agricultural Economics* 65(1983), 1158–62.

SHANNON, FRED A., *American Farmers Movements.* Princeton: D. VanNostrand, 1957.

3

Agriculture's Public Problems

The purpose of this chapter is to identify those problems that are likely to bring forth demands for government intervention in agriculture. A problem falls in this category when distress becomes widespread or substantial numbers of citizens express dissatisfaction with what is occurring as a result of market forces. Private problems become public problems when the proportion of the population in distress reaches a critical level. This was demonstrated during the 1920s and 1930s and again in the 1980s. When 1 or 2 farmers out of 100 are delinquent in loans, debt repayment is mainly a private matter, but when 10 or 20 out of 100 are in default and banks are in danger of failing, debt repayment becomes a public problem.

Publicity can change what was once thought to be mainly a private problem into a public problem. The loss of small farms, hunger and malnutrition, and working conditions for migrant labor are typical of the kinds of problems that become public issues when given widespread media coverage.

The principal problems of agriculture that have led to demands for government action in the United States over the past half century can be conveniently grouped under four headings. First and foremost, farmers have been confronted with extended periods of low returns for their labor. This is commonly referred to as the "income problem." Second, farmers have had to contend with widely fluctuating incomes associated with variability in both prices and yields. While often called the "instability problem," the word "variability" more accurately describes the irregular ups and downs in income experienced by farmers. For this reason the problems associated with fluctuations in prices and income will henceforth be referred to as the "variability problem." A third set of problems concerns the disappearance of small-scale family farms and the concentration of production on large units, an issue economists refer to as the "structural problem." Finally, there is the "conservation problem," that is, the potential loss of productivity owing to soil erosion and the depletion of underground aquifers.

The foregoing list is by no means exhaustive. Critics of modern agriculture, for example, consider food safety, overuse of herbicides and pesticides, and contamination of underground water as serious public problems, but thus far Congress has devoted relatively little time or attention to such issues. Farm policy debates are still dominated by the traditional issues, namely what to do about low incomes, unstable production and prices, the demise of family farms, and the loss of topsoil. The underlying causes of these problems and their current status are described in the pages which follow.

THE INCOME PROBLEM

Typically, farm incomes average somewhat below nonfarm incomes. This phenomenon is observable in most industrial nations, although the magnitude of the farm-nonfarm income gap varies greatly among countries. It tends to be wider in Southern Europe, for example, than in the United Kingdom, Australia, or New Zealand. Income differences are associated with variations from country to country in the size of farm units, the level of technical efficiency, and the availability of nonfarm jobs.

For substantial periods, the average per capita income of the U.S. farm population (from all sources including off-farm income) has remained below the average per capita income of the nonfarm population, but average farm-nonfarm income differences have been substantially less in recent years than during the 1930s. Just prior to World War II, per capita farm incomes averaged less than half of per capita nonfarm incomes (U.S. Department of Agriculture, 1983, p. 82). Prosperity brought on by World War II improved the relative income position of farmers. Another dramatic improvement occurred as a result of the export boom in the mid-1970s. In the late 1970s and early 1980s, the average per capita income of the farm population had risen to over 80 percent of the nonfarm coverage. At that time, successful farm operators were earning more than many of those employed in nonfarm occupations or owners of comparable nonfarm businesses. But during the 1950s and 1960s and again during the mid-1980s, the income difference widened with farmers as a group falling behind.

Average farm-nonfarm income comparisons probably are less useful today than a half century ago when farms were more homogeneous. Averages always hide a great deal of variability that occurs within groups. This is particularly true of modern agriculture. The spread in incomes among farmers has widened because of differences in managerial ability, the rate of adoption of new technology, the quality of soil resources, the availability of markets, and when an individual began farming. Even in periods of depressed farm prices, it is possible to identify farm operators who are doing relatively well because they have access to special markets or possess exceptional managerial ability. The time of entry and how the purchase of land and machinery was financed also affect the income of farmers. An operator who began farming in the late 1970s when both land prices and interest rates were high obviously is in a less favorable income position than one who purchased land much earlier or inherited the farm.

The persistence of relatively low average farm incomes for extended periods cannot be explained by one factor alone. Farm-nonfarm income differences are related to a combination of factors including unfavorable price relationships, lags in adjustment, and the willingness of farmers and new entrants to accept modest returns because of their preference for farming as a way of life. The principal causes of lagging farm incomes in industrialized countries are as follows:[1]

1. Slow growth in population and a low propensity to spend additional income on food (low income elasticity of demand). This results in only a modest rate of growth in aggregate demand for food products.

2. A chronic tendency for growth in aggregate supply to outstrip growth in demand owing to rapid changes in agricultural technology (improved varieties, cheap fertilizer, better pest control methods, etc.).

3. The unresponsiveness of aggregate food consumption to a change in price (low price elasticity of demand). This means that a small percentage increase in output results in a large percentage decline in average farm prices (in the absence of government intervention).[2]

---

[1]This list is based on a succinct summary drafted more than twenty-five years ago by J.R. Bellerby.

[2]Price elasticity of demand is defined as the percentage change in comsumption associated with a one percent change in price. For example, if the price elasticity of demand for grain is assumed to be − 0.4, it will require a 25 percent reduction in price to induce

4. Low mobility of factors of production or farm inputs, especially family labor and land, which means that such factors, once committed to agriculture, tend to remain in production.

5. The lack of major barriers to entry into agriculture and the willingness of potential entrants to compete for farms that become available despite the prospect of modest returns to labor and management.

6. Competition for farm land, both by farmers who want to expand and by new entrants, as well as by those seeking a hedge against inflation. This leads to overvaluing land, thus depressing current returns to labor and management.[3]

Periods of unfavorable prices for agriculture have been associated with slow growth of demand (item 1) and rapid changes in agricultural technology (item 2). These are the conditions that characterized U.S. agriculture in the 1950s and 1960s and again in the mid-1980s. Farm prices declined during those periods while the cost of nonfarm-produced inputs continued to rise.

Slow growth in demand would not be so serious for agriculture if consumers could be induced to purchase more food at lower prices. But this does not occur. Unfortunately for farmers, demand is price inelastic (item 3), that is, the percentage change in price for most farm products exceeds the percentage change in quantity. As a result, the total revenue obtained by farmers from the sale of farm products declines with an increase in the amount of food available per capita.

The combined effects of a shift in demand relative to supply and in-elastic demand and supply curves are illustrated in Figure 3.1. Assume that over a ten-year period the aggregate supply schedule shifts from S to S' owing to improvements in technology, while the demand schedule shifts only from D to D'. In the absence of support programs, average farm prices will fall from an index of 100 to 88, a decline of 12 percent; consequently, even though technical efficiency has improved, net returns for all farms combined may be depressed.

The adoption of yield-increasing technology in agriculture is both a cause and an effect of low prices. The competitive nature of agriculture provides an incentive for the individual to increase yields because all the

---

consumers to increase use by 10 percent. Consumption and price almost invariably move in opposite directions; hence the sign of the elasticity coefficient is negative.

The algebraic relationship can be expressed as follows:

$$E_d = \frac{\text{Percent change in consumption}}{\text{Percent change in price}} = \frac{+10\%}{-25\%} = -0.4$$

For a more complete explanation of price elasticity and its implications for agriculture, see Tomek and Robinson, pp. 44–48.

[3] If inflation persists, low current returns can be more than offset by long-run appreciation in the value of the farm.

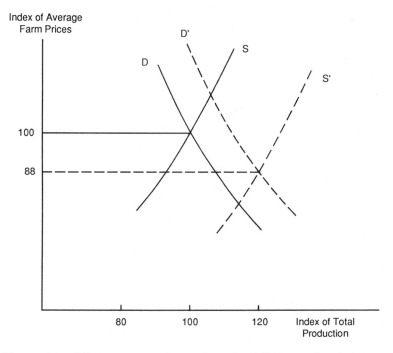

Figure 3.1   Effect on average farm prices of a shift in supply relative to demand.

additional output can be sold at existing market prices (the demand curve facing the individual firm is horizontal at the current market price).   If the added output is small, the innovator clearly gains, but when farmers collectively adopt output-increasing technology, the effect is to depress aggregate returns unless demand is elastic or prices are supported by the government.   In response to lower prices, farmers who have not heretofore adopted the new technology will be forced to do so in order to maintain their income.   Thus, there is pressure on everyone to take advantage of innovations in agriculture, even though the ultimate effect may be to make all but the early adopters worse off.   The progressive farmer looks to the agricultural colleges and experiment stations to find ways of increasing yields so that he or she can remain one step ahead. But for the majority of farmers, technology becomes what Willard Cochrane, a former Assistant Secretary of Agriculture, calls the "agricultural treadmill." Farmers must run with new technology if they are not to fall behind.

Depressed prices will result in only a temporary loss of income if alternatives are available and farmers refuse to work for low returns.   The exodus of those dissatisfied with low returns will enable the remaining farmers to divide the income pie into fewer slices.   Furthermore, competition for farms will decline, thus reducing the cost of entry. It is the immobility of land and labor (item 4) which prevents prices from recovering and keeps average farm incomes relatively low. If more farmers had refused to continue cultivating their land in the 1950s and 1960s, production would have declined and prices would have recovered. Many did leave agriculture, but the exodus was not sufficient to achieve income equality for farmers. Even if a farmer is forced to quit or decides to retire, his or her land is likely to be purchased by a neighbor. Thus, land tends to remain in production despite low prices. Aggregate farm output will respond to lower prices, but only if alternatives are available for both land and labor. In the short run, adjustments are difficult to achieve. Families committed to agriculture tend to remain on the farm, especially those who are older and have limited experience in nonfarm occupations. Resource adjustments in agriculture typically occur between generations, that is, when the farmer gets ready to retire or is forced to do so because of ill health.

Labor earnings in agriculture will remain depressed as long as potential entrants are willing to work for less than they could obtain in nonfarm occupations (item 5). Ultimately, it is the "supply-price" of labor, that is, the level of returns that potential entrants are willing to accept, that determines the ratio of farm to nonfarm incomes. As long as substantial numbers of new entrants are willing to pay a premium for being their own boss and working at a job they like, the price of farms will be bid up to a level that will make it difficult for farm operators to earn a current rate of return for their labor and capital equal to that prevailing in other occupations or comparable to that earned by entrepreneurs operating nonfarm businesses of a similar size.

High land prices depress current returns, but farmers are often willing to pay a premium for farmland because it may appreciate in value. In periods of inflation, many farmers do indeed "live poor and die rich." Annual gains from the appreciation of assets in a number of years during the 1970s were so great that they exceeded net returns from farming operations. This was particularly true in grain-producing areas of the Midwest. Those who sold their farms in the late 1970s gained enormously from asset appreciation, while many of those who purchased land at that time found it impossible, with the level of commodity prices prevailing in the early 1980s, to meet their financial obligations. Incomes were not sufficient to enable new entrants to earn a competitive rate of return on both their own capital and labor.

One of the reasons that land is overpriced (relative to its current earning potential) is that successful farmers with low debts can afford to bid relatively high prices for additional land, especially if they have underutilized labor and equipment. The marginal return from adding another 50 or 100 acres to an existing farm may be much higher than the average net income that one might obtain from the same land farmed as a separate unit. Potential new entrants are forced to bid against successful farmers who want to expand. The land frequently is worth more to the expansion-minded farmer than to the new entrant.

The tendency to bid more for land when returns increase has important policy implications. Government efforts to raise average labor returns to farmers by supporting prices, making payments to farmers, or offering credit on more liberal terms will not be successful in the long run if potential entrants are willing to pay for the privilege of obtaining these benefits. Any improvement in returns will accrue to current owners of land. If gains from subsidies or higher farm prices are offset by a proportionate increase in land costs, new entrants will be no better off. Gains in income, whether they are the result of improved market conditions or government subsidies, can be transferred to the next generation of farmers only by restricting entry or imposing ceilings on the price of farm land.

THE VARIABILITY PROBLEM

Incomes may be depressed in a particular year or for several years in succession because of low yields, low prices, or some combination of the two. Normally high prices help to compensate for low yields, but this is not always the case. In 1984, for example, yields of major crops were very low in parts of Iowa, Nebraska, and Missouri owing to a succession of natural disasters (too wet in the spring and too dry in the summer), but prices at harvest time were depressed because of large carryover stocks and higher yields elsewhere. The combination of low prices and low production forced many farmers to default on their loans, thereby threatening the solvency of local credit institutions. Just as in the 1930s, distress became so widespread that local merchants and bankers joined farmers in seeking government assistance.

Fluctuating prices are a major cause of income variability in agriculture. Price changes do not follow a consistent or regular pattern. Several years of depressed prices may be followed by a sudden increase brought about by a shift in demand such as occurred in the 1970s. Export demand tends to be more unstable than domestic demand, although feed ingredient demand may shift from year to year because of changes in the profitability of feeding livestock. As the principal residual supplier of grains, cotton, and soybeans on world markets, U.S. agriculture has become much more vulnerable to decisions made in other countries. The entry or exit of large buyers or sellers on world markets such as the Soviet Union, China, and the European Community has become a major source of instability. U.S. farm prices can be influenced as much by policy decisions made in Moscow, Beijing, and Brussels as those made in Washington. Significant shifts in export demand can also occur as a result of changes in production in competing exporting nations such as Canada, Australia, Argentina, and Brazil. Weather in the Southern Hemisphere has become almost as important to grain traders and U.S. grain farmers as that in the Midwest.

In some instances, the U.S. government has become a contributor to instability, or at least has added to the uncertainty confronting farmers and agribusiness firms. The decision to embargo soybean exports in the 1970s, for example, had a major impact on prices. Production, and hence prices, likewise may be influenced by an announcement to alter set-aside requirements or to introduce a new supply adjustment program, such as the PIK program in 1983. Macroeconomic decisions which affect interest rates and the value of the dollar relative to other currencies are another potential source of instability for agriculture.

The magnitude of income changes that can occur as a result of sudden shifts in demand or changes in production are illustrated by what happened to aggregate net farm income in North Dakota during the 1970s. Net farm income for the state as a whole (before inventory adjustment) rose from an average of just under $300 million per year in the early 1970s to a peak of $1.3 billion in 1974 (U.S. Department of Agriculture, 1986, ECIFS 4-5, p. 28). By 1977, the aggregate net income had slipped back to less than $300 million. Such extreme fluctuations in farm income obviously have important secondary effects on agribusiness firms, creditors, and communities serving farmers.

The response to income variability tends to be asymmetric, that is, a sudden decline in income is much more likely to bring forth demands for government intervention than a corresponding rise in income. Agribusiness firms as well as farmers find it extremely difficult to cope with a loss in sales once production capacity has been expanded to meet an increase in demand; however, the response of nonfarm sectors of the economy to a downward shift in demand is likely to differ from that of agriculture. Manufacturing industries are likely to cut production and to lay off workers in response to a decrease in orders. In the case of agriculture, the principal effect of a downward shift in demand is to reduce prices in the absence of government intervention.

THE STRUCTURAL PROBLEM

The term "structural problem" is now commonly used to identify a collection of issues related to land tenure and the size distribution of farms. Among the areas of concern are the loss of small-scale family farms, the tendency for production to become concentrated on larger units, and a decline in the proportion of land farmed by owner-operators.

Economic forces are pushing agriculture in most industrial countries toward a kind of dual structure. The disappearance of farms in the middle has resulted in a large number of part-time farms concentrated at the lower end of the size distribution, and a relatively small number of large-scale units at the upper end. Small-scale family farms tend to become either a part-time unit or to become larger by acquiring more land. The result is increasing concentration of production on farms that are still largely family-owned, but not operated exclusively by family labor. Typically, the larger than family-sized farm hires more labor and rents additional land.

Small-scale farm units are by far the most numerous, but they contribute relatively little to total production. In 1985, the U.S. Department of Agriculture estimated that there were over one million farms with sales of farm products valued at less than $10,000 annually (Table 3.1). Such farms accounted for 51 percent of the total number of farms in the United States in 1985, but only for 3 percent of gross farm receipts. At the opposite end of the size distribution, farms with sales in excess of $500,000 per year accounted for less than 1 percent of all farms but nearly one-third of gross farm receipts in 1985. Small-scale family farms (roughly defined as those with sales of $10,000 to $100,000 each year) account for approximately one-third of all farms and nearly a quarter of gross farm receipts.

More than half the farms in the United States sell farm products valued at less than $40,000 annually. In the mid-1980s, farms in the under $40,000 sales category depended mainly on off-farm income to sur-

TABLE 3.1 Number of Farms, Proportion of Gross Farm Receipts, and Percent of Income from Off-farm Sources, by Sales Classes, 1985

Sales Class	Number of Farms (1,000s)	Percent of Farms	Percent of Gross Receipts	Percent of Total Net Income From Off-farm Sources
Under $10,000	1,164	51	3	100[b]
$10,000–$39,999	473	21	7	100[b]
$40,000–$99,999	323	14	16	34
$100,000–$499,999	287	13	42	6
$500,000 & over	27	1	32	(c)
Totals	2,275[a]	100	100	

[a]Figures do not add to total due to rounding.
[b]Net loss from farming reported for this group.
[c]Less than 1 percent.
SOURCE: U.S. Department of Agriculture, 1986a, pp. 42–49.

vive. Aggregate net earnings from their farming operations were negative for this group in 1985, although undoubtedly some operators with gross sales of less than $40,000 earned a reasonable income from farming. Changing the census definition of farms to exclude those selling farm products valued at less than $10,000 annually obviously would have a major impact on public perceptions of the farm problem. Half the farms would disappear, which, of course, would have important political implications for the allocation of funds to states where small farms predominate. Funding for research and education is commonly based on formulas linking state allocations to the number of farms.

Raising the level of farm prices benefits mainly the 300,000 farms with sales in excess of $100,000 per year. These farms account for almost three-quarters of gross sales. Income from off-farm sources is a negligible part of the total net income on such farms. Many large-scale farms earn rates of return to labor and capital equal to those prevailing among nonfarm businesses.

Large-scale nonfamily corporate farms are important in only a few areas. Contrary to the impression one gains from reading urban newspapers, corporate farms are not taking over American agriculture. The number of corporate farms has risen over the past two decades, but the majority of such farms are owned by families. Larger family farms often choose to incorporate to facilitate the transfer of property between generations and, in some cases, reduce tax liabilities. Few nonfarm corporations have invested in agriculture in recent years, because returns from farming have not been attractive enough to encourage such investment. Some corporations that purchased farms earlier have sold their operations because they were unprofitable. In the early 1980s, nonfamily corporations with significant sales of farm products accounted for only about 1 percent of all farms and less than 5 percent of gross sales (Krause, p. 3). Such farms, however, control large areas of land and employ substantial numbers of hired farm workers in parts of California, Arizona, Hawaii, Texas, and Florida.

Agriculture is unique among major U.S. industries in maintaining a structure which is still dominated by family-operated units. Even in the summer months when seasonal labor is hired, farm operators and members of the operator's family provide over 60 percent of the labor force on farms in the North Central states, the Great Plains, the Intermountain states, and the Northeast (Figure 3.2). In only a few states does the proportion of labor which is hired exceed 50 percent. These states are mainly ones which specialize in the production of fruits and vegetables. For example, only 25 percent of those employed on California farms in July of 1984 were family workers; 75 percent were hired. The proportion of family workers is somewhat greater in Florida and North Carolina than in California, but still below 50 percent of the total

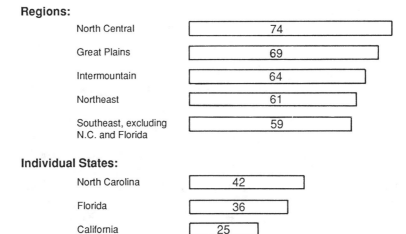

Figure 3.2   Family labor as a percent of the total labor force on farms, July, 1984. (Source: U.S. Department of Agriculture, 1985, p. 383.)

labor force. Seasonal or migrant labor is a social problem in relatively few states. Most hired workers on dairy and other livestock farms are employed throughout the year rather than seasonally. The typical large-scale family farm (over $100,000 gross sales annually) employs only one or two full-time hired workers and a few students or other temporary entrants into the labor force to help during periods of peak labor demand.

Farm tenancy is another area of concern. The plight of tenants and sharecroppers attracted a great deal of attention in the 1930s. Over the preceding three decades, the proportion of farms operated by tenants had gradually risen. By 1930, 42 percent of all U.S. farms were operated by tenants. A high proportion of these were in the South. Tenancy among black farmers was mainly a legacy of plantation agriculture and slavery. Following the Civil War, many of the plantations were sub-divided into small-scale units and rented on shares to former slaves. The families that operated these units were seldom out of debt to the plantation owners, who supplied them with seed, fertilizer, and even the food required for subsistence. At harvest time, the landlord took a large share of the crop in payment for what had been provided to tenants. Typically, leases were unwritten and the bargaining position of tenants was weak owing to the lack of alternative employment opportunities.

The wave of farm foreclosures that engulfed agriculture in the 1920s and 1930s added to the tenancy problem. Banks and insurance companies that had acquired land as a result of foreclosures became reluctant landlords. Most would have preferred to sell the land for cash, and did so when land values recovered. During the Depression, however, they had no alternative but to rent the land to someone who knew how to farm. Consequently, many farm operators who were unable to pay their debts became tenants, either on the farm they had once owned or on a neighboring farm.

Over the past fifty years, farm tenancy has become a less important issue, mainly because of changing economic conditions. By 1970, sharecropping had all but disappeared, and the proportion of farms operated by tenants had dropped to less than 13 percent. Both push and pull factors contributed to the decline in tenant farming, particularly in the South during the 1940s and 1950s. Sharecroppers were pushed out of agriculture by farm mechanization and pulled out by the military draft during World War II and by the availability of off-farm jobs.

Land tenure remains an issue not so much because of concern about the welfare of tenant farmers, but because absentee ownership of land is increasing. A substantial proportion of cropland, mainly in the Great Plains and in the Corn Belt, is no longer owned by those who farm it. The typical large-scale farm operator in that area is now a part owner, that is, he or she owns some land and rents additional acreage. Over half the agricultural land in the U.S. in 1982 was farmed by part owners. Farmland has been retained by the heirs of an earlier generation of farmers or has been acquired as an investment by those seeking a hedge against inflation.

Absentee land ownership is not viewed by everyone as a public problem. Farmers like the flexibility of being able to rent additional land. Letting someone else own the land also reduces the farmers' need for capital and shifts the risks associated with fluctuating land prices to others. The common charge that absentee owners are less concerned about making long-term improvements in the land or conserving soil is not convincingly supported by empirical evidence (Bills and Heimlich, pp. 13–16, and Lee).

The threat of foreign control of U.S. farmland surfaced briefly as an issue during the 1970s. Land became an attractive investment for foreign buyers because it was cheaper in the U.S. than in Europe and was rising rapidly in value. Reports of large-scale purchases by aliens led to expressions of concern by farmers and members of Congress. The response of Congress was to enact legislation compelling aliens to report the amount of land owned or purchased. As a result of this legislation, the U.S. now has reasonably accurate information on the extent of foreign ownership of land. The results of this survey have served to allay fears that aliens would eventually own a substantial proportion of U.S. agricultural land. Less than 1 percent of all privately owned agricultural land (including commercial forest land) was reported to be owned by foreign nationals or foreign corporations in 1987 (U.S. Department of Agriculture, 1988). A substantial proportion of the foreign-owned land is in forests, principally in Maine, Oregon, and the southeastern states.

THE CONSERVATION PROBLEM

The conservation problem, like the structural problem, encompasses a number of subissues. Among the areas of concern are soil erosion, the conversion of agricultural land to nonfarm uses, plowing up grassland to grow export crops, and depletion of underground aquifers. No one would deny that future production potential is adversely affected by these changes. The question at issue is whether the potential losses are so serious as to require government intervention on a larger scale than at present, and, if so, what kinds of policies would be effective in curbing such losses.

Over the past half century total agricultural output has more than kept pace with the growth of demand despite the loss of topsoil and cropland to nonfarm uses. Improvements in agricultural technology have succeeded in masking the effect of these changes. Agricultural scientists are divided over the issue of whether or not the U.S. can continue to rely on new technology to sustain growth in output. Those who are optimistic about the future argue that soil losses are not so serious as to impair future productivity and that yields will continue to rise as they have in the past.

Losses in productive capacity are extremely difficult to estimate. Soil scientists cannot agree among themselves on answers to the question of whether the loss of topsoil is accelerating or declining. In some areas, erosion probably has increased because more fragile grassland has been plowed up to produce crops for export, while in other areas soil losses have declined because farmers have adopted minimum tillage techniques (Gibbons, p. 382). Even in areas where rates of erosion are relatively high, losses in productivity over a 100-year period may be small because the next layer of soil is almost as productive as the top layer (Larson, Pierce, and Dowdy).

Soil scientists emphasize the diversity of the problem. There are areas of very high soil loss, but on much of the nation's cropland the average rate of erosion is well below that which presumably would sustain production over a long period of time. Soil losses are especially high in parts of Texas, Colorado, Iowa, Missouri, the Palouse area of Washington, and the Southeast (Gibbons, p. 360). For the nation as a whole, however, the average calculated rate of soil loss in 1982 was 4.8 tons per acre per year, just under the 5-ton per acre figure which the Soil

Conservation Service has designated as the tolerable upper limit.[4] Furthermore, the average rate of soil loss was slightly lower in 1982 than it had been five years earlier (U.S. Department of Agriculture, 1984).

The U.S. has more options to meet future food requirements than many other countries because it is much more richly endowed with potentially arable land. Land is not likely to be a limiting factor in producing the nation's food requirements for at least the next two or three generations. Many of the developing countries in Asia and some of those in Africa are not so fortunate. The man/land ratio is already much higher in Europe and Asia than the United States, and the area of potentially arable land on which expansion might take place much smaller.

Large areas of land now in grass or trees could be converted into cropland in the United States provided there were sufficient economic incentives to do so. Only about one-third of all the land in farms is planted to crops in a typical year (Figure 3.3). The Soil Conservation Service estimates that as much as 100 million acres of land that was idle, used for grazing or in forests in the early 1980s, could be converted into cropland at modest cost. The conversion of such land would increase the cropland base by around 25 percent. Some of the land now in grass and trees was farmed a generation or two ago. It is no longer farmed because it is uneconomic to do so. If farm prices rose sufficiently, some of this land would be brought back into cultivation. The availability of over 700 million acres of grazing and forest land on farms (Figure 3.3) helps to insure against future food shortages but obviously does not justify misuse of existing land resources.

Land lost to suburban development, superhighways, and shopping centers is also a potential threat to future food supplies. While the proportion of land in built-up areas is relatively small in the United States (only 74 million acres out of a total land area of over 2 billion acres in 1982), the rate at which land was being taken over for nonfarm uses became a public issue, particularly during the 1970s when there

---

[4]Erosion rates have to be estimated because it would be prohibitively expensive to install measuring devices on all fields or waterways to measure runoff and the amount of sediment produced. A formula has been devised by soil scientists to estimate the amount of erosion that occurs on a particular field. The formula is based on data obtained from fields on which actual erosion was measured. The Universal Soil Loss Equation which is used to compute losses from water erosion takes account of what crops are grown on the field, the length and slope of the land, the type of soil, the amount and intensity of rainfall, and the kinds of conservation practices adopted. Formulas also have been devised to estimate soil losses due to wind erosion. For additional details on the problems involved in measuring soil losses, see Larson, and others, pp. 460–62.

The five-ton per acre standard chosen as the upper limit of acceptable soil erosion must be interpreted with caution. It is not equally applicable to all areas. A loss of five tons per acre would severely depress the production capacity of a farm with thin topsoil, but not one located in areas where there are very deep soils.

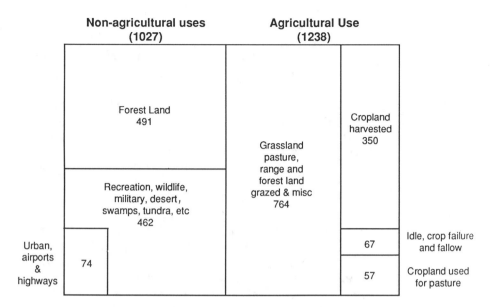

Figure 3.3 Major uses of land in the United States, 1982 (figures in millions of acres).

was great concern about food shortages. At that time, it was estimated that farm and forest land was disappearing at the rate of nearly a million acres per year. Not all the land used for transportation or suburban development was cropland, but the trend was viewed as ominous.

Much land obviously has been paved over or submerged under reservoirs during the past four decades; however the effect on agricultural production appears to have been minor because of offsetting additions to cropland in nonmetropolitan areas. As much land was brought under cultivation in the 1960s and 1970s as was lost to nonfarm uses. Much of the cropland that was added is located in the South and the West. Low-lying areas along the Mississippi River were cleared and wetlands were drained. Some land formerly devoted to grazing was plowed up for dry-land farming or brought under irrigation. Despite urban encroachment and the construction of a vast network of superhighways and airports, the total acreage defined as cropland by the Soil Conservation Service has not changed appreciably during the past four decades.

Projected changes in land use over the next two or three decades are not likely to pose a serious threat to future food production. Raup, a land economist at the University of Minnesota, points out that the rate of conversion of agricultural land to nonfarm uses is likely to be less in the immediate future than in the recent past because of a slower rate of population growth and the construction of fewer new shopping centers, highways, or reservoirs (Raup, p. 53).

Another area of concern has been the depletion of underground aquifers. This poses a threat to future agricultural production, particularly in parts of the Great Plains and the Southwest. A substantial proportion of the increase in agricultural output in the West during the past three decades is attributable to expansion in the area under irrigation. If water were no longer available, or too costly to use, total U.S. agricultural production undoubtedly would decline. Water tables in the West are falling, but apparently underground reserves are still substantial (Sloggett). The major short-run impact of declining water tables has been to raise pumping costs. If recent trends continue, pumping water in some areas may soon become uneconomic. This will lead to changes in land use, with more acreage devoted to crops that require less water or those that are tolerant of drought, such as grain sorghum. Economic pressures are already forcing farmers to make some adjustments in the use of both land and water. The critical policy issue is whether to rely mainly on economic pressure to bring about the adjustments or to force more rapid changes through taxation or government regulation.

CONCLUSIONS

The nature and extent or severity of the farm "income problem" in the future, as in the past, will be strongly influenced by external events. If slow growth persists in export demand and yields continue to rise owing to improvements in technology, the terms of trade of farm products are unlikely to improve. Under these circumstances it will be difficult to persuade Congress to abandon farm price and income support programs. On the other hand, if export demands rise and/or production increases less rapidly because of shortages of key inputs, environmental constraints, or adverse weather, the income problem in agriculture will become less severe. Congress may then be willing to consider major modifications of existing support programs. No one can be certain which scenario will prevail.

Income variability will remain a public problem even if the average level of prices rises to more acceptable levels. Increased dependence on export markets has made producers of grains and soybeans more vulnerable to conditions abroad. Changes in the exchange rate, dry weather, or a severe winter in the Soviet Union, Argentina, and Brazil, or decisions made by the Soviet Union or China to increase or decrease grain imports, can have a major impact on both the volume of U.S. exports and the prices of wheat, feed grains, and soybeans.

The changing structure of agriculture has made it more difficult to design equitable farm programs. Farms are now much less homogeneous than they were when price-support programs were first introduced. A smaller proportion of farms remains in the middle-size group, and a higher proportion is to be found at the upper and lower ends of the size distribution. The majority of farms (as defined by the census) now obtain more of their income from off-farm sources than from agriculture.

Concentration of production on the larger, mainly family-operated farms is likely to continue. In the absence of substantial changes in existing policies, most of the food purchased by consumers in the years ahead will be produced on farms with sales exceeding $100,000 annually. Such farms already account for roughly three-quarters of all farm products sold. There is little likelihood that successful family-operated farms will be displaced by large-scale corporate farms. The expanding sector of American agriculture is comprised mainly of family farms that have grown larger by acquiring additional land and hiring more labor.

Neither the conversion of cropland to nonfarm uses nor the loss of topsoil due to erosion is likely to result in a significant reduction in food production, at least over the next several decades. Unlike many other countries, the U.S. possesses abundant land resources. Losses in productive capacity due to erosion or conversion of land to nonfarm uses can be offset by converting land now in grass or trees to cropland. But doing so will cost money, and eventually consumers may be compelled to pay somewhat higher prices for food and fiber.

The policy issues relating to nonrechargeable underground aquifers are similar to those pertaining to the conversion of cropland to nonfarm uses. Congress is confronted with the difficult task of deciding whether to let market forces dictate water use or to impose unpopular regulations or taxes on users in order to conserve the remaining supplies for future generations.

DISCUSSION QUESTIONS

3.1. What accounts for the persistence of relatively low average returns to capital and labor employed in agriculture? How can long-run average returns to farmers be increased?

3.2. Under what demand and supply conditions are improvements in agricultural technology that lead to higher yields likely to result in higher average incomes for farmers?

3.3. What are the principal causes of variability in farm prices and incomes? Is the "internationalization" of U.S. agriculture likely to reduce or exacerbate the variability problem?

3.4. What effect would changing the census definition of a farm to exclude non-commercial units that obtain most of their income from nonfarm sources have on the number of farms and on average income figures for the agricultural population?

3.5. Large areas of land that were once in farms are now covered with airports, highways, shopping malls, and suburban houses. Why have these changes in land use, at least thus far, had little impact on the capacity to produce food in the United States?

REFERENCES

BELLERBY, J. R., "Agricultural Economic Theory and Policy," *The Indian Journal of Agricultural Economics* 14(1958), 1–3.

BILLS, NELSON L., and RALPH E. HEIMLICH, *Assessing Erosion on U.S. Cropland: Land Management and Physical Features*, Agricultural Economics Report Number 513. Washington, D.C.: Economic Research Service, 1984.

COCHRANE, WILLARD W., "The Agricultural Treadmill," *Farm Prices: Myth and Reality*. St. Paul: University of Minnesota Press, 1958.

CROSSON, PIERRE R., *The Cropland Crisis: Myth or Reality?* Baltimore: The Johns Hopkins University Press/Resources for the Future, 1982.

FREY, H. THOMAS, and ROGER W. HEXEM, *Major Uses of Land in the United States, Preliminary Estimates for 1982*, Staff Report No. AGES840712. Washington, D.C.: Economic Research Service.

GIBBONS, BOYD, "Do We Treat Our Soil Like Dirt?" *National Geographic* 166(1984), 351–88.

KRAUSE, KENNETH R., *Corporate Farming, 1969-82*, Agricultural Economic Report No. 578. Washington, D.C.: Economic Research Service, 1987.

LARSON, W.E., F.J. PIERCE, and R.H. DOWDY, "The Threat of Soil Erosion to Long-Term Crop Production," *Science* 219, no. 4584(1983), 458–65.

LEE, LINDA K., "The Impact of Landownership Factors on Soil Conservation," *American Journal of Agricultural Economics* 62(1980), 1070–76.

RAUP, PHILIP M., "Competition for Land and the Future of American Agriculture," *The Future of American Agriculture as a Strategic Resource*, edited by Sandra J. Batie and Robert G. Healy. Washington, D.C.: The Conservation Foundation, 1980.

SLOGGETT, GORDON, *Prospects for Ground-Water Irrigation*, Agricultural Economic Report No. 478. Washington, D.C.: Economic Research Service, 1981.

TOMEK, W.G. and K.L. ROBINSON, *Agricultural Product Prices*, 2nd ed. Ithaca, N.Y.: Cornell University Press, 1981.

U.S. DEPARTMENT OF AGRICULTURE, *Economic Indicators of the Farm Sector: Income and Balance Sheet Statistics, 1982*, ECIFS 2-2. Washington, D.C.: Economic Research Service, 1983.

————, "Less than 1 Percent of U.S. Agricultural Land is Foreign-Owned." News Release, April 7, 1988.

————, "More Land Protected from Soil Erosion." News Release, April 5, 1984.

————, *Agricultural Statistics, 1985.* Washington, D.C.: U.S. Government Printing Office, 1985.

————, *Economic Indicators of the Farm Sector: National Financial Summary, 1984,* ECIFS 4-5. Washington, D.C.: Economic Research Service, 1986.

————, *Economic Indicators of the Farm Sector: National Financial Summary, 1985,* ECIFS 5-2. Washington, D.C.: Economic Research Service, 1986.

4

Price Support Issues

For over fifty years price-support programs have been the dominant farm policy issue in Congress. These programs have been the most expensive and among the most controversial of all government activities relating to agriculture. In the United States as elsewhere, debates over farm policy have centered around the level of support to maintain on a selected group of commodities. In addition, Congress has had to decide what method or combination of methods should be used to make supports effective. The basic issue, of course, is whether or not the U.S. government should attempt to enhance farm prices, and, if so, for which commodities and by how much. Similar issues confront any government considering support programs for agriculture.

COMMODITIES TO SUPPORT

Very few countries attempt to support the prices of all farm products. In some countries, such as Japan, Switzerland, and Norway, the proportion of total farm output which is supported or protected from lower-priced imports approaches 100 percent. In the European Community it is around 90 percent; in Australia and New Zealand it is much lower. Only about 50 percent of the total value of agricultural output in the United States receives significant protection or support from the government. The prices of wheat, corn, cotton, rice, tobacco, peanuts, wool, sugar, and dairy products have been supported almost continuously since 1933, whereas the prices of fruit, vegetables, and most livestock products other than milk have not been supported or have been supported only intermittently and indirectly.

Politics and administrative feasibility have strongly influenced the decision to support or not to support the price of a particular commodity. The selective support system that has prevailed in the United States during the past fifty years reflects the coalition of regional interests that led to enactment of the Agricultural Adjustment Act of 1933. Political support for government intervention in pricing farm products during the 1920s and 1930s came mainly from states in the Midwest (the Corn Belt), the Great Plains (the wheat states), and the South. Support programs for a number of minor commodities such as honey, peanuts, potatoes, eggs, and tung nuts were added later as a result of political deals or to encourage production during World War II.

The objective of reducing dependence on imports has played a role in the decision to support particular commodities in the United States, just as in Europe and Japan. It is much easier to raise the prices of commodities which a country imports than those which it exports. Prices can be enhanced simply by imposing a quota or a tax on imports. Sugar and wool are among the commodities supported in this way in the United States.

Other factors which have contributed to the adoption of a selective support system in the United States include the storability of commodities and the willingness of producers to accept acreage restrictions or other measures designed to reduce output. The physical problems of making supports effective and handling surpluses are more easily solved for nonperishable commodities, such as grains and cotton, than for perishable commodities such as fruits, vegetables, and eggs. Storage costs also are much lower for grains and cotton than for perishable commodities.

Experience has demonstrated that unless producers are willing to accept controls, the costs of supporting prices can rise to unacceptable levels. A majority of farmers growing wheat, cotton, tobacco, and peanuts have been willing to accept measures designed to limit production in return for higher prices, but this has not been true of those producing broilers, eggs, pork, or beef. One of the reasons for Congressional resistance to adding new commodities to the compulsory support list in recent years has been the reluctance of producers of nonsupported commodities to accept effective control measures.

LEVEL OF SUPPORT

The level of support may be determined by formulas or by compromises worked out between opposing forces in Congress. For the most part, the U.S. has moved away from formula pricing towards what might be described as "political equilibrium pricing." In recent agricultural acts, Congress has mandated minimum support prices or has specified a range over which they can be adjusted by the secretary of agriculture. The prices specified in these acts represent a compromise or balance between opposing political forces. Some groups (and some members of Congress) want to maintain or raise support prices. Others representing agribusiness, consumers, and feed users want to hold down or reduce support prices, partly to encourage use, but also to cut government costs. Support prices will be raised or lowered depending on the relative strength of these opposing forces.

Formula pricing has the advantage of being impersonal and somewhat less subject to political manipulation once the formula is adopted. But the formula itself will inevitably be influenced by political considerations. The principal mechanical methods of establishing support prices that have been adopted or proposed are: (1) indexing formulas which adjust prices up or down on the basis of an index or mover (such as the "parity" formula); (2) basing support prices on some percentage of recent average market prices, and (3) basing prices on an estimate of cost of production, or adjusting support prices for changes in costs.

Indexing Support Prices

For many years, support levels in the United States were tied to "parity prices." The parity standard was adopted in 1933 in an attempt to define "fair" prices for farm products. Parity prices are those prices which give agricultural commodities the same purchasing power with respect to articles farmers buy as they had in some previous period. The base chosen in 1933 for establishing the standard of fairness was the five-year period immediately preceding World War I (1910-1914). There was no more recent period (just prior to 1933) that was thought to be "normal." A standard based on prices prevailing during and immediately after World War I was thought to be too high, while a pricing standard based on relationships prevailing in the 1920s and early 1930s was thought to be too low. Thus, the 1910-1914 standard became embedded in legislation.

With few exceptions, farm prices in the United States have never been supported at 100 percent of parity. During the 1930s, support levels for corn, wheat, and cotton averaged less than 60 percent of parity. In order to spur production, Congress raised support levels for many commodities to 90 percent of parity during World War II. As pointed out in Chapter 2, they were retained at this level for a brief period following the war, but thereafter were gradually reduced. During the 1950s and 1960s, support levels for most commodities were maintained within the range of 75 to 90 percent of parity.

The parity formula is simply a method of "indexing prices," that is, adjusting prices in a manner similar to the way in which Social Security benefits are linked to changes in the Consumer Price Index. The mechanics of calculating a parity price is straightforward. All one needs is the average price prevailing in 1910-1914 (or the adjusted base-period price) and a current index of prices paid by farmers on the 1910-1914 base (that is, with 1910-1914 = 100). The base-period price is multiplied by the current index of prices paid and divided by 100. For example, if the current index of prices paid by farmers is 1000 (10 times what it was in the base period), and the price of commodity X was $1.00 per unit in the base period, the current parity price for commodity X would be $10 ($1.00 x 1,000/100 = $10).

The critical factors, which determine support prices under the parity formula (or any formula in which prices are tied to an index), are the base period and the composition of the index or mover. Because the price of each commodity in the base period is multiplied by the same index, the effect of indexing is to maintain support prices in the same relationship to each other as prevailed during the base period. Whether support prices are favorable or unfavorable to farmers depends in part on the base period selected. If the base period chosen is one during which the prices received by farmers were low relative to those paid for key inputs, future support prices, even if indexed, will still be relatively unfavorable. Support prices will be favorable to farmers if linked to a base period when farm prices were relatively high. For this reason, the selection of base years for indexing prices is always a sensitive political issue.

Support prices can be raised not only by linking them to a more favorable base period but also by adjusting the index of prices paid by farmers, that is, the mover in the parity formula. If items whose prices have gone up more than the average are added to the index (or given greater weight in constructing the index), the effect will be to raise the overall index and, hence, support prices. For example, if farm wages have gone up more than other items, the index could be raised simply by adding farm wages as one component of the index or by giving this item greater weight in calculating the index.[1]

---

[1]For a more complete explanation of how index numbers are constructed and the ways in which they may be manipulated so as to produce a higher or lower level of support prices, see Tomek and Robinson, pp. 195-96 and 204-9.

Continued use of an indexing formula to establish support prices can lead to serious problems. Adjusting all base-period prices by the same index perpetuates whatever relationship between commodity prices existed in that period. This may not be fair to some producers. If, for example, the price of corn was high relative to beef during the base period, indexed support prices will continue to be unfair to beef producers. Intercommodity price relationships can be altered by selecting a new base period, provided, of course, that market prices have changed during the intervening period. But problems of equity between producers will arise regardless of which base period is selected.

Indexed support prices will gradually become out of date if they are not adjusted to reflect changes in demand. An attempt to maintain an indexed support price for a commodity that must compete with lower-priced exports from other countries or substitute products will result in a severe loss of markets. Cotton suffered this fate in the 1940s and 1950s when synthetic fibers began making inroads into cotton use. Similar problems now confront sugar producers because of increasing use of corn sweeteners.

Support prices which are adjusted by a common mover such as the index of prices paid by farmers reflect changes in the *prices* of items purchased by farmers, but not *costs* of production. Production costs are a function of changes in efficiency (output per unit of input) as well as changes in prices. If output per unit of input doubles with no change in input prices, producers can survive with farm prices that are 50 percent lower than those prevailing before the new techniques of production became available. Indexing support prices without adjusting for changes in efficiency will lead to generous profits on those farms that are able to adopt the new technology.

The parity formula ultimately was abandoned as a basis for establishing support prices because of its failure to allow for changes in technology or demand. A return to support prices based on 90 percent or even 80 percent of the 1910-1914 parity standard would greatly overprice commodities such as wheat and corn.[2] Farmers would be willing to produce far more than could be sold at such prices. Maintaining prices at a high percentage of parity (as originally defined by Congress) would necessitate either more effective controls on farm output or very large export subsidies to enable U.S. farm products to compete with those offered by other low-cost producers such as Canada and Australia.

---

[2]In December 1987, the parity price for wheat was $6.89 per bushel. This was around 2 1/2 times the average market price of wheat during that month ($2.71 per bu.) and more than 50 percent above the 1987 target or guaranteed price paid to farmers who agreed to set aside 27.5 percent of their base acreage for wheat (U.S. Department of Agriculture).

Supports Based on Recent Average Prices

An alternative to indexing is to base support prices on some percentage of recent average market prices. This method has the advantage of allowing support prices to change with market conditions, provided past prices have been permitted to respond to shifts in demand and/or supply. Supporting the price of a commodity at, for example, 80 or 90 percent of a three- or five-year moving average of past prices would allow support prices to adjust gradually to changing market conditions. In the absence of supports, price adjustments obviously would occur more rapidly. Thus, the principal effect of basing supports on an average of past prices would be to delay price adjustments. Market forces ultimately would dictate support levels, but adjustments from year to year presumably would be more gradual than would occur if prices were not supported. Such a method of establishing support levels would not necessarily lead to prices acceptable to producers. Support prices based on some percentage of recent market prices would continue to fall in a generally declining market. Farmers would not be protected against income losses; however, such prices would be less likely to perpetuate overproduction or lead to the displacement of U.S. farm products by substitutes or similar products offered by foreign suppliers.

Supports Based on Cost of Production

Another alternative to indexing support prices is to base them on an estimate of average production costs. Per unit production costs, if properly calculated, reflect changes in efficiency as well as changes in the prices of major input items. For this reason, support prices based on cost studies are less likely to lead to serious overpricing than indexed prices. The principal limitation of basing support prices on farm costs is the difficulty of deciding which costs or whose costs should be used in the calculations. Costs vary widely among farms, not only because of differences in efficiency and resource endowment, but also because of differences in the time at which major input items were acquired and how they are valued. If land, for example, has appreciated in value, costs of production calculated on the basis of current land prices will be much higher than those calculated on the basis of land prices prevailing a decade or two ago. Similar problems arise in valuing old buildings and equipment. How the farmer values his or her own or his or her family's labor also greatly influences production costs. Even if consistent values are applied to labor and land, average costs per bushel or per hundredweight will differ between years and between farms, depending on yields. Unit costs are likely to be low when yields are high, and vice versa. Average costs from samples of farms typically vary among regions or between farms of different sizes or on different types of soil. Thus, even when accurate cost of production data are available (and it is difficult and expensive to obtain such data), administrators are left with the task of deciding where within the array of calculated costs one should establish the support price. A support price that will barely cover costs on some farms will produce generous profits on others. The problem of deciding just whose costs to cover is, of course, not unique to this method of establishing support prices. The equivalent decision with an index-based pricing formula is to decide at what level of parity to establish the support price, for example, at 70, 80, or 90 percent of the parity price. In all cases, judgment is required in deciding the appropriate figure to use.

Congressionally Mandated Support Prices

Disenchantment with formula pricing has led Congress in some instances to give the secretary of agriculture discretion in determining the level of support or to specify minimum support levels in legislation. Support levels determined in this way, as pointed out earlier, are usually the result of political compromises worked out between senior members of the Senate and House agricultural committees. Such prices are likely to be strongly influenced by economic conditions prevailing at the time new legislation is considered. If the outlook is optimistic, Congress may raise support prices, while if exports are declining and government support costs are high, Congress may reduce them.

Designating support prices four or five years in advance is a risky business. Economic conditions may change and the resulting support prices may turn out to be too high or too low. Overpricing will lead to the loss of markets and/or to excessive government costs. If inflation accelerates and demand rises, the mandated support prices may turn out to be irrelevant or so low as to provide no benefits to farmers.

In recent years Congress has mandated two support levels for such commodities as wheat, corn, and cotton—a target price and a loan rate. Target prices have no bearing on market prices; their sole function is to guarantee farmers a minimum return. They simply trigger income or deficiency payments to farmers. This occurs whenever the average market price falls below the target price. The loan rate does not necessarily determine market prices, but tends to put a floor under such prices. This is the price at which an eligible farmer can take out a price-support loan. The loan need not be repaid (hence it is called a nonrecourse loan), but the farmer has the option of doing so. If average market prices rise above the loan rate, the farmer may sell the stored commodities and repay the loan, but if market prices remain depressed, the farmer will keep the money, and the government will take title to the commodities pledged as security for the loan.

Market prices may dip below loan rates when crops are large and storage space is limited. This also can occur if substantial numbers of farmers fail to qualify for price-support loans. To be eligible for price-support loans (and government payments) farmers may be required to divert or set aside (keep idle) a minimum proportion of their base acreage. Some may elect not to do so and, consequently, must sell their commodities for whatever they will bring.

Market prices also can fall below price-support loan rates if the government releases a sufficient volume of commodities from storage. This was done in the mid-1980s by offering farmers payment-in-kind (PIK) certificates for idling land and as a substitute for cash payments to bridge the gap between target prices and loan rates. The certificates represented claims on government-held stocks. Surplus commodities acquired with PIK certificates could be sold but could not be recycled under price-support loans. Partly as a result of such sales, corn prices for the 1986/87 season averaged well below price-support loan rates.

Loan rates under the Food Security Act of 1985 were established at levels designed to make U.S. farm products competitive on world markets; target prices were fixed at a level designed to sustain farm incomes. The difference between these two prices determined the maximum level of deficiency payments. The payment per unit of product was less than this difference whenever the market price rose above the loan rate.

The relative levels of the parity price, the target price, the loan rate, and the market-clearing or equilibrium price are shown schematically for a hypothetical commodity (X) in Figure 4.1. The hypothetical demand and supply curves for commodity X illustrate how the gap between production (determined by the supply curve) and consumption (determined by the demand curve) would change if support levels were raised or lowered. The equilibrium or market clearing price is assumed to be $2.20 per unit. At any price above this level the government will be forced to accumulate surplus stocks and/or make payments to farmers.

The relative price levels illustrated in Figure 4.1 are representative of those prevailing for the major supported commodities in the mid-1980s. Average market prices for grains and cotton during that period were typically less than 50 percent of parity prices. Target prices at that time were well below parity prices but still above market-clearing or equilibrium prices. For some commodities, the price-support loan rate was below the equilibrium price, but in Figure 4.1 the loan rate is shown to be above that price; however, a shift in demand to the right, perhaps resulting from an increase in exports, might move the equilibrium price

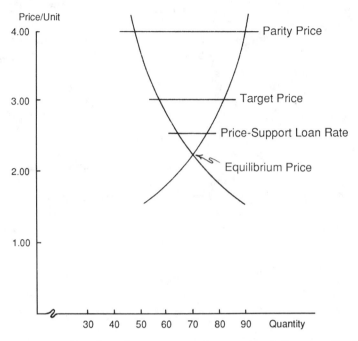

Figure 4.1   Hypothetical parity price and support levels for commodity X.

above the loan rate. The equilibrium price would have to rise to the target price or above to eliminate government payments to farmers.

METHODS OF SUPPORT

Direct costs to consumers and to the government of supporting farm prices above equilibrium levels will depend on the methods adopted to make supports effective as well as on the level of support. Because the slopes (or elasticities) of demand and supply curves differ between commodities, the optimum support method will not be the same for all commodities. Under some circumstances, a combination of support methods may be appropriate. As pointed out earlier, the simplest method of supporting domestic prices is to restrict imports, but this is feasible only if domestic consumption exceeds production at the support price. If production exceeds what can be sold at the support price, the most popular alternative from the point of view of farmers is to subsidize consumption or exports and, thus, eliminate the surplus. This is unlikely to be a viable option, however, if markets are weak and other countries match whatever subsidies are being offered. If surpluses persist, the principal options are: first, to purchase and store excess production; second, to let market prices fall to whatever level is necessary to clear the market and then make deficiency payments to producers; and third, to restrict production to what can be sold at the support price.

Government Purchases

The magnitude of government purchases required to maintain minimum guaranteed prices is illustrated in Figure 4.2. The support price is designated as P_s on the vertical axis. At that price, according to the supply schedule, producers will be willing to offer Q_2 units for sale; however, as the demand schedule indicates, consumers will be willing to purchase only Q_1 units at the support price. Thus, the support price can be maintained only by withholding Q_2 minus Q_1 units from the market. Producers will obtain gross returns equivalent to P_s multiplied by Q_2. Government expenditures will then account for the difference between what consumers spend (P_saQ_10) and what farmers receive (P_sbQ_20). If

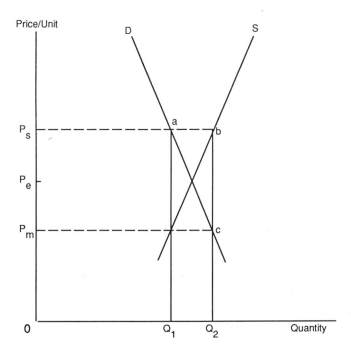

Figure 4.2 Government and consumer costs of supporting prices above equilibrium.

the government decides to hold the surpluses for possible future use, it will incur additional storage and handling costs. The alternative is to destroy whatever surpluses are acquired or to find a secondary market where the surpluses can be sold or "dumped" without undercutting the internal market price.

Deficiency Payments

An alternative method of support is to make up the difference between the market-clearing price and the support or guaranteed price with a check from the government. Because the support level is assumed to be above the equilibrium price, production will exceed the equilibrium quantity and, consequently, the market-clearing price will fall below the long-run equilibrium price. Thus, under a deficiency payment scheme, consumers will benefit from low market prices. This method of support also enables the government to avoid storing and handling surplus commodities.

The economic effects of an unlimited deficiency payment program (that is, one in which no limits are imposed either on production or total payments to producers) can be illustrated by referring again to Figure 4.2. Assume the guaranteed price to producers is P_s. At the guaranteed price (P_s) production will be Q_2, the same as with a government purchase program. Under a deficiency payment program, the total quantity produced will be sold, thus depressing the market price to P_m. This is the price at which the quantity produced at P_s will be consumed. Thus, there are no surpluses, but the government must pay an amount equivalent to the price gap (P_s minus P_m) multiplied by the total quantity produced (Q_2). Consumers obtain a larger quantity at a lower price than they would under a government purchase program; however, they may pay more in taxes, depending on how government payments are financed. The market value of the commodities purchased by consumers is represented by the rectangle P_mcQ_20. The gross revenue of producers is equal to the rectangle represented by P_sbQ_20. Government payments make up the difference, represented by the rectangle P_sbcP_m.

The cost to the government of an unlimited deficiency payment program depends on the level of support in relation to the equilibrium price and the slopes of the demand and supply curves. Costs are likely to be high if: (1) the guaranteed price is substantially above the equilibrium price; (2) the supply curve is relatively flat which implies that small increases in the guaranteed price will result in relatively large increases in output; and (3) the demand curve is relatively steep (implying a low price elasticity of demand). Under such circumstances, the gap between the guaranteed and market-clearing prices will be very large. A low level of support combined with an inelastic supply curve will result in relatively low government costs. When analyzing the consequences of a deficiency payment program, it is important to keep in mind that the total revenue obtained by farmers will be the same regardless of how much consumers pay directly and how much they pay indirectly in taxes. The slope of the demand curve determines how expenditures will be divided between consumers and the government. The flatter the demand schedule, the more consumers will pay, and the less the government will have to contribute in the form of deficiency payments.

The slope of the demand schedule also determines whether it will be cheaper for the government to make deficiency payments to producers or to purchase surpluses, assuming the same support level is to be maintained. As pointed out previously, production will be the same as long as the level of support remains the same. The slope of the supply curve influences total production and consequently the absolute level of government costs, but not *relative* costs.[3] Relative costs are determined solely by the slope of the demand curve. If demand is inelastic (between 0 and −1.0), it will be cheaper for the government to purchase the surplus than to make deficiency payments. If demand is price elastic (a larger number than -1.0 in absolute value), it will cost the government less to make deficiency payments.

The relative costs of government purchases and deficiency payments for a hypothetical commodity are illustrated in Figure 4.3. Because the demand curve is relatively flat, the gap between P_s and P_m is not large. Deficiency payments are represented by the horizontal rectangle P_sbcP_m. The cost to the government of buying surpluses to maintain the price at P_s is represented by the vertical rectangle abQ_2Q_1. The vertical rectangle is larger than the horizontal rectangle, thus indicating that a government purchase and storage program will cost more than a deficiency payment program. For most agricultural commodities, demand is price inelastic; consequently, government purchases are likely to be a less expensive method of supporting prices. Of course, consumers will have to pay more for a smaller quantity consumed.

The government's liability for deficiency payments can be limited by paying producers for only a certain quantity of output or by imposing a ceiling on the amount of money that will be paid to large producers. Each producer may be allocated a quota or a share of total output on which payments will be made (Ritson, p. 371). When payments are restricted in this way, the marginal price for each unit produced in excess of the quota is the market-clearing price (P_m in Figure 4.3). The quota price, including the payment, remains at P_s, but this price no

---

[3]The flatter (or more elastic) the supply curve, the higher government costs will be, regardless of the support method adopted.

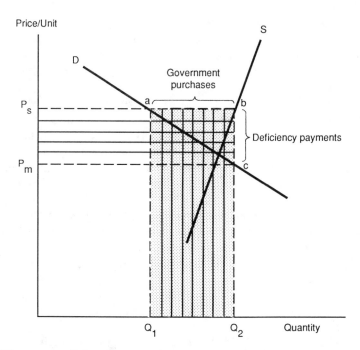

Figure 4.3   Relative cost to the government of deficiency payments and government purchases to maintain the same level of support.

longer determines production. Farmers will be less likely to increase output at the lower market-clearing or over-quota price than at the guaranteed price. For this reason, total production is likely to be less with a deficiency payment program constrained by a quota than with an unrestricted payment program.

The total cost of a deficiency payment program also can be limited by imposing a ceiling on the amount paid to any one producer.[4] If payments are unrestricted, the amount each farmer receives is proportional to his or her sales. Payments will be less unequally distributed if a ceiling is imposed on payments per farm. On grounds of equity, one can make a persuasive case for restricting the amount of money paid to operators of very large farms, but it is difficult to prevent such farms from circumventing the intent of the law. This can be done by subdividing farms to qualify for payments or by making several members of the family separate owners for the purpose of collecting deficiency payments.

A more equitable distribution of payments can be achieved by imposing an upper limit on payments per farm, but not without running

[4]Payment limitations of this type have been in effect in the United States since 1970.

the risk of undermining incentives to limit output. Deficiency payments have been used in recent years as an incentive to encourage participation in voluntary supply adjustment programs. Large producers will have little incentive to participate in supply control programs if they cannot qualify for payments. The effectiveness of such programs in limiting total output will be reduced if large producers elect not to participate. Thus, there may be a conflict between restricting payments to avoid pyramiding benefits on large farms and achieving supply control objectives.

The problems of administering an unlimited deficiency payment program are likely to be somewhat more complex than those involved in carrying out a government purchase or storage program. Under an unlimited deficiency-payment program, there is a built-in incentive for producers to inflate their sales so they can qualify for larger payments. Buyers may collude with farmers to issue fraudulent receipts. Commodities also may be sold several times to qualify for payments. For example, farmer A could sell his grain to farmer B even though he planned to feed what grain he produced to his own cattle or hogs; farmer B could then sell his grain to farmer A. Both could produce receipts from the sale of grain, thus enabling them to obtain payments. There is likely to be less fraud in making payments on milk and other commodities that are sold directly to handlers for processing. It is relatively easy to check receipts for commodities that are sold to a few handlers or established buyers.

One method of avoiding the problem of inflated sales receipts is to base deficiency payments on an estimate of *production* on each farm rather than on total *sales*. This might be difficult to do for livestock products, but it works reasonably well for crops. Deficiency payments can be calculated for each farm by multiplying a uniform payment rate per unit of product (for example, per bushel or per pound) by an average yield estimated for each farm. Total payments are then determined by multiplying the payment rate per acre by the maximum number of acres which the farmer is allowed to plant. In this way, cash grain producers and those who feed grain on the farm can be treated equally without forcing the latter to sell their grain.

One of the obvious advantages of supporting agriculture by using deficiency payments is that it tends to keep food prices relatively low. This will be an advantage to consumers provided they do not have to pay more money in taxes to cover the cost of deficiency payments. Whether consumers gain depends on how the payments are financed. If the additional revenue is obtained by imposing sales taxes on nonfarm products, low-income consumers are unlikely to be net winners. On the other hand, if the payments are financed by raising income taxes, especially if they are added to the taxes imposed on upper-income groups, the poor will come out ahead. At some point along the income scale, the additional tax burden will exceed the savings from lower food costs. Just where this will occur depends on the tax rates and how much of the lower-cost foods each family purchases.[5]

A deficiency payment program is preferable to a high loan rate when one of the objectives is to avoid losing markets. This is particularly important for products faced with close substitutes, such as cotton, or those which must compete with exports from other nations. One of the reasons for introducing target prices and deficiency payments for grains and cotton in the United States in the 1970s was to make it politically acceptable to reduce price-support loan rates. By establishing two support prices—one price for farmers and another price for buyers—agricultural incomes can be maintained without sacrificing sales.

From the point of view of producers, the principal objection to deficiency payments is that the subsidies paid to them are highly visible. Although the total cost to society of supporting prices by means of deficiency payments is no higher than with alternative support methods (taking account of food costs as well as public costs), appropriations for deficiency payments are readily identifiable in government budget figures and may become the target of public criticism. Moreover, the public image of farmers is not improved if they are placed in the position of receiving government checks, and sometimes very large ones. The combination of high public costs and/or the publicity given to farmers who receive large payments is likely to make a support program based on deficiency payments more vulnerable than one based on disguised methods of raising prices. Opposition to large payments may force the government to restrict payments or to impose controls on output so as to raise the market price and, thereby, reduce treasury costs.

Under a deficiency payment program, surpluses will be sold rather than stored by the government. This means that total carryover or reserve stocks are likely to be smaller if prices are supported solely by making deficiency payments to producers. Consumers will not be as well protected against a price increase if there is a shortfall in production or demand suddenly increases. Farmers and private storage operators, however, will have a greater incentive to store part of the crop following years of good harvests in anticipation of higher prices when supplies are short. The amplitude of price fluctuations may be greater with a deficiency payment program than with a government storage program. To help stabilize prices, the government may come under pressure to

[5]For an analysis of the effects on different income classes of a deficiency payment program confined to livestock products, see Sisler, pp. 29–32.

augment a deficiency payment program with some sort of reserve scheme.

Limiting Supply

A third method of making supports effective is to limit output or sales to what consumers will purchase at the support price. If production were restricted to Q_1 (Figure 4.2), there would be no need for government purchases or deficiency payments. The most common method of attempting to restrict agricultural output is to impose acreage allotments or to pay farmers for keeping land idle. Destruction of commodities once they have been produced is highly unpopular; consequently, this is not considered by most governments to be a viable policy option. In emergency situations, however, this may be done. As noted earlier, young pigs were killed and cotton was plowed under in the United States in the early 1930s. Brazil also has destroyed coffee from time to time.

A sales quota applied to each farm would be the least-cost method of supporting prices if such quotas could be enforced. Certificates authorizing sales might be distributed to producers with the requirement that each unit sold be accompanied by a certificate. The records of buyers would have to be audited to make sure they purchase no more from a farmer than he or she is authorized to sell. Any government seeking to control sales in this way obviously would encounter difficult political and administrative problems in deciding how many certificates should be issued and how these should be allocated among farmers. Under a sales-quota scheme, no public costs would be incurred in buying or storing commodities or in making deficiency payments to producers, although administrative costs could be quite high.

Whether producers collectively would gain from a sales quota depends on the price elasticity of demand and on how much costs can be reduced by curtailing output. If the demand for a commodity is price inelastic, farmers will obtain more total revenue by selling less. If demand is price elastic, producers as a group will gain only if costs decline by more than the loss in total revenue. Sales quotas or production control programs are most likely to benefit producers of commodities with an inelastic demand. In the short run, the demand for most agricultural commodities is price inelastic, but there are exceptions. The demand for broilers and some kinds of fruit, for example, may be elastic. This also may be true in the longer run for agricultural commodities faced with competition from substitutes such as cotton, jute, and sugar.

Farmers who would like to expand or bring a son or daughter into the business generally oppose sales quotas. In most cases, quotas have been allocated among farms on the basis of past records of production or sales. If no provision is made for augmenting quotas for those seeking to expand, historical patterns of production will be frozen. This can be avoided by permitting farmers to buy and sell quotas or annual marketing certificates. Farmers seeking to expand could then purchase sufficient quotas or certificates to cover their additional output. Those planning to retire from agriculture presumably would be willing to sell their quotas. Thus, production would eventually shift to farms in the more favored areas or those with lower costs. Such farms are the ones most likely to be successful bidders for whatever quotas or certificates are offered for sale. Returns from higher prices that might result from limiting sales would most likely be capitalized into the value of certificates or quotas, thus raising selling costs by an equivalent amount for new or expanding producers. If quotas could be freely bought and sold, the original owners of quotas would be the principal winners.

Under a quota scheme, income is transferred directly from buyers to producers through higher prices. Representatives of consumers fear that giving producers the right to limit sales would enable them to extract "monopoly profits" and, hence, to exploit consumers.

Any attempt to limit production or sales is likely to be opposed by those supplying inputs to farmers as well as those processing or handling farm products. Profits in agribusiness are strongly influenced by the volume of sales and, consequently, firms supplying services to farmers often join with consumer groups in blocking attempts to restrict sales.

In practice, the U.S. has found it more acceptable to limit the acreage planted to certain supported crops than to restrict sales.[6] This has been done either by imposing compulsory acreage allotments or by offering farmers compensation for keeping land idle. Under a compulsory allotment program, bases for specific crops such as wheat or cotton are allocated to individual farms. Such bases traditionally have been tied to the farm's previous history of production. If an allotment program is in effect, only those farmers with allotments can plant certain crops. Farmers must pay substantial penalties if they plant more than the allotted acreage. The "leftover" acreage, however, can be planted to any

---

[6]Tobacco is an important exception. Owing to higher yields, the acreage control program became progressively less effective in the 1960s and 1970s. Moreover, quality deteriorated as producers sought to raise yields on their restricted acreage. Ultimately, producers were persuaded to accept poundage quotas. This gives tobacco growers an incentive to improve quality, because better grades bring substantially higher prices. Growers now seek to maximize gross revenue rather than yields.

uncontrolled crop. In contrast, under a land set-aside program, cropland cannot be diverted to another crop; it must be kept idle.

The major reason for restricting land rather than such inputs as fertilizer or credit is that land use can be policed much more effectively. The acreage planted to a particular crop can be observed over a period of several months. Land use can be checked easily with maps and aerial photographs. Nonland inputs are much more difficult to measure and control.

Acreage allotment programs are often ineffective in reducing total output. This is the result of what is frequently referred to in Washington as "slippage" (Ericksen and Collins, p. 172). An acreage control program will not be very effective as a supply control measure if farmers inflate their base or raise yields on the acreage that remains in production. Political pressure from farmers combined with weak local administration contributes to inflating the base for establishing allotments. Farmers tend to overestimate how much land they planted to a particular crop in the past. Sometimes farmers will increase plantings in anticipation of an allotment program. If the base is inflated, the actual acreage planted in a given year, even with a substantial cut in the allotment, may still produce surpluses. Farmers also will keep the highest-yielding land in allotment crops and retire or divert the poorer land to other crops. By using more fertilizer, they will be able to offset at least a part of the effect of reduced acreage. It is possible to compensate for an inflated base and higher yields by imposing additional cuts in the allotment, but often there is political resistance to doing so.

Changes in land use and the consolidation of farms may be retarded if allotments are based on historical patterns of production. Low-cost producers will be prohibited from expanding or may be able to do so only at substantial cost (if allotments can be purchased from other farmers). Interregional shifts in production that could lead to increases in efficiency may be retarded. This was one of the consequences of the cotton allotment program in the 1930s.

Under the acreage allotment programs that were in effect during the 1930s and again in the late 1940s and early 1950s, substantial areas of land were diverted from crops subject to allotments such as cotton, wheat, and corn to nonallotment crops such as barley, grain sorghum, and soybeans. This resulted in increased production and lower prices for nonallotment crops. Understandably, producers who obtained most of their income from such crops were annoyed. From their point of view, no useful purpose was served by shifting surpluses from one group of commodities to another.

Beginning in the 1960s, compulsory acreage allotments were replaced by voluntary set-aside programs for most supported crops including wheat, corn, and cotton. This was done partly to give farmers greater freedom of choice in deciding whether or not to expand and partly to avoid the diverted acreage problem. By making supply control programs voluntary, the Department of Agriculture also was relieved of the requirement that it conduct a referendum among producers of crops subject to allotments.[7] A two-thirds vote of approval among producers was required before a compulsory acreage control program could be put into effect. It was not always possible to obtain a two-thirds majority in favor of allotments. In addition, the diverted acreage problem was solved by paying farmers to keep land idle. Under voluntary land-retirement or set-aside programs, the land taken out of production must be kept idle; it cannot be planted to another crop.

A voluntary land-retirement program costs more than a compulsory allotment program because farmers must be paid to keep land idle. Payments per acre must be high enough to attract participation. Experience during the 1950s and 1960s demonstrated that payments equivalent to 50 percent or more of the gross value of output per acre are required to induce farmers to set aside acreage (Robinson, p. 25). To attract participation, the government must pay at least as much as the farmer would have earned if he or she had planted the additional acreage. The marginal returns from planting this additional acreage are likely to be quite high for farmers who have underutilized equipment and family labor. For this reason, many farmers will prefer to plant the additional acreage rather than rent it to the government.

Voluntary acreage-reduction or set-aside programs have proved to be the most politically acceptable (or the least unacceptable) of all supply management programs in the United States. Such programs have been continued under both Democratic and Republican administrations. Farmers like the flexibility of participating or not participating, depending on weather conditions prevailing at planting time and price prospects. It is looked upon as an alternative enterprise, that is, "farming the government."

Experience has demonstrated that if the government is prepared to make payments sufficiently attractive to farmers, enough land can be idled to achieve the required adjustments in production. Costs are high, but retiring land is likely to be less expensive than acquiring surplus stocks and then trying to dispose of them. Besides taxpayers, the prin-

---

[7]From the beginning, Congress mandated that a referendum be conducted among all allotment holders and that a two-thirds vote of approval be obtained before a compulsory allotment program could be put into effect. Many producers failed to vote, but generally producers of cotton, tobacco, rice, and peanuts who participated in the referendum voted in favor of allotments. This was less likely to be true of wheat and corn producers. Many corn farmers feed most of what they produce to their own livestock. They tend to vote against allotments.

cipal losers from idling acreage are agribusiness firms, particularly those providing crop inputs such as fertilizer, seed, and herbicides.

CONCLUSIONS

Inequities among farmers inevitably arise because of political decisions made to support the prices of some farm products but not others. Differences in support levels also result in favoring some producers relative to others. No method of establishing support prices is equally "fair" to all producers.

Economic forces have compelled Congress to lower the real level of support prices (that is, support prices adjusted for inflation) for nearly all farm products over the past forty years. Improvements in agricultural technology have made it impossible for farmers or the government to live with the consequences of maintaining high support prices. Loan rates and government purchase prices have been reduced in an attempt to preserve markets and to discourage overproduction; however, a substantial degree of overpricing has persisted, especially for commodities with effective supply controls such as tobacco. The degree of overpricing (relative to long-run equilibrium or free-market prices) varies greatly among commodities.

Prices can be maintained above equilibrium by any one or a combination of support methods including import restrictions, supply controls, a government purchase and storage program, or deficiency payments. The U.S. government has made use of all these methods of supporting prices over the past fifty years.

No one support method is ideal for all commodities and all situations. In general, those methods that are more effective in holding down government costs, such as compulsory supply controls, are least acceptable to farmers and to agribusiness firms. Those that are more acceptable to farmers, such as voluntary land retirement schemes or deficiency payments, tend to be more costly to taxpayers.

DISCUSSION QUESTIONS

4.1. What would be the consequences of reverting to the old parity formula as a basis for establishing support prices for farm products?

4.2. What would be the effect on consumer food costs, returns to farmers and treasury or government costs of: (1) raising target prices without changing price-support loan rates or (2) raising loan rates without changing target prices?

4.3.   Under what conditions will it be less costly to the government to support farm incomes by making deficiency payments to producers rather than buying and storing surplus commodities at the support price? What are the principal criticisms of relying on deficiency payments to support farm incomes?

4.4.   Why has Congress opted for relatively costly voluntary set-aside programs to cope with surplus capacity rather than less costly compulsory acreage allotments?

4.5.   Assume a sales quota scheme has been proposed for commodity X. Under what conditions is such a scheme likely to enhance returns to producers of commodity X? If quotas can be bought and sold, how are any gains likely to be distributed among producers? Who or what groups might be expected to oppose the proposed quota scheme?

REFERENCES

ERICKSEN, MILTON H., and KEITH COLLINS, "Effectiveness of Acreage Reduction Programs," *Agricultural-Food Policy Review: Commodity Program Perspectives,* Agricultural Economic Report No. 530. Washington, D.C.: Economic Research Service, 1985.

RITSON, CHRISTOPHER, *Agricultural Economics—Principles and Policy.* Boulder: Westview Press, 1977.

ROBINSON, K.L., "Cost and Effectiveness of Recent Government Land Retirement Programs in the United States," *Journal of Farm Economics* 48(1966), 22-30.

TOMEK, W.G., and K.L. ROBINSON, *Agricultural Product Prices,* 2nd ed. Ithaca, N.Y.: Cornell University Press, 1981.

SISLER, D.G., *Direct Payments as a Policy Tool in the Feed Grain Livestock Sector,* Agricultural Experiment Station Bulletin 1011. Ithaca, N.Y.: Cornell University, 1966.

U.S. DEPARTMENT OF AGRICULTURE, *Agricultural Prices* (December 31). Washington, D.C.: National Agricultural Statistics Service, 1987.

5

Economic Consequences of Supporting Farm Prices

The consequences of supporting agricultural prices depend on the commodities supported, the level of support, and the methods used to make supports effective. Just how much producers have gained or consumers have had to pay in the form of increased prices or higher government costs is difficult to estimate precisely. Gains and losses vary greatly among commodities and from year to year, depending on underlying economic conditions, the size of the harvest, and support levels. While precise estimates of benefits and costs cannot be obtained, it is possible to identify the major effects of programs designed to enhance farm prices. In this chapter, the consequences of the somewhat unique set of support policies that the U.S. has adopted and maintained over the past fifty years are summarized.

The primary objective of attempting to identify winners and losers of U.S. support programs is to provide a guide to thinking about the consequences of pricing policies. A secondary objective is to help answer the kinds of questions raised by editorial writers, TV commentators, and those who have the responsibility of making policy decisions. They want to know how much farm incomes might fall in the absence of support programs, whether large farms benefit disproportionately from government payments, how much price supports have cost consumers, and why current farm programs are so expensive. The next section describes the effects of U.S. support programs on the level and distribution of income within agriculture. Subsequent sections deal with the effect of support programs on output and efficiency, food prices, and government costs.[1]

EFFECTS ON RETURNS TO FARMERS

Support programs can be used successfully to transfer income from the nonfarm sector to agriculture by raising prices and thus extracting more money directly from consumers or by making payments from the treasury. The amount of income transferred directly from consumers to farmers is especially difficult to estimate, because no one can be sure what prices would have been in the absence of government intervention. Income transfers in the form of direct government payments can be determined much more precisely, but not all the benefits to farmers from government intervention take this form. Price-support loans and purchases also help to raise farm incomes; however, the long-run benefits to farmers may be less than the short-run effects of government acquisitions. Some of the commodities acquired may eventually be resold, thereby depressing returns to farmers at a later date. The short-run effects of government intervention on farm prices and incomes are first described. This is followed by an assessment of the longer-run consequences.

In most years since the early 1950s, U.S. support programs have held the prices of grains, cotton, milk, peanuts, tobacco, and a few other commodities above where they otherwise might have been. Prices have been raised more for commodities with effective supply-control measures, such as tobacco and peanuts, than for commodities with weak controls or no constraints on production, such as soybeans and milk. For most supported commodities, the degree of price enhancement has been modest. In recent years support programs have raised average U.S. farm prices by no more than 10 to 20 percent.[2] This is substantially less than the degree of price enhancement that prevailed in Japan and the

---

[1]Economists sometimes refer to the net social cost of support programs. The concept of social cost (or welfare losses) is useful in ranking alternative support methods. It is not a concept that is understood by most elected representatives or commonly used in making policy decisions. For those interested in the more technical aspects of policy analysis, a brief appendix is included at the end of this chapter. The effects of two alternative support methods on consumer and producer surplus and net social costs are described to illustrate the principles involved and how the concept of net social cost may be used to rank alternative support methods.

[2]In a study prepared for the Trilateral Commission, D. Gale Johnson estimated the increase in value of U.S. farm products at domestic prices over world prices at 12 percent in 1979/80 and 19.8 percent in 1982/83 (Johnson, Hemmi, and Lardinois, pp. 76–77).

European Economic Community during the late 1970s and early 1980s (Johnson, Hemmi, and Lardinois, p. 20; Miller, pp. 27–31).

Gains from price-support programs in the United States have been unequally distributed among regions and farms because supports have been tied to particular commodities. Most of the direct or "first-round" benefits of higher prices have gone to farmers producing grains, cotton, tobacco, peanuts, milk, and sugar. Regionally, the benefits have been concentrated in the Great Plains, the South, and the Midwest where supported crops account for a high proportion of the cash receipts of farmers. Government payments, either for retiring land or for bridging the gap between target prices and market prices or loan rates, also have gone mainly to producers of wheat, cotton, corn, and rice.

Within agriculture, the benefits of higher commodity prices have been distributed roughly in proportion to sales. This is not quite true, however, for government payments. Some of the largest farms that produce wheat, corn, cotton, or rice may elect not to participate in the voluntary set-aside program offered in a particular year. As a result, they do not qualify for price-support loans and/or government payments. Farm operators may decide to forego benefits because of payment limitations or because they find it uneconomic to keep a substantial proportion of their acreage idle.[3] For example, if a farmer wanted to double-crop wheat and soybeans, he or she might elect not to participate in the wheat program so as to be able to plant more soybeans.

If the benefits of support programs were distributed strictly in proportion to sales, the largest 14 percent of all farms (those with sales of $100,000 or more in 1985) would obtain approximately three quarters of the total benefits (Table 5.1). Farms with gross annual sales of less than $40,000, the sales category which accounted for 72 percent of all farms in 1985, would receive only 10 percent of the total benefits. Actual benefits probably are distributed somewhat less unequally than these figures imply because many of the farms with gross sales exceeding $100,000 per year produce commodities such as beef, pork, broilers, fruits, and vegetables, which are not supported.

Government payments are less unequally distributed than gross sales. Farms with gross sales of $500,000 or more accounted for 32 percent of all farm product sales in 1985 but only 13 percent of government payments in that year (Table 5.1). Farms in the $100,000 to $500,000

---

[3]In the early 1980s, payments were limited to $50,000 per farm. Payment limitations at that time applied to price-support and acreage-diversion payments (if offered), but not to price-support loans or payments in the form of commodities offered in 1983 under the payment-in-kind program. Payments made under the so-called "marketing loan program," included as one of the options authorized by the Food Security Act of 1985, also are exempt from the $50,000 payment limitation.

TABLE 5.1   Distribution of Farms, Gross Cash Farm Income, and Government Payments by Sales Classes, 1985

Sales Category (dollars/farm)	Percent of Farms	Percent of Gross Cash Farm Income	Percent of Government Payments
Less than $40,000	72	10	10
$40,000 to $100,000	14	16	22
$100,000 to $500,000	13	42	55
Over $500,000	1	32	13
Total	100	100	100

SOURCE: USDA, 1986, pp. 42, 45, and 46.

sales category, however, received 55 percent of government payments, a substantially higher percentage than their proportion of total sales. The under-$40,000 sales category received about the same percentage of government payments as gross farm receipts in 1985. Payments made to large farms obviously are much greater than those made to small farms, but, proportionately, government payments have added as much or more to the incomes of medium- and small-scale farms as to the very large farms. This was true in 1985, and apparently in earlier years as well (Browning and Reinsel).

Initial gains to farmers from raising or supporting prices tend to diminish with the passage of time. This occurs for two reasons: First, markets are lost because of overpricing; and second, benefits become embedded in the sale price of farms. Cotton was one of the early losers from overpricing because it led to increased use of synthetic fibers (Paarlberg, p. 1165). More recently, U.S. tobacco farmers have been displaced from world markets by lower-priced tobacco offered by competing exporters. U.S. imports of tobacco also have risen because foreign supplies are cheaper. U.S. support programs have encouraged other countries to produce more wheat, cotton, rice, and soybeans as well as tobacco. In response to these developments, Congress has found it necessary to reduce price-support loan rates. High support prices cannot be sustained in the face of rising production abroad and the threatened loss of markets. Initial gains tend to be eroded because of lost sales and/or forced reductions in support prices.

Long-run net returns to farmers will be no higher with support programs than without such programs if the price of farms rises by an amount that reflects the difference in anticipated returns. Capitalizing the value of program benefits raises production costs for new entrants or those buying additional land. As a result, succeeding generations of farmers will gain very little from government efforts to raise prices. Most of the benefits accrue to original owners of farms with allotments or the right to receive payments. The capitalization of benefits is observable wherever or whenever the right to receive such benefits is attached to a particular piece of property. The willingness of individuals to pay for the privilege of obtaining higher returns explains why taxi medallions (the right to operate a taxi) command such high prices in New York City. It also explains why tobacco allotments are so valuable. Farms with allotments sell for much higher prices than those in the same area without allotments. In the late 1970s and early 1980s, renters were willing to pay as much as 30 percent of the support price for the opportunity to grow tobacco (Sumner and Alston, p. 15).

EFFECTS ON AGRICULTURAL OUTPUT AND EFFICIENCY

U.S. support programs have had a mixed effect on agricultural output and efficiency. Somewhat higher and more stable prices have given farmers an incentive to use more fertilizer on supported crops and also have made lenders more willing to finance the expansion plans of successful farm operators. Acreage control programs have given farmers an additional incentive to raise yields. But some of the output-increasing effects of support programs have been neutralized by paying farmers to keep land idle. The mixed signals have resulted in less than optimum use of resources—farmers have purchased more yield-increasing inputs than would have been justified under free-market conditions but have underutilized land. The net result probably has been to raise average costs of production.

Voluntary land retirement programs and the dairy buy-out program have succeeded in reducing output or at least holding production below where it otherwise might have been. Increases in yields per acre and production per cow have offset a substantial part of the effect of reduced acreage and fewer cows. Nonparticipants in the voluntary programs offered in recent years have in some cases increased the area planted to supported crops. The long-term land retirement programs adopted during the 1950s and 1960s did little to reduce total output because landowners rented mainly low-yielding or marginal land to the government. Some of the land signed up was already on its way out of production. A Department of Agriculture historian summarizes the effects of U.S. supply reduction programs on farm output as follows:

> Acreage control programs over the past half century have served more to slow the increase in production than truly keep it in check. None of the different methods tried has been without problems. Voluntary acreage reduction programs..., while generally reducing acreage to the desired

level,...have failed to cut production enough to balance supply and demand. Participants have responded to voluntary programs by farming their permitted acreage more intensively. Nonparticipants have planted without restriction... (Bowers, p. 45).

Historically-based allotment and set-aside programs have retarded regional shifts in production (at least during certain periods) that might have led to greater efficiency. In the absence of cotton allotments, for example, production undoubtedly would have expanded more rapidly in low-cost areas of the West during the 1930s and 1950s. Tobacco and peanut allotments also have prevented production from shifting to lower-cost farms as rapidly as might otherwise have been the case. Mechanization of tobacco production probably was retarded by small farm allotments, although when mechanization became feasible the program was modified to allow those who wanted to expand to purchase or rent allotments from others.

The potential adverse effects of allotment and set-aside programs tied to historical bases have been minimized by shifting to voluntary programs and by freeing farmers from controls at various times. Low-cost producers have had ample opportunity to increase production of wheat, corn, and cotton in recent years. Many did so when prices rose during the 1970s and set-aside programs were abandoned. The only commodities subject to allotments without periodic breaks have been tobacco and peanuts. Losses in efficiency from freezing patterns of production and keeping acreages small have been greater for these commodities than for other supported farm products. Support programs have had little adverse effect on output and efficiency for those commodities without supply reduction programs, such as milk and soybeans.

EFFECTS ON LIVESTOCK FEEDERS AND AGRIBUSINESS FIRMS

The distribution of income between livestock feeders and producers of feed ingredients unquestionably has been influenced at times by support programs. Changes in *relative* support levels for feed grains and milk sometimes benefit milk producers and sometimes grain producers. Livestock feeders often criticize support programs because, at times, they have raised the cost of feed. In the short run, profit margins of hog producers and cattle feeders may have been depressed because of higher feed ingredient costs, but, in the long run, production tends to respond to the price of feed. If livestock production becomes less profitable, farmers cut back on the number of animals they feed. This tends to increase prices, thus offsetting the effects of higher feed costs. Long-run average profit margins for commodities like broilers, eggs, and hogs probably have been influenced relatively little by support programs; however, the prices of livestock products may have been somewhat higher and total livestock output a little lower because of reduced supplies and higher prices for feed. On a few occasions livestock feeders have benefited from the release of government-held grain stocks.

The effect of support programs on agribusiness firms has been mixed. They have benefited from increases in production induced by support programs (and the opportunity to store surplus commodities), but have been adversely affected by subsequent efforts to limit output. It is not clear whether, on balance, they have been net gainers or losers. In years when farmers have been compelled to set aside substantial areas of land to qualify for price supports and government payments, the negative impact of acreage restrictions has more than offset the beneficial effects of higher input use per acre. Suppliers of fertilizer and herbicides have been especially vulnerable to changes in set-aside requirements for wheat, cotton, and corn.

EFFECTS ON CONSUMERS

Overpricing farm products has raised the average cost of food in the United States, but only modestly. This contrasts sharply with the situation prevailing in Japan and a number of European countries, such as Norway and Switzerland, where consumers have borne a much higher proportion of the cost of supporting agriculture. The substantial cuts in price-support loan rates authorized for wheat, corn, and rice in the Food Security Act of 1985 reduced the degree of overpricing in the late 1980s relative to what it had been earlier. Under provisions of the 1985 Act, the proportion of income transferred to agriculture in the form of government payments rose relative to that obtained through higher prices.

The percentage increase in consumer food costs owing to overpricing farm products has been modest for two reasons. First, raw-product price enhancement has been limited to a relatively small group of commodities. Second, the degree of price enhancement has been modest. For many of the supported commodities such as wheat, corn, and rice, the proportionate effect on consumer food costs of higher farm prices is very small because the raw product accounts for such a small fraction of the end product which the consumer buys. With a product such as wheat, a 20 percent increase in the farm price will add only about one cent to the cost of a loaf of bread, a rise of only 1 percent to 1 1/2 percent in the retail price. The effect on consumer food costs of overpricing such commodities as wheat, corn, and rice is also small because so little of the total food budget is spent on these items. A substantial fraction of what the consumer spends on food is not affected by U.S. support programs because the raw products are not supported (for example, fruits and vegetables), or are imported.

The principal food items affected directly by support programs have been wheat, corn, dairy products, and sweeteners (sugar, corn syrup, etc.). Indirectly, higher grain prices have added to the cost of livestock products. The indirect effects of higher grain prices outweigh the direct effects, because U.S. consumers purchase nearly three times as much grain in the form of livestock products as they do in the form of bread, bagels, pizza, breakfast food, and other products derived directly from grain. Support programs have had little or no influence on the prices of fruits, vegetables, margarine, and cooking oils.

The figures presented in Table 5.2 illustrate how one can obtain a rough estimate of the impact of higher farm prices on the aggregate cost

TABLE 5.2 Estimated Effect of Eliminating Price Supports on Consumer Expenditures for Domestically Produced Food, 1981

| Major Food Expenditure Categories | Estimated Farm Value | | Estimated Consumer Savings (percent) |
	Actual (1981) (billions of dollars)	Without Supports (billions of dollars)	
Meat, poultry and eggs	39.6	37.0[a]	7
Dairy products	16.8	15.5[b]	8
Grain and bakery products	4.9	4.2	15
Fruits and vegetables	13.3	13.3	0
Miscellaneous	7.7	7.2[c]	6
Total farm value[d]	82.4	77.2	6
Marketing bill	202.1	202.1[e]	0
Total retail cost of food	284.5	279.3	2

[a]Meat, poultry, and egg prices are not supported, but the cost of these items is influenced indirectly by support programs on feed ingredients. The estimated change in costs is determined by deducting the savings in aggregate feed costs that might be achieved if supports on grains were eliminated. The average saving is assumed to be $15 per ton of feed multiplied by the total amount of grain fed to cattle, hogs, and poultry. The estimate also includes an allowance for the effects of eliminating restrictions on meat imports.
[b]Based on the assumption that prices to producers would fall by about $1.00 per cwt. of milk. The estimate also includes an allowance for the indirect effects of eliminating supports on feed grains.
[c]Includes the estimated effects of eliminating supports on sugar, peanuts, and soybean oil.
[d]Column values may not add to total due to rounding.
[e]Marketing, transportation, processing, and packaging costs are assumed to remain constant; only raw product costs are affected by the elimination of support programs.
SOURCE: USDA, 1982, p. 84.

of food and the percentage change in retail food prices. First, one must identify the supported commodities and estimate the farm value of all commodities purchased by consumers. These estimates are shown in the second column of Table 5.2. Changes in the cost of each commodity group, assuming no support programs, must then be estimated. The changes indicated in the last column are based on informed guesses as to what might have happened to raw product costs if support programs had been eliminated in the early 1980s. When combined, the figures in column three suggest that without supports, the farm value of all food of domestic origin would have declined by about 6 percent in 1981. Assuming no change in marketing and transportation costs ($202 billion in 1981), retail food expenditures in the absence of supports would have declined by only about 2 percent.

The foregoing estimates of savings to consumers should not be considered as definitive or precise, but they indicate the general order of magnitude of possible savings. Even if one assumes that farm prices would fall by another 10 percent or even 20 percent, the corresponding percentage reduction in average retail food prices would still be small (less than 5 percent).[4] The obvious conclusion is that U.S. consumers should not expect a large percentage reduction in average food prices from eliminating farm price supports.

The aggregate income transfers from consumers to farmers through price enhancement also can be estimated from Table 5.2. According to the figures in the first two columns, the total farm value of foods without supports would have been around $77 billion in 1981, $5 billion less than the value with supports. As these figures imply, even a modest tax on consumers in the form of higher raw-product prices can result in substantial direct income transfers to farmers.

Direct income transfers from consumers to farmers declined after 1985 because price-support loan rates for grains and cotton and purchase prices for surplus dairy products were reduced. The decline in direct income transfers from consumers was more than balanced by higher government payments in the late 1980s. In 1986 and 1987, such payments added substantially more to gross farm income than the amounts transferred to farmers by overpricing farm products.

---

[4]The maximum savings in percentage terms can be estimated very simply. Assume supported commodities account for 50 percent of all farm products sold, and that 30 percent of what the consumer spends for food goes to farmers. Based on these assumptions, changes in support prices would affect only 15 percent of retail food costs (50 percent supported commodities, multiplied by 30 percent farm value). Overpricing supported commodities by 20 percent would add only 3 percent to the retail cost of food (15 percent farm value of supported commodities multiplied by 20 percent).

GOVERNMENT COSTS

Total government support costs exceed the amount of income transferred to farmers because the government incurs administrative costs and must pay for storing and disposing of surplus commodities as well as making price-support loans and deficiency payments. Not all the $25.8 billion that was reported in 1987 as the cost of supporting farm prices and incomes in the preceding fiscal year went to farmers. Some of it went to agribusiness firms for storing and handling surplus grain. Other payments were made to exporting firms to make U.S. farm products competitive on world markets. Indirectly, farmers benefit from subsidized exports, but they are not the ones who receive the payments.

Net costs may be less than gross outlays for support activities. The government incurs an outlay in making price-support loans to farmers, but it may recover all or part of the initial outlays if prices subsequently rise. Net government costs depend on how long the commodities are held in storage before being sold or given away, and the price at which they are sold if commercial markets are available. If commodity prices are generally rising, the government may even profit from the sale of previously acquired commodities. This is likely to be a rare event, but it did occur when surplus commodities were sold during and immediately after World War II.

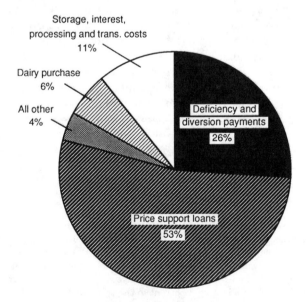

Figure 5.1   Percent of commodity credit corporation outlays by activity, fiscal 1986. (Source: USDA, 1987, p.25.)

Price-support activities are carried out by the government-owned Commodity Credit Corporation (CCC). The principal components of net CCC outlays for all price-support activities in 1986 are shown in Figure 5.1. In that year, payments to farmers and price-support loans accounted for three-quarters of net CCC outlays. Costs associated with handling and storing surplus commodities account for a high proportion of the remaining outlays.

The total cost of support activities as well as the relative importance of different cost elements varies from year to year. These costs are influenced by the size of the crop, the relationship of market prices to target prices, and whether or not programs to compensate farmers for keeping land idle are in effect. The high degree of variability in support costs is illustrated in Figure 5.2, which shows total outlays for support activities by fiscal years from 1960 through 1986 in constant (1982) dollars. Short crops and favorable market conditions led to a decline in outlays for support activities in the mid-1970s and again in the early 1980s. Thereafter, outlays rose dramatically owing to the reemergence of surpluses and the decision to rely more on deficiency payments to maintain farm incomes. Total outlays (in 1982 dollars) for support activities in

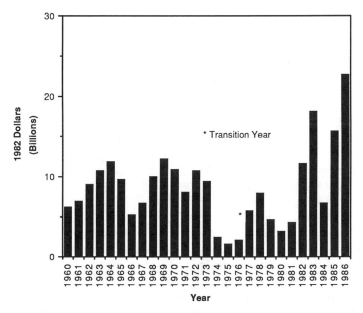

Figure 5.2 Price-support outlays in constant (1982) dollars, 1960–1986. Annual outlays by fiscal years in current dollars converted to 1982 dollars using the GNP price deflator for personal consumption expenditures. (Source: Johnson, Hemmi, and Lardinois, p. 65 for the years 1960–1975 and USDA, 1987, p. 25 for the years 1976–1986; GNP deflator from U.S. Department of Commerce, 1987.)

1986 were more than twice the average level of outlays in the 1960s and nearly four times the corresponding figure for the 1970s. Net support costs in 1986 averaged a little over $100 for every man, woman, and child in the United States. While large in aggregate value and in relation to outlays in earlier years, support costs in the mid-1980s were still relatively small in relation to the total federal budget. In 1986 and 1987, two of the peak years, they added less than 3 percent to combined government expenditures for all activities.

The open-ended commitment to support prices has made it extremely difficult to control treasury costs. The only way in which the government's liability can be significantly reduced is to lower support prices or to introduce compulsory measures to restrict production or sales. More effective payment limitations to individual farm operators also would help to reduce costs, but only marginally. Exemptions from payment limitations and loopholes in the law have enabled a few very large farms to receive checks from the government totaling more than a million dollars in some years. Closing these loopholes, however, would not have a major impact on the total cost of support activities, because most of the money goes to farmers who legitimately qualify for payments of less than $50,000 in a typical year.

CONCLUSIONS

Experience over the past forty years demonstrates that support programs can be used successfully to transfer income from the nonfarm sector of the economy to agriculture; however, the amount of money that can be transferred to agriculture by raising farm prices or making payments to farmers is subject to political constraints. Congress is constrained in its attempts to enhance farm incomes by consumers who object to paying more for food, by farmers who are strongly opposed to compulsory controls, by agribusiness firms who would like to sell more to farmers, and by taxpayers who complain about the high cost of supporting agriculture. Fewer political constraints exist in countries that must import food. Politically and technically, it is much easier to overprice commodities that are imported than those that are exported.

The distribution of benefits from U.S. support programs has been extremely unequal among farms and regions because supports and payments have been linked to particular commodities. A high proportion of the benefits has gone to those who have the most to sell or those with the largest bases or allotments. Support programs tend to reinforce existing income inequalities. This tendency can be avoided only by divorcing payments from current output.

The net benefits for succeeding generations of farmers have been limited because gains have been capitalized into the value of farmland. The original owners of farms with allotments or bases receive most of the benefits. Once benefits are incorporated in the value of farms, it becomes difficult to reduce the level of support because of the adverse effect this would have on farm incomes and land prices. Creditors, as well as those who have overpaid for farmland, acquire a vested interest in continuing support programs.

Farmers run the risk of losing markets, particularly for commodities that are exported, if support levels are maintained very far above long-run equilibrium levels. The internationalization of U.S. agriculture has made farmers more vulnerable to overpricing. High support prices encourage producers in other countries to expand and capture a larger share of world markets.

Consumers would benefit, but only marginally, from any reductions in price-support loan rates for grains and cotton or purchase prices for surplus dairy products below those already authorized in the Food Security Act of 1985. The major effect of lowering loan rates without simultaneously reducing target prices would be to increase the potential cost of deficiency payments. One of the major consequences of the 1985 Act has been to shift more of the cost of supporting agriculture from consumers to taxpayers.

DISCUSSION QUESTIONS

5.1. Who or what groups have been the principal beneficiaries of U.S. support programs?

5.2. Why have deficiency payments been somewhat less unequally distributed among farms than gross farm receipts?

5.3. What factors tend to limit long-run gains to producers from supporting farm prices?

5.4. Assume price-support loan rates and purchase prices for surplus commodities are to be raised 10 percent. How might one estimate the percentage impact on average food costs of the increase in support prices?

5.5. Why were U.S. government support costs so much higher in the mid-1980s than they had been earlier? Is it correct to assume that net CCC outlays represent the amount of income transfered directly from taxpayers to farmers?

Appendix 5-A:
Effects of Alternative Support Methods
on Consumer and Producer Surplus
and Net Social Costs

The concepts of consumer and producer surplus are employed by economists to describe how alternative support programs transfer income between consumers and producers. Net social cost is a technical term that measures the difference between changes in producer and consumer surplus (or between marginal social cost and marginal social benefit). These concepts are useful to economists, but seldom are of interest to policymakers. The latter are unlikely to be familiar with the terminology and, in any event, are more interested in the effects of farm programs on such variables as the volume of exports, consumer food costs, the magnitude of surpluses, and the federal deficit than on consumer and producer surplus.

Consumer and Producer Surplus in the Absence of Government Intervention

In the absence of government intervention, price and production will be simultaneously determined by the intersection of the demand and supply curves. The equilibrium price is identified as P_e in Figure 5.3, and the equilibrium quantity, Q_e. Consumer surplus is equal to the area under the demand curve and above the equilibrium price (the darkly-shaded area in Figure 5.3). The area under the demand curve represents the marginal utility of each additional unit consumed. The shaded area identifies the region where the marginal utility exceeds the cost of each additional unit (the equilibrium price). Technically, the demand curve assumes the marginal utility of money remains constant, a condition which is not strictly fulfilled if prices rise or fall; however, the area under a static demand schedule above the equilibrium price can be regarded as a reasonable approximation of consumer surplus.

Producer surplus is equal to the area above the supply curve and below the equilibrium price (the lightly-shaded area in Figure 5.3). The supply curve identifies the marginal cost of producing each additional unit of output. Thus, the shaded area indicates the amount by which total revenue (price × quantity) exceeds the sum of marginal costs.

At the equilibrium price, the marginal cost of the last unit sold just equals the marginal utility to consumers. When prices are at this level, there are no net social costs. With support prices held above equilibrium levels, however, there will be a net social cost, because the marginal cost of producing an additional unit (in response to the higher support price)

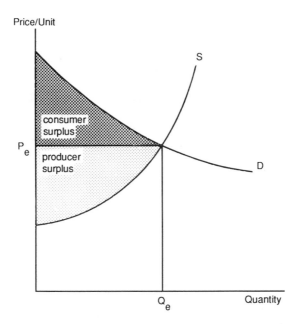

Figure 5.3   Consumer and producer surplus in the absence of government intervention.

will exceed the marginal utility of the units produced in excess of equilibrium quantities.

Changes in producer and consumer surplus and in net social cost associated with overpricing are described in the following sections. In the first section, it is assumed prices are raised by limiting supply; in the second section, it is assumed that prices to producers are maintained at the support level by deficiency payments.

Effect of Limiting Supply on Producer and Consumer Surplus

With an effective supply control program, consumer surplus will decline and producer surplus will increase. The effects are shown in Figure 5.4. By limiting output to Q_1, prices can be raised to P_s (the support level). The loss in consumer surplus is equal to the triangle *abc* plus that part of the lightly-shaded area which lies between the equilibrium price and the support price (P_sabP_e in Figure 5.4). This rectangular area represents the direct income transfer from consumers to producers. Producer surplus increases by this amount; however, these gains are offset in part by the loss in producer surplus represented by the triangle *bcd*. This loss occurs because producers are compelled to

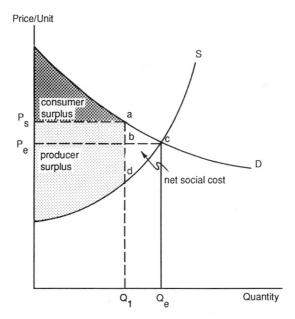

Figure 5.4   Consumer and producer surplus and net social cost with an effective supply reduction program

reduce output from Q_e (the equilibrium quantity) to Q_1. If the price increase were small and the required reduction in output were very large, losses in producer surplus from selling less could exceed gains from higher prices. But the result usually is as shown in Figure 5.4, namely, a net gain in producer surplus at the expense of consumers.

The net gain in producer surplus in Figure 5.4 is less than the loss in consumer surplus. Consequently, there is a net social cost. The area *abc* is the loss in consumer surplus; the area *bcd* is the loss in producer surplus. The two areas combined are equal to *acd*, sometimes referred to as the "welfare triangle." This area also represents the difference between the loss in marginal utility and the savings in marginal cost from producing less. Consumers lose marginal utility, represented by the area under the demand curve bounded by Q_1 and Q_e (acQ_eQ_1); cost savings are represented by the area under the supply curve (dcQ_eQ_1). The net loss in marginal utility exceeds gains from freeing resources for other uses by the area *acd*.

The size of the welfare triangle, representing net social cost, will vary depending on how high prices are supported above equilibrium and the slopes of the demand and supply curves. If the demand curve is very steep (inelastic), a small reduction in output will result in a substantial increase in the average price received by producers. This will result in a large income transfer from consumers to producers. The net social cost of such an income transfer will be relatively small, however, because of the inelastic demand schedule. The steeper the demand schedule and the flatter the supply schedule, the smaller the social cost associated with a given transfer of income to farmers. If the demand curve is flat, the social cost of transferring income to farmers by restricting supply will be very high. Thus, if the objective is to minimize social costs, supply reduction programs should be introduced only for commodities with inelastic demand (and preferably a relatively elastic supply schedule which implies that resources withheld from agricultural production can be readily transferred and profitably used to produce other goods and services).

Effect on Consumer and Producer Surplus of a Deficiency Payment Program

The effect of a deficiency payment program is to increase *both* consumer and producer surplus, but at the expense of taxpayers. Gains to consumers in the form of lower prices and to producers in the form of price-support payments are more than offset by higher government costs. These changes are illustrated in Figure 5.5. Again, it is assumed

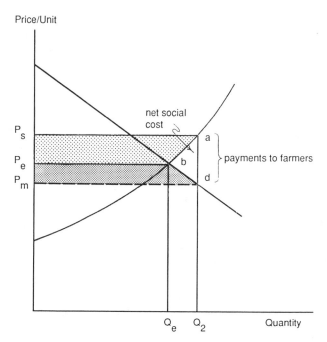

Figure 5.5   Changes in consumer and producer surplus and the cost of government payments to farmers under a deficiency payment program

that the support price is at P_s. This is the price guaranteed to producers. At this price, producers will increase output to Q_2. The additional output will cause prices to fall from the equilibrium level (P_e) to the market-clearing level (P_m). The government will be obligated to make up the difference between P_m and P_s by payments equal to the area P_sadP_m.

In Figure 5.5, only changes in producer and consumer surplus are identified. Producer surplus increases by the amount of the lightly-shaded area. This is the result of raising the support price to P_s and permitting unlimited production. The increase in producer surplus (the area above the supply curve) is equal to P_sabP_e. Consumers gain because prices fall in response to the increase in output. The gain in consumer surplus is represented by the darkly-shaded area which is bounded by the demand curve. This is equal to P_ebdP_m.

Net social costs are incurred because government payments to producers exceed the combined gains in producer and consumer surplus. The difference is equal to the area abd. The loss in welfare is the result of producing the additional output (Q_2–Q_e). The marginal cost of producing this additional output is equal to the area under the supply curve (baQ_2Q_e); the marginal utility to consumers of this increment in output is equal to the area under the demand curve (bdQ_2Q_e). The area abd identifies the net social cost, which is the difference between the marginal cost and the marginal social benefit of increasing output.

The net social cost (or the size of the welfare triangle) for a deficiency payment program also depends on the level of support in relation to the equilibrium price and the slopes of the demand and supply curves. In this case, the steeper the demand schedule, the greater will be the net social cost of supporting farm prices above equilibrium. With an inelastic demand curve, market prices will fall substantially. This will increase consumer surplus, but the gains in consumer surplus will be more than offset by higher government costs. Net social costs will be small if a deficiency payment scheme is used to support commodities with a relatively elastic demand and an inelastic supply schedule. Under these conditions, farmers will increase production very little in response to higher prices, and only a small reduction in the market price will be required to move the additional output into consumption. The welfare triangle will then be relatively small.

If one knows something about the slopes or elasticities of demand and supply schedules, equilibrium prices and quantities, and the relationship of the support price to the equilibrium price, numerical values of changes in producer and consumer surplus can be obtained.

One also can estimate the net social cost. These estimates are useful mainly in comparing alternative support methods.[5]

REFERENCES

BOWERS, DOUGLAS E., "USDA Acreage Reduction Programs, 1933–1987," *Policy Research Notes,* Issue 23. Washington, D.C.: Economic Research Service, 1967.

BROWNING, T. L., and E. I. REINSEL, "Distribution of Farm Program Payments by Income of Sole Proprietors," *Agricultural Economics Research,* 25 (1973), 41–44.

COUNCIL OF ECONOMIC ADVISERS, *Economic Report of the President.* Washington, D.C.: Government Printing Office, 1987.

JOHNSON, D. GALE, KENZO HEMMI, and PIERRE LARDINOIS, *Agricultural Policy and Trade: Adjusting Domestic Programs in an International Framework,* A Report of the Trilateral Commission: 29. New York: New York University Press, 1985.

PAARLBERG, DON, "Effects of New Deal Farm Programs on the Agricultural Agenda a Half Century Later and Prospects for the Future," *American Journal of Agricultural Economics* 65 (1983), 1163–67.

SUMNER, DANIEL A., and JULIAN M. ALSTON, *Consequences of Elimination of the Tobacco Program,* North Carolina Agricultural Research Service Bulletin 469. Raleigh, N.C.: North Carolina State University, 1984.

U.S. DEPARTMENT OF AGRICULTURE, *Economic Indicators of the Farm Sector—National Financial Summary, 1984,* ECIFS 4-3. Washington, D.C.: Economic Research Service, 1986.

U.S. DEPARTMENT OF AGRICULTURE, *Food Consumption, Prices, and Expenditures 1960–1981,* Statistical Bulletin Number 694. Washington, D.C.: Economic Research Service, 1982.

U.S. DEPARTMENT OF AGRICULTURE, *Agricultural Outlook,* AO-129 (April). Washington, D.C.: Economic Research Service, 1987.

WALLACE, T.D., "Measures of Social Costs of Agricultural Programs," *Journal of Farm Economics* 44 (1962), 580–94.

[5]The relative social costs of supporting prices by imposing supply controls or making deficiency payments are a function of the *relative* elasticities of demand and supply. For a more detailed explanation of net social costs and the conditions under which deficiency payents may be preferable to supply controls, see Wallace.

6

Coping with Variability

Variability in prices and production is a common problem faced by producers of raw materials. The important policy issue is to what degree the government should intervene in an attempt to moderate fluctuations in prices or attempt to compensate for losses in income due to either low prices or low yields. Demands for government intervention reflect dissatisfaction with existing market mechanisms or the actions of farmers and private traders who seek to protect themselves from the effects of unstable prices and production. These protective or compensatory devices include storing commodities in years of high production and low prices for resale later, saving income earned in high-return years to cover losses in other years, and hedging on futures markets or dealing in commodity options. Hedging is an alternative only for producers of certain commodities, mainly grains, cotton, and beef, and provides protection against adverse price movements for only a limited period of time, usually twelve months or less. These protective devices or compensatory mechanisms are considered by many elected representatives to be inadequate. Political pressure to do something to moderate price fluctuations usually rises following periods of unusually high prices or a sudden collapse in farm incomes. Producers, as pointed out in Chapter 3, are most likely to seek government assistance when prices and/or yields fall sharply. Consumers, on the other hand, are more likely to demand stabilization programs following a period or rapid inflation or the threat of food shortages. Creditors also may join in supporting stabilization measures when land values collapse.

While there is a broad measure of support for government action designed to moderate price fluctuations and to compensate for losses in income, conflicts arise over precisely where or over what range prices should be stabilized, what policy instruments should be used to achieve the desired objectives, and who should bear the cost. These and related issues are addressed in this chapter.

The policy instruments that have been proposed or are most likely to be considered in implementing a program to reduce the amplitude of price fluctuations or to compensate for a sudden loss in income are as follows:

- publicly-financed storage or reserve schemes, mainly for grains, cotton, and tobacco
- insurance schemes to compensate farmers for losses in production or income
- export restrictions or variable export taxes to protect domestic consumers and stabilize internal prices
- bilateral contracts or agreements to stabilize export sales
- marketing restrictions or set-aside requirements to prevent flooding markets in years of high production.

Storage or reserve policies have received the most attention, and therefore the issues involved in designing and implementing reserve schemes are discussed first. A brief analysis of crop and income insurance schemes follows. Measures designed to insulate the domestic economy from instability in the export market or to stabilize export demand are reviewed in the final section. Marketing or sales restrictions and other measures designed to control the flow of commodities to markets are discussed in the next chapter.

STORAGE OR RESERVE POLICIES

Storage policies are useful as a price stabilization device for only a limited number of commodities, mainly grains, cotton, tobacco, and a few tropical products such as coffee and sugar. The costs of storage are much too high to make this a feasible policy instrument to reduce interyear fluctuations in the prices of livestock products, fruits, and vegetables. Prices can always be raised by destroying or diverting part of what is produced, but they cannot be lowered in years of short crops unless supplies can be stored from one season to the next.

Proposals to strengthen U.S. reserve policies and/or create international reserves of grain received a great deal of attention in the 1970s. Food deficit countries feared they would be unable to obtain the food they needed if additional reserves were not created and placed under international control. Critics of past U.S. reserve policies maintained that rules for buying and releasing commodities needed to be spelled out more clearly to protect livestock feeders. They also argued that storage holdings were unlikely to be large enough to insure that the U.S. would be a reliable supplier on world markets unless additional incentives were offered to increase reserves. National and international conferences were held to address the food security issue, but attempts to negotiate an international reserve scheme failed to produce significant results. Interest in the issue declined as surpluses once again began to build up in the late 1970s.

There are a number of technical issues that must be addressed in designing a storage or reserve scheme.[1] One is whether storage decisions should be based on price rules or quantity rules. If governed by price rules, reserves will be acquired at some lower price boundary and released at a predetermined upper price. If quantity rules are adopted, decisions to acquire and release commodities will be based on deviations from trends in production or the ratio of storage stocks to current or anticipated use (Halcrow, pp. 123–24). Price rules rather than quantity rules have generally governed storage decisions in the United States, although price stabilization has been a secondary objective to supporting or raising prices.

The analysis which follows is based on the assumption that price stabilization is the principal objective. If a country decides to use reserves as an instrument to stabilize price, it then must decide how much stability is desired, that is, the range over which prices will be allowed to fluctuate. The width of the price band will influence the size of storage stocks required to keep market prices from exceeding the upper price boundary or falling below the minimum price. Other issues that must be addressed are where to store commodities and who should pay for the

---

[1]Economists have developed complex theoretical models to determine optimum storage rules. In theory, the welfare of society as a whole can be maximized by storing additional commodities up to the point where the marginal social benefit just covers the marginal social cost. Both costs and benefits are difficult to quantify. One can estimate annual storage costs, but judgement is required in projecting how long commodities will have to be stored before they can be released. It is even more difficult to estimate the potential gains to society from reducing the amplitude at price fluctuations, especially when there is a threat of losing markets to substitutes or competitors abroad if prices rise above a certain level.

cost of storage, that is, consumers, in the form of higher prices, or the government.

How Much Price Flexibility?

The size of reserve stocks and, indirectly, government costs, are closely linked to the width of the price band a country wishes to maintain; the wider the price band, the smaller the reserves required. With a wide price band, there will be more incentive for private storage and less need for a government storage program. Provided high production years precede years of low output, prices can be kept within acceptable limits by acquiring stocks at the lower end of the price band and releasing them at the upper end. If insufficient stocks have been acquired, however, it will not be possible to prevent prices from rising above the upper boundary. Likewise, the floor cannot be defended if the government buying agency has insufficient funds or storage space to handle the surpluses that exist at the support price.

Some, but not too much, flexibility in prices is desirable. Prices that fluctuate over a wide range make it difficult for farmers and agribusiness firms to plan. There may be overadjustments in either direction. Sharply rising prices lead to overinvestment in land and sales of equipment that cannot be sustained when prices subsequently decline. Excessive price instability also may lead processors or manufacturers to seek substitutes which may depress future sales.

Price stability, however, can be overdone. If prices are held within too narrow a band, there will be little incentive for private storage and, consequently, the government will be compelled to carry most of the burden of acquiring and holding stocks. Price signals also may be distorted. Some flexibility is necessary if prices are to perform the important functions of rationing consumption in poor crop years and guiding future production. An attempt to maintain a stable price when demand is either rising or falling will delay the needed adjustments. Furthermore, stable prices will result in unstable farm incomes as long as production continues to fluctuate from year to year. With stable prices, total revenue is higher with large crops than with small crops. If incomes are to be stabilized, prices must be allowed to rise in years of low production by an amount equal to the percentage decline in output; for example, the average price must rise by 20 percent to compensate for a 20 percent reduction in yield.

During the 1960s and early 1970s, grain prices in the United States were held within a band that, in retrospect, appears to have been too narrow. During much of that period, the government held large stocks acquired as a result of defaults on price-support loans. The government was authorized to sell commodities from storage whenever the market

price rose above the price-support loan rate by 15 percent or more. Because of this commitment, neither U.S. nor foreign grain users had any
incentive to store grain. They assumed, quite reasonably, that additional supplies always could be obtained at the resale or release price from
government-held stocks. The narrow price band also inhibited adjustments in production and use that might have occurred more promptly in
response to changing market conditions (Robinson). The lower price
boundary, for example, perpetuated the surplus problem in the 1960s,
while the attempt to defend the upper price boundary in the mid-1970s
(unsuccessfully after stocks were depleted) delayed changes in grain consumption that might have led to less extreme price fluctuations later.

Congress responded to criticisms of the government storage
program as it operated during the 1960s and early 1970s by widening
the price band. Legislation adopted during the late 1970s prohibited the
government-owned Commodity Credit Corporation from selling stocks at
less than 150 percent of the price-support loan rate.[2] A price band of
this width is sufficient to encourage private traders to hold stocks, but
only for a period of two or, at most, three years. Some producers would
prefer an even wider price band and smaller government-held stocks.
They argue that the presence of large reserves in the hands of the
government tends to depress market prices. Raising the release price for
government-held stocks (or the price at which farmer-held reserves can
be sold without incurring penalties) would shift more of the cost of carrying reserves from the government to consumers.

The U.S. government absorbed a high proportion of storage costs in
the 1950s and 1960s. Taxpayers had to pay for handling and transporting large quantities of grain as well as storage and interest charges. In
some years, the government had to move older grain from one area to
another in order to free space for the new crop. The government was
also forced to cover losses resulting from deterioration in quality.
Spoilage of grain, however, has not been a major problem in the United
States. With proper storage facilities and good management, grain and
cotton can be stored without loss almost indefinitely. The government
has been able to avoid serious storage losses by rotating older stocks,
that is, by selling old grain and replacing it with grain from the most
recent harvest.

---

[2]While government-owned grain cannot be sold at less than the release price, the
Commodity Credit Corporation has made grain available in exchange for payment-in-kind
(PIK) certificates. PIK certificates have been given to farmers in part payment for idling
land and also to cover part of the cost of deficiency payments. Grain exchanged for PIK
certificates has been sold. One of the effects of using PIK certificates to compensate
farmers in 1986 and 1987 was to depress the market price for corn below the price-support
loan rate in those two years, thus widening the price band (Kennedy, p. 16). This also
resulted in converting government-owned grain into free stocks.

How Much to Store?

The size of storage stocks required to keep U.S. prices within the upper and lower boundaries targeted for a stabilization program will depend on the width of the price band established and the response of other nations. Larger stocks obviously will be needed to keep prices within a narrow band than a wide band. Still larger reserves will be required if other countries rely on the U.S. to stabilize international as well as domestic prices. The burden on the U.S. will be much less if other countries create and maintain their own reserves and/or permit prices to rise in years of short crops so as to ration consumption, thereby helping to ease pressure on world markets. Pooling reserves or coordinating national reserve policies makes sense economically if not politically. The same degree of price stability could be achieved at lower cost if reserves were internationalized rather than managed independently by each of the principal exporting and importing nations (Huddleston, p. 300; Johnson, 1981, p. 257).

The pricing policies of importing countries are an important variable influencing the size of reserves required to achieve a given level of stability in world grain prices. If importing countries allow their internal prices to rise when international supplies are short, there will be less need for reserves. The higher prices will ration internal use by making it less profitable to feed grain to livestock. If, on the other hand, importing countries attempt to preserve a greater degree of internal price stability than that prevailing on world markets, someone will need to carry larger reserves. Internal price stability can be achieved, but only at the cost of importing more or less. If internal prices are not permitted to rise following a short crop, more grain will need to be imported, thus placing greater pressure on residual markets. This was demonstrated during the 1970s. Japan, the European Community, and the Soviet Union all sought to prevent prices from rising internally by importing more grain. This added to world demand at a time when supplies were short. World prices rose more than would have been the case if the rationing effect of higher prices had been spread more broadly among major importing countries (Johnson, 1975).

The amount of grain reserves required to achieve a given level of stability in U.S. prices cannot be determined precisely because of the uncertain reaction of other countries to whatever policy the U.S. adopts. Past changes in production or the decisions of major importers such as the Soviet Union, China, and Japan to purchase more or less grain from the United States are not necessarily good guides to what may happen in the future. Reserve requirements to achieve a given degree of price stability will depend not only on political decisions and weather conditions prevailing in other countries but also on anticipated fluctuations in U.S. production. All these variables are difficult to predict. For this reason, one can only guess at what might be a reasonable level of reserves to maintain.

Since 1970, U.S. carryover stocks of grain (consisting mainly of wheat, corn, and grain sorghum) have ranged from a low of just over 30 million tons to a high of around 200 million tons (USDA, 1987, p. 22).[3] Almost everyone agrees that 30 million tons provides too little security, while 200 million tons is more than adequate. Stocks of 30 million tons are barely sufficient to keep the pipelines full, that is, to keep exports moving and to sustain output of livestock feed and food products derived from grain. Taking account of both costs and probable variations in yields, a target for grain reserves of somewhere between 70 and 100 million tons appears to be a reasonable compromise. Carryover stocks of this magnitude should enable the United States to compensate for all but the most extreme shortfalls in production or shifts in export demand.

Who Should Bear the Costs of Storage?

The width of the price band that a country seeks to maintain influences not only the size of stocks required but also total storage costs and how such costs will be shared between users and the government. As emphasized previously, larger stocks will be required to keep prices within a narrow range. Thus, total storage costs will be greater if a narrow rather than a wide price band is maintained. The share of costs borne by the government is also likely to rise as the width of the price band narrows. There is a simple explanation for this. Private traders will be reluctant to hold stocks unless prices are expected to rise by enough to cover storage costs. If private traders do not store sufficient grain, the government will be compelled to do so.

The annual costs of storing commodities are not insignificant, even for a commodity which is relatively cheap to store such as bulk grain. In the mid-1980s, such costs averaged slightly more than 20 percent of the

---

[3]Carryover stocks of grain in the United States have been determined by price-support decisions, shifts in demand, and changes in production, not by a conscious decision to build and maintain a certain level of reserves. By acquiring commodities at price-support loan rates and releasing stocks at resale prices, the U.S. has, in effect, operated a price-stabilization program, but the accumulation of stocks has been mainly a by-product of measures adopted in an attempt to support or enhance farm incomes rather than simply to stabilize prices. Except for a brief period in the 1970s, the lower price boundary (loan rate) exceeded the equilibrium price. This made it difficult to empty bins once they had been filled.

purchase price of grain.[4] Either consumers or the government must cover these costs. If prices rise by only 30 percent over a two year period, neither the government nor private storers will be able to recover their costs. Prices must rise by at least 20 percent per year to make storage of grain profitable. If prices rise by this amount, the full cost of carrying reserves will be paid by grain users. If the government stores grain and sells it at prices that rise by less than 20 percent per year, the taxpayer will bear a substantial part of the costs.

The relationship that is likely to prevail between government costs and total carryover or reserve stocks of grain is illustrated in Figure 6.1 using hypothetical data. Annual government storage costs (shown on the vertical axis) are assumed to be zero with carryover stocks of only 40 million tons, and to rise to $2 billion per year if stocks reach 100 million tons. When stocks are relatively small, it is assumed that most will be held by farmers, cooperatives, and private traders, and that prices can be expected to rise by an amount sufficient to cover storage costs, either for private traders or for the government. Large stocks are likely to hold

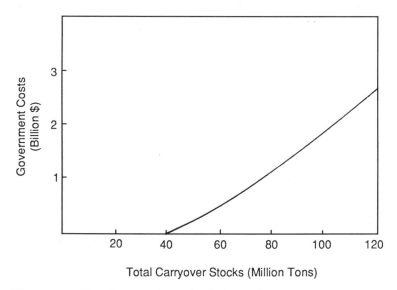

Figure 6.1 Hypothetical relationship between the size of grain carryover stocks and government costs.

[4]Commercial storage could be rented at that time for around $14 per ton of grain. In addition, grain storers must cover the interest on the capital tied up in stored grain. If grain costs $100 per ton and the prevailing interest rate is 10 percent, interest on the money invested in grain (or foregone interest on money that might have been invested elsewhere) will amount to $10 per ton. Thus, the annual cost of storing grain at that time was around $24 per ton.

down prices. Under these circumstances, users will be protected from substantial price increases, but will have to pay for such protection indirectly through higher taxes. Government costs can be expected to rise slightly more than proportionately with an increase in the size of carryover stocks because private traders and farmers will shift more of the burden of holding stocks to the government as prospects for a significant price increase diminish.

Where to Store Reserves?

From an economic perspective, it makes sense to maintain reserves as close as possible to where storable commodities are produced, that is, on farms or in storage facilities located in surplus-producing regions (Johnson, 1947, p. 175). Storage costs are generally lower on farms than in urban areas. By storing grain near where it is produced, unnecessary hauling costs also can be avoided. Grain that is stored far from producing areas frequently turns out to be in the wrong location when needed. As a result, additional costs may be incurred in moving it to areas where it ultimately will be consumed.

The major argument for maintaining reserves in consuming areas, and especially in potential food deficit countries, is to reduce risks associated with acquiring and moving grain when world supplies are short. Shipping space may not be available when needed, or embargoes may restrict the availability of grain. For this reason, importing countries usually prefer to have reserves available locally and under their own control; however, few of the major importing countries now carry reserves in excess of those required to even out supplies between harvests.

Net Producer Gains or Losses from Acquiring and Releasing Reserves

The amplitude of price fluctuations obviously can be reduced by acquiring reserves at low prices and releasing them at high prices. More stable prices can help to reduce risks for both farmers and those selling services to farmers. If survival is threatened, a farmer may be willing to forego potential price gains later in return for maintaining a floor under current prices. Producers gain from somewhat higher prices when commodities move into storage, but they will lose when the stocks acquired previously are sold.

Whether producers collectively gain or lose from storing commodities in years of low prices and then selling the stored commodities in years of high prices depends on storage costs, how long the commodities are held in storage before being sold, and the slope of the demand curve (or its elasticity) at the time of sale relative to the slope or elasticity at the time commodities are withdrawn from the market (Tomek and Robinson, pp. 277–80). Ignoring for the moment storage costs during the intervening period, producers will receive more total revenue from storing commodities only if the demand curve is steeper (less elastic or more inelastic) at the time commodities are stored than when they are sold. To put it another way, the percentage increase in price resulting from withholding commodities from the market must exceed the percentage decrease in price associated with the release of stored commodities.

The foregoing principles are illustrated in Figure 6.2. Assume a monopoly marketing board or the government decides to raise prices in year one by storing an amount equal to d (current production) minus c. This raises the average price from P_1 to P_2. Assume two or three years later, production falls to a. In that year reserves equal to b minus a (the quantity previously stored) are placed on the market. This leads to a fall in prices from P_4 to P_3. In the diagram on the left (Situation A), demand is relatively elastic at low prices but inelastic at high prices. This leads to an increase in price associated with withholding commodities, which is much less than the decrease in price following release of the stored commodities. The opposite situation is illustrated in Situation B. When demand is relatively inelastic at low prices, the rise in price resulting

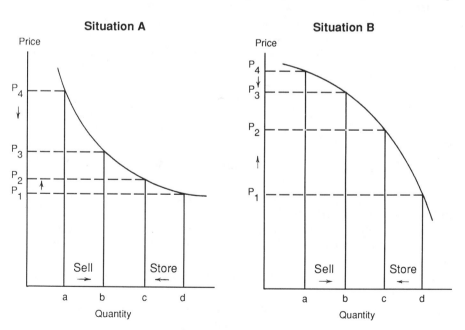

Figure 6.2 Effect of alternative demand assumptions on producer returns from storing commodities.

from withholding a given quantity exceeds the decrease in price associated with release of an equivalent amount when prices are high (P_2
minus P_1 in Situation B is greater than P_4 minus P_3). Under these conditions, farmers gain from storing part of the crop in a year of low prices
and releasing stocks in a year of high prices. Producers will not gain if
demand conditions are similar to those shown in Situation A.[5]

In both situations depicted in Figure 6.2, the amplitude of price
fluctuations is reduced (from P_4 minus P_1 without storage to P_3 minus
P_2 with storage); however, the same quantity stored in Situation B as in
Situation A will not produce similar price effects. The amplitude of price
fluctuations is reduced more in Situation A than in Situation B. This is
a function of the differing shapes of the demand curves. Thus, it is important to know something about the elasticity of demand at various
points along the demand curve in order to predict the effects of a storage
program on prices as well as aggregate returns to producers.

Net gains or losses to farmers from a storage program designed to
stabilize prices will depend not only on the shape of the demand curve
but also on how long commodities are stored and who pays for storage.
In Canada, farmers (not taxpayers, as in the United States) have borne
the cost of storing wheat. The Canadian Wheat Board deducts storage
costs from revenue obtained from wheat sales before distributing net
returns to producers. Storage costs can more than offset any gains from
withholding stocks and selling them later at higher prices. This was
demonstrated by Gislason. Wheat stored in the 1930s was eventually
sold during World War II at relatively favorable prices, but the gains
were not sufficient to cover all the storage costs incurred in the years
during which stocks were being held off the market. Canadian farmers
would have obtained more total revenue over the twenty-six-year period
from 1929 to 1955 if they had sold all the wheat they produced each
year, even at the low prices prevailing in the 1930s (Gislason, p. 599).

Quantity vs. Price Rules for Storing Commodities

The foregoing analysis assumes stocks will be acquired and
released at certain prices. These are the management rules that have
dictated the size of government-owned grain stocks in the United States.
Wheat and corn have been acquired at price-support loan rates and sold
at release prices. The size of grain carryover stocks probably would have
been much less in the 1980s if the acquisition and release of stocks had

---

[5]In general, the effects of stabilization policies on consumers are the opposite of
those on producers. Consumers gain from withholding stocks in low-priced years and
releasing them in high-priced years, when demand is inelastic at high prices and/or the
demand curve shifts to the right.

been based on quantity rules rather than price rules (Halcrow, pp. 124–25). Quantity rules could be based on the size of storage stocks in relation to use or on deviations from trends in production. For example, if production in any year exceeded some percentage of the five-year moving average of past production, the government (or some authorized agency) would be required to purchase a specified fraction of the surplus. Similar rules would govern the release of stocks if production fell below the five-year moving average. Such action would help to even out supplies, but would not necessarily keep prices within politically acceptable limits. Under quantity rules, prices would play a greater role in guiding production.

YIELD AND INCOME INSURANCE

Insurance schemes do nothing to eliminate the causes of instability, but may be used successfully to compensate producers for losses from drought, hail, other natural disasters, or even low prices. Such schemes may be financed by premiums paid by producers, government subsidies, or a combination of the two. The U.S. has operated a selective crop-insurance program since 1938.[6] Income insurance schemes have been discussed but not implemented in the United States. Canada, however, has experimented with several types of income-payment schemes designed to augment the incomes of farmers in years of low returns.

Most crop-insurance schemes compensate farmers for some fraction of losses associated with a crop failure or low yields. The U.S. crop-insurance program is voluntary rather than compulsory. Farmers who participate in the program are eligible for benefits whenever actual yields fall below a specified percentage of average yields calculated for the farm or the county. The guaranteed percentage may be as low as 50 percent or as high as 75 percent of the average county yield. Premiums paid by participating producers vary, depending on the percentage of yield that is guaranteed and the history of yield losses in the area. Indemnities paid to those incurring losses are based on the difference between the harvested yield (if any) and the guaranteed yield. The yield difference is multiplied by an estimate of the average cost of production per unit, for example, per bushel or per hundredweight. The indemnity rate per unit of output typically covers about 90 percent of production costs and is adjusted each year to reflect changes in costs.

---

[6]An all-risk crop insurance program is now available in all important agricultural counties in the United States. Most major crops, including wheat, corn, cotton, grain sorghum, rice, barley, and soybeans can be insured. Government subsidies amount to approximately 25 percent of the total cost of operating the program.

The following example illustrates how the total indemnity is calculated. Assume the guaranteed yield is seventy-five bushels of corn per acre, and the farmer harvests only fifty-five bushels per acre. The indemnity rate for that year is estimated at $2.50 per bushel. Based on these assumptions, the calculated indemnity rate per acre would be as follows:

Average county yield of 100 bushels
per acre multiplied by 75 percent
(the guaranteed percentage)   =   75 bu. per acre

Actual yield   =   55 bu. per acre
                                                            ─────────────────
                                  Difference   =   20 bu. per acre

Payment rate (based on 90 percent
of estimated production costs)   × $2.50 per bushel
                                                            ─────────────────
                        Total indemnity $50.00 per acre

In the majority of years, the crop-insurance program has operated at a loss.[7] Participation tends to be selective. Farmers in high-risk areas are more likely to participate and, consequently, losses tend to be high. Raising premiums to the level necessary to avoid losses would reduce participation and make the program less effective as an income-stabilization measure. To encourage participation, the government subsidizes premiums and absorbs losses not covered by premium income.

Proponents of subsidizing a crop-insurance program argue that it is less expensive to underwrite part of the costs of such a program than to compensate producers in other ways. When disaster strikes, the government is often pressed to make additional payments to farmers or to extend credit on favorable terms. Losses on disaster loans may turn out to be very high. If most farmers are covered by crop insurance, the government will be under less pressure to fund disaster relief programs that could prove to be more costly than crop insurance subsidies.

Farm-revenue insurance has been proposed as an alternative to supporting farm prices (Congressional Budget Office, 1983, pp. 17–25). Such a scheme would protect farmers against severe losses whether from adverse weather or depressed prices. A revenue-insurance program for major crops could be operated in a manner similar to the present crop-insurance program. Participants would be eligible for payments when-

----

[7]For the thirty-one-year period 1948–1979, the total cost of the crop-insurance program, including administrative costs and indemnities paid to farmers, exceeded premiums by 24 percent (Hazell and Valdes, p. 3).

ever the gross revenue per acre (yield multiplied by the current market price) fell below a guaranteed level of return. The gross revenue guaranteed to farmers most likely would be based on some percentage of recent average revenue, for example, 75 percent of average gross revenue per acre over the preceding five years. The program could be either voluntary or compulsory. If voluntary, only those farmers who paid premiums in high-return years would be eligible for benefits. Premiums charged producers would be based on estimated losses; however, these would be very difficult to forecast.

An income-insurance program financed entirely by premiums paid by farmers would not raise the average level of returns but could save a farmer from bankruptcy during a period of low prices or crop disasters. The principal effect would be to alter the distribution of income between years. Premiums paid in good years would be equivalent to forced savings; the income from premiums would then be returned to farmers in years of low returns.

An income-insurance program could be financed by direct appropriations from the treasury rather than producer assessments. If so, it would resemble a deficiency-payment scheme; however, payments would be based on the difference between guaranteed revenue per acre and actual revenue, not the difference between target prices and loan rates or market prices. Payments based on the revenue gap would cover losses resulting from either low production or low prices. Deficiency payments based on target prices compensate only for low prices, not low production. Payment limitations similar to those imposed on deficiency payments could be implemented by restricting eligibility for income insurance to a maximum number of acres or livestock units.

An income-insurance program is more likely to be acceptable to farmers and administratively feasible if income fluctuations are modest and the interval between periods of relatively high and low returns is brief. Under such conditions it would be possible to even out the flow of income with modest producer assessments and payments. If the program is to be financed by producers, it must begin in a period of prosperity for agriculture; otherwise, the revenue available for augmenting incomes will be inadequate.

Creditors and agribusiness firms would benefit indirectly from an income-stabilization program for farmers, but such a program would not reduce the amplitude of price fluctuations. One of the advantages of an income-stabilization program over a price-support program is that it would not distort price signals. Producers might be more willing to accept lower price-support loan rates if they knew that any loss in income resulting from a decline in market prices would be made up by income payments. But payments might keep more farmers in business, thereby delaying resource adjustments.

An income-stabilization program is relatively easy to administer in countries where farmers are compelled to sell to a monopoly marketing board. The board can even out the income stream of farmers simply by withholding part of the earnings from sales in years of high prices for distribution in years of low prices. Some inequities among producers will arise from such a scheme, especially if there is a long interval between the time income is withheld and payments are made. New entrants will gain at the expense of those who left farming during the intervening period. In some cases, the accumulation of funds by marketing boards, especially those handling export crops in Africa, has been a temptation for the government to divert the funds to other uses. The net effect has been to depress returns from export crops.

Compensatory payment schemes have been adopted in Canada in an attempt to stabilize farm incomes. Under both provincial and federal enabling legislation, voluntary income-stabilization programs are now in effect for a number of livestock products as well as for crops. Costs are shared by the government and producers. Payments are made only in years when prices fall below recent trend values. Hog farmers, for example, are eligible for payments whenever the average market price falls below the previous five-year average price adjusted for changes in costs of production (USDA, 1984, p. 18).

The Western Grain Stabilization Program is designed to stabilize the aggregate income for prairie farmers as a whole, not for individual farmers (Congressional Budget Office, 1984, p. 40). Indemnity payments are made to participating farmers (those who have paid premiums into the fund) whenever the aggregate cash flow calculated for the region falls below the average of the preceding five years. Aggregate cash flow is estimated by deducting cash expenses for all farms combined from gross sales. Farmers contribute a proportion of gross sales (1.5 percent in 1985) up to a maximum per farm. In addition, the government contributes to the stabilization fund; these contributions have exceeded the premiums collected from farmers. Payments are limited to a maximum amount per farm. Thus, the program helps to maintain cash flow in the region whenever average returns decline because of low production or low prices, but an individual farmer will not be eligible for compensation if his or her income declines in a year when the aggregate income for the region exceeds the five-year moving average. Payments are based exclusively on regional shortfalls in income.

TRADE RESTRICTIONS

Import restrictions can be used as a price stabilization device as well as a method of protecting producers. By relaxing or tightening import controls or quotas, supplies can be augmented or curtailed to reduce the amplitude of domestic price fluctuations. The U.S. made use of this option in the mid-1970s, in an attempt to check the upward spiral in the prices of dairy products and sugar. Such a policy can be effective if the additional volume of imports is small relative to the quantities normally sold on world markets. If, however, residual supplies are limited and many countries try to buy more, the cost of imports will rise. This was demonstrated in 1974 when many countries simultaneously relaxed import restrictions and sought to purchase additional sugar. The increase in demand was so large in relation to available supplies that prices tripled within a few months.

Trade embargoes can be used to ease internal inflation when export demand is driving prices upward. The effect of an embargo is to curtail exports. The additional supplies that otherwise might have been exported are then available to domestic consumers. The United States exercised the embargo option in the 1970s when the price of soybeans suddenly rose from around $4 to $10 per bushel. Domestic consumers and feed users pressured the government to restrict exports to hold down prices. The embargo succeeded in achieving this objective, but alienated soybean producers and foreign buyers who complained about the unreliability of the U.S. as a supplier in times of critical world shortages. Japan sought alternative sources of supply and vowed to reduce its dependence on the U.S. A partial embargo also was imposed briefly on wheat exports in the 1970s, again with the objective of holding down internal prices.[8] Export embargoes are most useful as a price stabilization device when export demand is strong. Relaxing or eliminating an embargo is unlikely to raise internal prices if export demand is weak.

The decision to impose an export embargo on grain or soybeans involves a trade-off between the short-run interests of domestic consumers and feed users and the long-run interest of grain producers and perhaps society as a whole. If an embargo encourages other countries to increase production, future export sales will be lost. Capricious or unexpected changes in rules governing the release of commodities or exports obviously can adversely affect a country's long-run competitive position on world markets.

Variable export taxes also can be used to insulate the domestic market, at least partially, from changes in world prices. An export tax, collected on products sold abroad, tends to discourage exports and leave

[8]The 1980 partial embargo on grain exports to the Soviet Union was imposed for a different reason. In this instance, export restrictions were used as an instrument of foreign policy (that is, to retaliate against the Soviet Union for its decision to invade Afghanistan) rather than to curb inflation.

more of the crop available for internal consumption. When export demand is weak, export taxes may be reduced. Thailand and Argentina are among the countries that have used such taxes, not only to raise revenue, but also to influence the allocation of supplies between home sales and exports. Producers obviously complain when export taxes are raised in an attempt to hold down internal prices.

BILATERAL TRADE AGREEMENTS

Bilateral trade agreements are another policy instrument that can be used in an attempt to stabilize exports (Groenewegen and Cochrane). If importing countries could be persuaded to purchase about the same quantity each year, one of the major sources of instability would be eliminated. Bilateral agreements typically specify that an importing country will purchase a specified minimum quantity each year. Such agreements help to stabilize the volume of trade, but not prices. Sales are made each year at prevailing world prices. Obviously, these will fluctuate depending on demand and supply conditions.

A substantial proportion of world trade in grains and sugar is now carried out under bilateral agreements. Canada, Australia, and Argentina, as well as the U.S., have negotiated such agreements with the U.S.S.R., China, and a few other countries. Under a succession of agreements, the Soviet Union has made commitments to purchase certain minimum quantities of grain each year from the United States; it may purchase additional quantities, but only if the U.S. permits it to do so. Prior to 1985, both parties honored their commitments. The U.S. did so even in 1980, when the partial embargo on grain shipments to the Soviet Union was imposed. The embargo applied to additional quantities above the minimum amount spelled out in the agreement. In most years between 1975 and 1983, the Soviet Union purchased more than the required minimum quantities of wheat and corn. They did not do so in 1985 and 1986. In those years, the Soviet Union fulfilled its commitment to purchase corn but not wheat. The Soviet government maintained that it was not obligated to buy U.S. wheat, because the price was too high.

The bilateral agreements negotiated in the late 1970s and early 1980s have not succeeded thus far in reducing the volatility of exports or the prices of internationally traded commodities such as wheat and sugar. Such agreements are difficult to negotiate and to enforce. As an alternative to bilateral agreements, it has been suggested that more comprehensive multilateral market-sharing agreements be negotiated.

The issues involved in attempting to use international commodity agreements as an instrument to stabilize prices are discussed in Chapter 13.

CONCLUSIONS

Price-support and storage or reserve policies in all probability will continue to be the principal policy instruments employed in the United States in an attempt to reduce price instability. Other policy instruments that might be used to moderate fluctuations in prices and farm incomes have failed to win widespread support or are unlikely to be effective. Income insurance schemes, export controls, and bilateral trade agreements fall into this category.

Price stabilization programs are feasible for only a small group of commodities which can be stored at modest cost for extended periods. The width and position of the price band is critical to the success of any price stabilization scheme. If the lower price boundary is set too high (as has generally been the case in the United States) the government will accumulate excess reserves. To avoid further accumulation and to reduce costs, the government is then forced to offer incentives to curtail production. A relatively wide price band centered on the long-run equilibrium price will necessitate little government intervention; under such circumstances private traders and farmers will carry most of the reserves required. The narrower the price band, the more likely it is that government storage will be substituted for private storage. With a narrow price band, the costs of storage will be shifted to taxpayers; with a wider price band, more of the costs of carrying reserves will be borne by users.

The benefits of price stabilization achieved by storing and releasing commodities are likely to accrue mainly to consumers rather than producers, especially if demand is highly inelastic at the upper price boundary. Price stabilization is likely to help farmers survive periods of low prices, but will not necessarily lead to an increase in total revenue.

Export embargoes are now widely condemned, both by grain producers and by most members of Congress. As a result, provisions have been included in recent agricultural acts that make it highly unlikely that any administration will impose embargoes on exports in the future except in extreme emergencies.

Bilateral trade agreements have not proved to be very effective in reducing export instability. They are difficult to negotiate and to enforce. Either side may fail to live up to the agreement, thus creating an additional source of uncertainty which may lead to less stable rather than more stable exports.

DISCUSSION QUESTIONS

6.1. Why is price stabilization a feasible objective for only a small number of farm products?

6.2. Assume the government of country X wants to stabilize grain prices by acquiring stocks at some lower price boundary and releasing stocks at an upper boundary. What factors would need to be considered in deciding on the width of the price band, that is, the difference between the acquisition and release prices?

6.3. Will farmers as a group gain if the government attempts to stabilize prices by acquiring stocks at the price-support loan rate and releasing stocks in years of short crops and high prices?

6.4. How does a yield-insurance program differ from a revenue-insurance program? Why is a voluntary yield-insurance program unlikely to be self-supporting, that is, premiums paid by participants are not likely to cover all costs? Should the U.S. government continue to subsidize the crop-insurance program?

6.5. What policy instruments might be used by exporting and importing countries to insulate the domestic market from extreme fluctuations in world prices?

REFERENCES

CONGRESSIONAL BUDGET OFFICE, *Farm Revenue Insurance: An Alternative Risk-Management Option for Crop Farmers.* Washington, D.C.: Congress of the United States, 1983.

CONGRESSIONAL BUDGET OFFICE, *Canada's Western Grain Stabilization Program: An Option for U.S. Farm Policy?* Washington, D.C.: Congress of the United States, 1984.

GISLASON, CONRAD, "How Much Has the Canadian Wheat Board Cost the Canadian Farmer?" *Journal of Farm Economics*, 41 (1959), 584–99.

GROENEWEGEN, J. R. and W. W. COCHRANE, "A Proposal to Further Increase the Stability of the American Grain Sector," *American Journal of Agricultural Economics* 62 (1980), 806–11.

HALCROW, HAROLD G., *Agricultural Policy Analysis.* New York: McGraw-Hill, 1984.

HAZELL, PETER, and ALBERTO VALDES, "Is There a Role for Crop Insurance in Agricultural Development?" *Food Policy Statement No. 5.* Washington, D.C.: International Food Policy Research Institute, 1985.

HUDDLESTON, BARBARA, "Responsiveness of Food Aid to Variable Import Requirements," *Food Security for Developing Countries,* edited by Alberto Valdes. Boulder: Westview Press, 1981.

JOHNSON, D. GALE, *Forward Prices for Agriculture.* Chicago: University of Chicago Press, 1947.

————, "World Agriculture, Commodity Policy, and Price Variability," *American Journal of Agricultural Economics* 57 (1975), 823–28.

————, "Grain Insurance, Reserves, and Trade: Contributions to Food Security for LDCs," *Food Security for Developing Countries,* edited by Alberto Valdes. Boulder: Westview Press, 1981.

KENNEDY, JOSEPH V., "Generic Commodity Certificates: How They Affect Markets and the Federal Budget," *Choices,* Third Quarter (1987), 14–17.

ROBINSON, K. L., "Unstable Farm Prices: Economic Consequences and Policy Options," *American Journal of Agricultural Economics* 57 (1975), 769–77.

TOMEK, W. G., and K. L. ROBINSON, *Agricultural Product Prices* (2nd edition). Ithaca, N.Y.: Cornell University Press, 1981.

U.S. DEPARTMENT OF AGRICULTURE, *World Grain Situation and Outlook,* FG8-87. Washington, D.C.: Foreign Agricultural Service, 1987.

7

Marketing
Orders

Marketing orders provide the legal authority for producers of certain designated commodities to act collectively in an attempt to improve returns. Legislation authorizing such action was first adopted in the 1930s in response to pressure from producers and, particularly, farm cooperatives. The objective of such legislation was to promote "orderly marketing." To producers, this meant raising prices in years of excess production, or at least reducing the amplitude of price fluctuations. Farmer-owned cooperatives sought marketing order legislation in an attempt to enforce classified pricing schemes for milk and to compel all producers (including nonmembers) to comply with regulations designed to raise or to stabilize farm prices. They had tried to enhance returns to their members in the 1920s and early 1930s by charging milk handlers higher prices for milk that was bottled and sold for fresh use or by withholding produce. Fruit and vegetable cooperatives were not successful in raising prices because they could not control sales by nonmembers and even found it difficult to enforce contracts with their own members when opportunities arose to sell at a higher price outside the agreement. Dairy cooperatives encountered resistance when they tried to extract more money from fluid milk handlers.

MARKETING ORDER ENABLING LEGISLATION

Federal legislation permits, but does not compel, producers of certain commodities to adopt an order. Congress has modified the enabling legislation from time to time to broaden the list of commodities eligible for marketing orders; however, the number of commodities for which federal marketing orders are authorized is still quite limited. The list of eligible commodities includes milk sold for fluid use, fresh fruits and vegetables, nuts, and certain specialty crops including raisins, hops, and cranberries. In some cases, federal legislation restricts marketing orders to certain geographical areas. For example, apple growers in the Pacific Northwest are permitted to adopt a marketing order, but not apple growers in Virginia. Fruits and vegetables sold for processing generally are excluded from federal orders. These restrictions reflect the opposition of agribusiness and processing firms to any measures which might limit the volume produced or sold.

The procedures that must be followed in adopting an order are spelled out in the enabling legislation. The first step is to draft a specific order identifying precisely the producers and areas to be covered, the types of action permitted under the order, and the composition of the advisory committee. Usually a producer organization or a cooperative representing producers takes the initiative in drafting a specific proposal. The Department of Agriculture plays only a passive role; it has the authority to reject a proposed order, but seldom initiates action.

Once a specific order has been drafted, public hearings are scheduled by the secretary of agriculture to enable all those who might be affected by the order to express their views. The hearing record serves as a basis for the secretary's decision to recommend or not to recommend that a special referendum be held. If there is a great deal of conflict or opposition to the proposed order, the secretary is unlikely to call for a referendum, that is, a vote among producers affected by the order.

Congress has specified that a proposed order must be approved by two-thirds of those voting in a special referendum (either by number or volume of production) before it can be put into effect. This is to insure that an order has widespread support among producers. A simple majority vote is sufficient to kill an order that previously had been adopted.

The final step under a fruit, vegetable, or specialty-crop marketing order is to select members of the advisory committee. Membership consists of representatives of both growers and handlers. The secretary of agriculture also may appoint someone to represent the public interest. Members of the advisory committee recommend whatever action to be taken in a particular year or crop season. The secretary of agriculture can, however, veto recommendations of the advisory committee. Market order regulations which apply mainly to handlers or marketing firms are issued by the secretary and enforced by the U.S. Department of Agriculture.

Various types of action are authorized under federal legislation that may make it possible to enhance producer returns as well as to stabilize prices. With few exceptions, however, marketing orders cannot be used to restrict entry of new producers or to curtail production.[1] The principal action taken under milk marketing orders is to establish minimum prices which buyers must pay for milk based on whether it is sold for fresh use or converted into dairy products such as butter or cheese. A major use of marketing orders for other commodities has been to collect money from producers for research and promotion. All but eleven of the forty-seven fruit, vegetable, and specialty-crop marketing orders in effect in 1983 were used mainly to fund advertising programs (Lindsey).[2]

Producers of fruits, vegetables, and specialty crops cannot fix minimum prices as can be done under milk marketing orders, but they are permitted to manage supplies. Under existing legislation, producers are authorized to:

1. pro-rate or allocate existing supplies among alternative uses or outlets;
2. prohibit shipments for brief periods to avoid a "market glut" (sometimes referred to as a "shipping holiday");
3. enforce minimum grade and size or maturity regulations; and
4. create a "reserve pool" by withholding and storing part of the crop marketed in a particular year.

The four types of action listed have been used mainly in an attempt to improve returns to producers of citrus fruits, nuts, raisins, and cranberries. Few vegetables, other than potatoes and onions, are covered by marketing orders. Marketing orders are not authorized for fruits and vegetables sold for processing, that is, canning, freezing or drying. Commodities subject to marketing orders in 1981, the area or region to which

[1]Among the few commodities for which allotments (which restrict entry of new producers) have been authorized are hops, Florida celery, and spearmint oil (USDA 1981, p. 38). The hop marketing order which made use of these provisions was terminated in 1986.

[2]Assessments for research and advertising are authorized under separate legislation for commodities not eligible for marketing orders. In 1986, such assessments were authorized for wool, cotton, eggs, wheat, milk, beef, pork, and honey. In that year, a total of over $150 million was being collected from producers (including assessments authorized under marketing orders) for research and promotion (Warman).

the orders apply, and the types of action authorized are listed in Appendix B.

One of the functions of marketing orders, especially those applied to milk, has been to legitimize discriminatory pricing, that is, to compel buyers to pay different prices for essentially the same raw product. One way this is done is to establish minimum buying prices for milk based on use. Another way is to withhold supplies or divert part of total production to a secondary market, thereby raising prices in the restricted market. Whether or not producers gain from this type of action depends on a complex set of factors. For this reason, it is necessary to review the principles of discriminatory pricing before attempting to assess the impact of marketing orders on producers and consumers.

POTENTIAL GAINS FROM DISCRIMINATORY PRICING

Provided certain conditions are met, producers can increase total revenue by charging buyers different prices for the same commodity depending on location, time, or use of the product (Tomek and Robinson, pp. 106–11). Producers will gain from price discrimination only if markets (or uses) with differing elasticities of demand can be identified and effectively separated so that sales in the lower-priced market (or use) do not displace those in the higher-priced market (or use).

A numerical example may help to illustrate how returns to producers can be enhanced by controlling the allocation of total supplies between markets. For simplicity, assume that total output of commodity X is 100 units and that a monopoly selling organization can allocate supplies between markets A and B. They have different demand schedules, as shown in Figure 7.1. The demand schedule in market A is much steeper than in market B. Because the assumed demand curves are linear, elasticity is not constant, but changes at all points along the demand schedule. Over the range in output between 40 and 60 units, demand in market A is price inelastic, while in market B it is elastic.[3]

Under free market conditions (assuming uncontrolled allocation of

---

[3]The average elasticity within this range can be approximated by dividing the percentage change in quantity by the percentage change in price. Assume ten units are withheld from market A and diverted to market B. This represents a 20 percent change in quantity from the initial level of sales (fifty units) in each market. Given the demand curves shown in Figure 7.1, the price will rise 50 percent in market A and decline 10 percent in market B. Thus, the average elasticity in each market represented by these changes is as follows:

$$E_A = \frac{-20\%}{+50\%} = -0.4 \quad \text{and} \quad E_B = \frac{+20\%}{-10\%} = -2.0$$

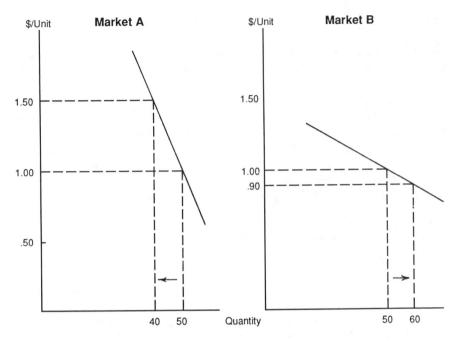

Figure 7.1 Price effects of diverting supplies from market A to market B.

supplies) the price would be the same in both markets; given the demand schedules shown in Figure 7.1, fifty units would be sold in A and fifty units in B. If it were possible to limit sales in market A and divert ten units of the total supply from A to B, the price would rise from $1.00 to $1.50 per unit in A; adding ten units to the supply in B would depress the price there from $1.00 to $.90 per unit. The total revenue before and after the diversion is:

	Initial Situation (Competitive Pricing)	Following Diversion (Discriminatory Pricing)
Market A	50 units × $1/unit = $50	40 units × $1.50/unit = $60
Market B	50 units × $1/unit = $50	60 units × $.90/unit = $54
	Total Revenue $100	$114

By diverting ten units from market A to B, producers could raise their total revenue from $100 to $114, a gain of 14 percent. It would be possible to increase total revenue even more by diverting additional units from market A to B. Revenue would be maximized by allocating supplies so as to equate marginal returns in both markets. (The added revenue obtained from selling the last unit in B should just equal the added revenue from selling the last unit in A.) These conditions are fulfilled when one-third of the total output is sold in market A and two-thirds in market B (see Appendix A for the algebraic solution). The optimum allocation of supplies between markets would raise total revenue to a maximum of $116.33, a gain of 16 percent over what producers as a group would have obtained under competitive conditions.

Gains from discriminatory pricing depend on a number of factors including:

- whether or not separate markets can be identified with differing elasticities of demand;
- how effectively supplies can be controlled to prevent undercutting prices in the primary or more inelastic market; and
- the volume sold in each market.

If the elasticities are similar, little will be gained by diverting supplies from one market to another. The decline in price in the market to which supplies are diverted (the less inelastic market) will about equal the gain in price in the primary market. Even if elasticities differ, gains will be modest if only small quantities can be sold in the market with the higher price. Large differences in elasticity combined with substantial sales in the higher-priced market will lead to significant gains. If these conditions are not fulfilled, gains will be small.

In the foregoing illustration the elasticity of demand in market B was assumed to be five times that in market A, a difference much greater than that likely to be found in most real-world situations. Substantial differences may exist, however, if the government is prepared to purchase any surpluses diverted from the primary to the secondary market. In this case, demand in the secondary market is infinitely price elastic at the support price.

Gains to producers from price discrimination will be greatest if demand in the primary market is highly inelastic and demand in the secondary market is elastic. Recall that total revenue increases with smaller supplies when demand is inelastic; total revenue also rises, but with an increase in the quantity sold when demand is elastic. Thus, revenue can always be increased by reducing sales in the inelastic market and increasing sales in the elastic market.

Price discrimination pays even if demand is inelastic in both the primary and secondary markets, provided there is a difference in elasticity. If demand is more inelastic in market A than in market B, it will pay to divert supplies from A to B; the gain in revenue from reduced supplies in A will exceed the loss in revenue from selling more in B. The smaller the difference in elasticity between markets, the less producers can expect to gain.

Markets can be separated on the basis of where commodities are sold, how they are used, or when they are sold. Geographical or spatial price discrimination is possible, for example, if domestic demand is more inelastic than export demand, or if the demand for a particular product such as citrus fruit is more elastic in Texas than in New York. Total revenue can sometimes be increased by restricting the quantity sold domestically and "dumping" the surplus abroad. In such cases, the domestic market must be protected by a tariff or an import quota. Separation of domestic markets is more difficult. If price differences between regions exceed transportation costs, truckers or handlers will buy the commodity in the lower-priced market and sell it in the higher-priced market.

Price discrimination is most commonly based on use. In the case of milk, buyers are charged different prices for the same raw product depending on whether it is bottled and sold as fluid milk or converted into butter, cheese, ice cream, or other dairy products. Fruits and vegetables also lend themselves to differentiation on the basis of use. Prices in the fresh market, for example, may be raised by diverting part of the supply to processing outlets (for example, a starch factory in the case of potatoes). A monopoly selling organization might go even further in differentiating markets for a commodity like apples. For example, a high price might be maintained for apples sold for fresh use, a somewhat lower price for those sold to canners or freezers, and a still lower price for those sold to cider or juice manufacturers. Preventing producers from diverting supplies from one market to another, however, would be a serious problem. Even a monopoly selling organization might not be able to maintain price differences given the economic incentive for processors to resell the raw product in a higher-priced market.

In a few instances it may be possible to differentiate markets based on time of sale. Operators of movie theaters typically charge more for first-run features than older movies. For such commodities as turkeys and cranberries, prices might be raised during holiday periods on the assumption that demand is more inelastic at that time than during the rest of the year. But the possibilities of maintaining higher prices during certain periods will be limited if the commodity can be processed or stored. The availability of frozen turkeys, for example, has undercut efforts by producers to raise prices at Thanksgiving or Christmas.

ECONOMIC CONSEQUENCES OF MILK MARKETING
ORDERS

Approximately 80 percent of all the milk produced in the United States is now regulated under provisions of federal orders; most of the remaining milk that meets fluid-grade standards (Grade A milk) is regulated under state marketing orders (Boynton and Novakovic, p. 2; Babb and others, p. 165). The principal function of milk marketing orders, as emphasized earlier, is to legalize discriminatory pricing. Buyers are compelled to pay different prices for milk of the same quality, based on use. The prices established under federal milk marketing orders are minimum prices; handlers can and sometimes do pay a premium above the minimum class prices, especially when supplies are short. Two and sometimes three class prices are fixed each month. The Class I price is charged for all milk sold in fluid form, whether whole, low-fat, or flavored milk. The Class II price is paid by handlers for milk used to make other dairy products such as cheese, skim-milk powder, and butter. Sometimes an intermediate pricing class is established for milk used to make what are usually referred to as "soft" dairy products, mainly cottage cheese, yogurt, and fresh cream.

Class I prices are invariably higher than Class II prices; however, the difference in price, commonly referred to as the "Class I differential," varies among markets. The differential is lower in markets such as Chicago and Minneapolis-St. Paul than in New England, Florida, and Texas. The size of the differential is mainly a function of the cost of moving milk from the upper Midwest (the major surplus-producing region) to other markets. Originally, Class I differentials were based on actual transportation costs, but in the 1960s and 1970s they were not adjusted by enough to reflect all the increases in costs that occurred during that period. Congress mandated new Class I differentials in the Food Security Act of 1985. Under this Act, the differential ranges from $1.20 per hundredweight in the upper Midwest to $4.18 per hundredweight in southeastern Florida (Congressional Record, H12255).

In some markets producer organizations have succeeded in charging buyers more than the minimum Class I prices mandated in the order. The ability of producers to collect such premiums or to engage in what is referred to as "over-order" pricing depends on whether or not a producer organization controls a major share of the total supply. If buyers can purchase milk from independent or unaffiliated producers, it will be impossible for a cooperative to charge buyers more than the prescribed minimum Class I price.

Class I and Class II milk prices in recent years have been determined by a formula which links prices in each market to the average price paid to farmers by butter and cheese manufacturing plants located in Minnesota and Wisconsin. The prices paid by these plants for manufacturing-grade milk (Grade B milk) is referred to as the Minnesota-Wisconsin (or M-W) series. Manufacturing-milk prices in that region are sensitive to small changes in the supply-demand balance. When supplies are short, the M-W price tends to rise above the national support level for manufacturing milk. This then raises Class I prices in all markets. At other times, the M-W price tends to follow the support price.

Basing milk prices in all federal order markets on the M-W series has been criticized, because the price series tends to be somewhat unstable. Small changes in residual supplies can lead to substantial changes in manufacturing-milk prices. Furthermore, the series is based on only a small sample of all the milk produced in the United States. It is based on manufacturing-grade milk which accounts for only about 15 percent of total production. As Grade B producers disappear and a higher proportion of milk is priced under federal orders, the base for pricing will become even less representative of total supplies. Eventually, the M-W series probably will have to be replaced as a standard for determining federal-order prices (Boynton and Novakovic, p. 5).

Class II or manufacturing-milk prices are approximately the same in all markets and are linked to the M-W price. Uniform pricing of manufacturing milk is necessary because products derived from surplus milk are easily transported between regions. Cheese, butter, and skim-milk powder produced in federal-order markets must compete with similar products manufactured from Grade B milk in Minnesota and Wisconsin. Handlers operating in federal-order markets will not purchase surplus milk if it is priced higher than what unregulated plants pay for manufacturing milk in the Midwest.

Milk handlers or processors can purchase as much or as little milk as they like and use it in ways they find most profitable. Total Class I and Class II sales are determined by the decisions of those buying milk, not by the marketing order administrator. Buyers must pay at least the minimum class prices established under the order. Records of milk handlers are audited to make sure they pay the appropriate prices.

Receipts from all sales are pooled or combined on a marketwide basis under most federal orders. An average price, often referred to as the "blend price," is calculated each month by dividing total receipts (less market-order expenses) by the volume of milk delivered by all producers. Under marketwide pooling, each producer receives the same blend price, plus or minus a transportation or location differential, and usually a seasonal adjustment as well. Nearby producers receive higher prices than more distant producers. In a few markets, individual handlers pool receipts. This can lead to large differences in the prices paid to farmers in the same area. A farmer selling to a handler with a high proportion of Class I sales will receive a higher average price than one selling to a handler with a low Class I utilization.

Federal marketing orders cannot be used to limit either the quantity produced or marketed. Nor can such orders be used to restrict the movement of milk between regions. In earlier years, local authorities sometimes tried to protect nearby producers by imposing sanitary regulations or by refusing to inspect dairy farms beyond a certain distance from the market. Courts have ruled against most of these restrictions or barriers to the movement of milk (Manchester, pp. 15–16). As a result the movement of milk between regions is now governed mainly by economic considerations. Farmers in Wisconsin, for example, could ship milk to New York or Georgia if it were profitable to do so. If a Wisconsin cooperative decided to enter the New York market, the price received for the milk shipped to New York would be the New York price less the cost of transporting milk to New York. Except in very unusual circumstances, the net price (New York price less transportation costs) would be less than the price they would obtain by selling milk locally or to handlers in Madison or Chicago. It is the cost of moving milk between regions, rather than market-order provisions or sanitary codes, that protects nearby producers in federal-order markets in the East and South from lower-priced Midwestern milk.

Producers pay all the costs associated with administering marketing orders, including auditing the records of milk handlers or buyers. These costs are deducted from gross receipts before the average or blend price is calculated. Indirectly, however, marketing orders may have added to support costs. By increasing returns to producers, marketing orders have encouraged excess production. Taxpayers have had to pay for the surplus milk produced. Thus, at least some of the cost of surplus removal can be attributed to the higher prices maintained as a result of milk marketing orders.

Long-run gains to producers from raising Class I prices have probably diminished with the passage of time. The higher cost of Class I milk to handlers has been passed on to consumers. This undoubtedly has had some adverse effect on consumption, at least in the long run. Per capita use of fluid-milk products has declined, but this is not due solely to the higher prices maintained in markets regulated by state or federal orders. Higher Class I prices have raised returns to producers, thereby providing an incentive to increase production. In a number of federal order markets, production has risen relative to Class I sales. With rising production, more milk is sold at the Class II price, thus lowering the blend price. The combined effect of reduced fluid-milk consumption and higher production has been to limit gains to producers. Federal-order pricing has raised the average or blend price paid to producers by no more than 10 percent in recent years, and probably closer to 5 percent.[4]

[4]A report commissioned by the American Agricultural Economics Association to review the literature relating to federal milk marketing orders concluded that the effects of such orders on producer returns were modest. Despite differences in elasticity estimates,

In a few state-regulated markets, it has been possible to restrict the entry of new producers or to limit production by imposing marketing quotas. By limiting production, producers can retain more of the gains from overpricing. Where this occurs, entry costs for new producers tend to be higher. Benefits to producers are reflected in the value of farms that possess the right to ship milk to the higher-priced market. The same is true of farms with bases or allotments. Benefits tend to be capitalized into the value of bases, thus forcing new entrants to pay for the privilege of obtaining higher prices.

Class I base plans are one of the policy instruments that have been proposed, and in a few cases adopted, in an attempt to neutralize the effects on production of raising Class I prices. The objective is to discourage expansion by paying farmers the Class II price rather than the blend price for any amount produced in excess of Class I requirements. Each farmer would receive a Class I quota based on his or her share of the total Class I market. The higher Class I price would be paid for that milk. Any milk produced in excess of that quantity would bring only the Class II price. The Class II price is lower than the blend price, because the latter is an average of Class I and Class II prices. Farmers presumably would have less incentive to increase production with a somewhat lower marginal price for any additional milk they produced.

The theoretical effects of a Class I base plan are illustrated in Figure 7.2. Farmers will maximize returns by producing up to the point where the marginal revenue equals marginal cost. Under pooled pricing, the marginal revenue for an additional unit of output is the blend price. Given the marginal cost curve shown in Figure 7.2, the farmer will produce 12,000 hundredweight of milk at the blend price which is assumed to be $13.25 per hundredweight (cwt.). At a Class I price of $15 per cwt., handlers will purchase 5,000 cwt. The remaining production (7,000 cwt.) will be sold to manufacturers of dairy products at the Class II price. Pooling all returns from the sale of Class I and Class II milk will yield an average price of $13.25 per cwt.

Under a Class I base plan, the Class I price remains the same; the amount sold at this price also would remain the same. The only difference is that now producers would be paid $12 per cwt. for any milk produced in excess of 5,000 cwt. Based on the marginal cost curve illustrated in Figure 7.2, production would fall from 12,000 cwt. at a price of $13.25 per cwt. to 10,000 cwt. at a price of $12 per cwt. The response of producers to a lower price depends on the shape of the marginal cost

the studies they reviewed indicated that average producer prices had been increased by no more than 10 percent. Most of the estimates based on prices prevailing in the 1970s were in the 2 percent to 5 percent range (American Agricultural Economics Association, p. 18).

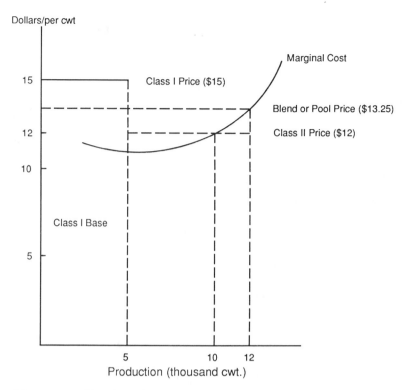

Figure 7.2 Hypothetical effects on prices and production of introducing a Class I base plan for milk.

curve. In Figure 7.2 it is relatively flat. If the curve had been steeper, the reduction in output would have been less.

The effect of introducing a Class I base plan depends on the difference between the blend price and the Class II price and the shape of the marginal cost curve. The smaller the price difference and the steeper the marginal cost curve, the less output will be affected.

Class I base plans of the type illustrated in Figure 7.2 do not limit what an individual farmer can produce; such plans simply alter the way farmers are paid for their milk. A farmer who does not increase production would receive precisely the same total revenue under a base-surplus pricing system as he or she would obtain with pooled returns. Only those who plan to increase production would be adversely affected.

A Class I base plan will effectively limit output only if bases are fixed. If new bases are assigned each year, farmers will have an incentive to increase production to build a larger base.

In practice, the production effects of a Class I base plan are likely to be quite small, because the difference between the blend price and the Class II price in most federal-order markets is no longer very large.

Where Class I utilization is low, the blend price typically averages no more than about 10 percent above the Class II price. Reducing the marginal price by 10 percent will not have a major impact on production unless the supply curve for the region is relatively flat (price elastic). If the typical firm's marginal cost curve is steep (reflecting the lack of more profitable alternative uses for labor and land), production will be little affected. The major impact of adopting a Class I base plan may be to discourage expansion, but the reduced marginal price may not be low enough to do so if technology is changing and incremental costs associated with expansion are modest.[5]

Policy Issues Related to Federal Milk Marketing Orders

Critics of milk marketing orders have proposed a number of reforms including reducing the Class I price and allowing handlers to produce reconstituted or "filled" milk with lower-cost ingredients.[6] These proposals obviously are designed to lower the cost of fluid-milk products to consumers. Federal milk marketing orders have had little or no effect on the cost to consumers of manufactured dairy products. The prices of butter, cheese, ice cream, and other Class II products are determined mainly by the support price for manufacturing milk, not by federal-order pricing.

Consumer groups, the Federal Trade Commission, and the Justice Department have been especially critical of over-order pricing, that is, charging buyers more than the minimum Class I price. As pointed out in the preceding section, it is possible for a producer organization occupying a monopoly position to extract premium prices from buyers. The Justice Department has sought to curb such practices where the effect has been to "unduly enhance prices."

Class I prices could be lowered very simply by reducing Class I differentials, that is, the difference between Class I and Class II prices. A somewhat higher price for fluid milk than for manufacturing milk can be justified because there are additional costs involved in meeting fluid re-

---

[5]Class I base plans were authorized for federal order markets under the Food and Agriculture Act of 1965; however, the authority for implementing new Class I base plans terminated on December 31, 1981. Such plans were adopted only in the Puget Sound area of Washington and in Georgia. They did not succeed in curbing production mainly because the marginal or Class II price was not low enough to discourage expansion. According to Nott and Hamm, who reviewed the literature relating to such plans, "quota plans didn't stop overproduction. . .because the prices paid to farmers for. . .overquota shipments were too high. . . . Marginal, and perhaps even average, costs of production were lower than the lowest price received by farmers" (p. 22).

[6]Reconstituted milk is made with skim-milk powder and water; filled milk has butterfat or vegetable oil added.

quirements; however, the differentials mandated in the Food Security Act of 1985 are higher in some markets than needed to assure adequate supplies of fluid milk. A differential of no more than $1.00 per hundred-weight probably would be sufficient to cover the incremental costs of meeting fluid-milk requirements (Dobson and Salathe, p. 215).[7] Reducing the Class I differential to $1.00 per cwt. would lower the cost of fluid milk to handlers by somewhere between $1.00 and $3.00 per cwt. A saving of one dollar in the cost of milk to handlers reduces the price to consumers by around two cents per quart (assuming marketing margins remain constant). Thus savings to consumers would range somewhere between two and six cents per quart, with savings in most markets probably averaging closer to two cents than to six cents. Potential savings would be greatest in markets more distant from surplus-producing areas of the Midwest, because Class I differentials are now much higher in those markets.

Producers of manufacturing or Grade B milk would benefit indirectly from a reduction in Class I price differentials. Sales of fluid products probably would increase slightly if these differentials were reduced. With lower prices for Class I milk, average returns to farmers in federal-order markets would decline. Thus, there would be less incentive to maintain or increase production. Any reduction in the quantity of surplus or Class II milk in federal-order markets would benefit producers of butter, cheese, and skim-milk powder. It also could lead to savings in support costs.

Consumer groups have attacked marketing-order provisions that make it uneconomic to reconstitute milk from low-cost skim-milk powder. Federal marketing orders do not explicitly restrict the manufacture or marketing of reconstituted milk, but the regulations which apply to pricing reconstituted milk ingredients tend to discourage the production and sale of such milk. Under existing regulations, handlers must pay the equivalent of the Class I price for all milk sold for beverage use, whether the products are made from fresh milk or powdered milk. Skim-milk powder can be purchased for less than fresh milk, because the price is based on Class II or manufacturing-milk prices. If skim-milk powder is reconstituted, however, it becomes fluid milk according to marketing-order regulations, and must be priced accordingly. If reconstituted milk could be made from cheaper ingredients, a lower-priced substitute could be offered to consumers. A change in the pricing regulations for reconstituted milk also would make it possible for

---

[7]Reducing the Class I differential to a dollar or less, however, would depress returns to producers in some markets to the point where production might be inadequate to meet local needs. In such markets, it would be necessary either to raise the Class I price or import milk.

markets short of milk during certain times of the year to augment supplies by adding water to powder imported from other regions. An acceptable product can be made by blending fluid whole milk with reconstituted milk and adding butterfat if necessary. Market-order producers resist changing regulations because this would reduce Class I milk sales and, consequently, lower their returns.

ECONOMIC CONSEQUENCES OF MARKETING ORDERS FOR COMMODITIES OTHER THAN MILK

The kinds of action taken under fruit, vegetable, and specialty-crop marketing orders are extremely diverse. For this reason, it is impossible to generalize about the effects of such orders. Only a few nonmilk orders have been used to control supplies and to enhance prices. Most have been adopted in an attempt to improve quality or to collect money for advertising and promotion.

The prices of a limited number of commodities have been influenced by exercising the power to manage supplies or to withhold shipments during certain periods. Among the commodity groups that have used marketing orders as a price-stabilization or price-raising device are those producing fresh oranges and lemons, almonds, filberts, walnuts, raisins, and cranberries. Supplies have been controlled by withholding part of the crop in years of high production or by regulating the flow of commodities to markets. The emphasis has been on controlled marketing, not production. Handlers, not producers, are regulated, unless the latter do their own marketing.

The set-aside program for raisins illustrates the way in which marketing orders may be used to even out supplies and take advantage of differing price elasticities of demand in separate markets. In years of large crops, the initial buyer of raisins (or first handler) may be compelled to set aside or withhold a specified proportion of the raisins purchased from growers. The set-aside raisins cannot be sold without the permission of the market order administrative committee. By withholding part of the crop, prices can be raised or maintained in the domestic market where demand presumably is price inelastic. Set-aside raisins may be exported, sometimes at much lower prices than those prevailing in the domestic market. If subsequent crops are short, they may be released for domestic use. Surpluses that cannot be exported may eventually be sold to wineries for conversion into alcohol, which is then used to fortify wines.

Marketing order administrative committees sometimes declare a "shipping holiday" when markets are glutted. This means that no shipments can be made by handlers during that period. The flow of commodities to market also may be restricted by issuing what amounts to shipping quotas for each handler. Produce that cannot be marketed because of excess supplies may be diverted to a secondary market, if available, or destroyed. At times, California oranges have been dumped on unused runways to dry in the sun (Crittenden). The dried product is then sold as livestock feed.

Still another way of limiting sales is to impose grade and size restrictions. Products that fail to meet the minimum standards, like the surpluses mentioned previously, may be destroyed or sold to processing outlets. By imposing grade and size regulations, marketing order administrative committees may succeed in restricting imports as well as domestic supplies. Under the existing federal marketing order enabling legislation, imported commodities must meet the same quality standards as those regulated under marketing orders. The objective of this provision is to prevent low-quality imports from undercutting domestic sales. Grade and size regulations have been imposed at times to make it difficult for foreign producers to sell fresh vegetables in the United States. Florida tomato growers, for example, adopted grade and size restrictions which were designed to limit imports from Mexico. Initially, the regulations achieved some success, but eventually Mexican growers changed production practices so as to meet the minimum grade and size provisions imposed on Florida growers.

The effects of market-order restrictions on prices and returns cannot be measured precisely, but the studies that have been made of commodities subject to orders suggest that benefits have been relatively small and confined mainly to the short run. Jesse and Johnson compared the stability of prices for a group of market-order commodities with nonorder commodities having somewhat similar characteristics. Their analysis was based on prices prevailing during the period from 1952 to 1979. They found little or no correlation between use of market order restrictions and price behavior. According to the authors:

> Even the strongest orders (for California almonds and walnuts), limiting both quality and quantity and applying to all U.S. production, showed no statistical significance in enhancing or stabilizing producer prices (Jesse and Johnson, p. iii).

The data did not permit them to test whether or not price stability had been reduced for market-order commodities (relative to what it would have been without an order). They did discover that price fluctuations were greater for some market-order commodities than for nonorder commodities. This, however, may have been the result of adopting marketing orders for commodities with an inherent tendency toward greater price fluctuations.

As with milk marketing orders, the effectiveness of orders for other commodities in raising returns to producers is constrained by the inability to control the use of substitutes or to limit production. If the market-order program succeeds in raising prices, producers operating under the order are likely to increase production. With few exceptions, marketing orders cannot prevent growers from planting more. The area devoted to grapes and citrus fruit, for example, has risen in response to more favorable returns, made possible in part by marketing order provisions. The longer-run effect has been to put pressure on prices. Marketed supplies have increased despite market pro-rates (shipping restrictions) and set-aside requirements.[8]

Growers not operating under marketing orders also may increase production. The enormous expansion of potato plantings in the West, for example, severely undermined the effectiveness of the Maine potato order. National orders are essential for total control of supplies, but few orders of this type are in effect. Many fruit and vegetable orders apply to only a part of total production. Interregional competition and differing opinions among growers about the need for orders or who would serve on the administrative committee have made it difficult to gain support for national orders.

The use of fruit, vegetable, and specialty-crop marketing orders to limit sales and raise prices has been questioned by many individuals both inside and outside of the government. A small group of California and Arizona citrus growers, for example, have voiced strong opposition to orange and lemon pro-rates (Crittenden; Lindsey; Bovard). These restrictions inhibit the freedom of aggressive growers to expand and increase their market share. Disenchanted growers also have accused Sunkist, the dominant marketing cooperative, of exercising undue influence over marketing-order decisions, discriminating against new and expanding producers and, in some cases, blocking the adoption of innovative marketing practices.

Marketing orders are not well regarded by those who advocate less government involvement in agriculture. Government agencies charged with protecting consumers against monopoly pricing or undue price enhancement, such as the Federal Trade Commission and the Justice Department, have been frequent critics of marketing orders. In 1982, the Office of Management and Budget prevented cherry growers in Michigan from implementing a plan to withhold and store canned or frozen sour cherries in an attempt to stabilize prices (Birnbaum). In the

---

[8]Thor and Jesse concluded on the basis of simulation studies that citrus orders led to increased plantings. In the absence of orders, their analysis indicated that the area planted to oranges (and production) might decrease "by as much as 20 to 30 percent especially in Southern California" (Thor and Jesse, p. 40).

same year, the secretary of agriculture issued administrative guidelines designed to prevent market order administrative committees from attempting to restrict production or the total quantity marketed (USDA, 1982). Another administration might reverse these decisions, but the threat of legal action against marketing orders serves as a check on their use as a mechanism for enhancing producer prices.

There is very little opposition to marketing orders that simply collect money from producers to fund advertising and promotion programs. This, of course, is the major activity carried out under marketing orders for commodities other than milk. Producers apparently are convinced that promotion pays and, therefore, are willing to tax themselves to support advertising programs. Studies of generic (nonbrand) advertising programs suggest that they do produce some gains to producers in the short run, but not necessarily in the long run. Advertising helps to increase sales (Forker, p. 52); however, gains may be eroded if producers increase output in response to the higher level of sales or more favorable prices.

CONCLUSIONS

Marketing orders have had a significant impact on the prices of relatively few farm products other than milk. Only ten or eleven of the forty-seven fruit, vegetable, and specialty-crop marketing orders in effect in the mid-1980s made use of provisions designed to regulate marketing or control supplies. Milk marketing orders have helped to stabilize prices and production of milk. Benefits to producers have been paid for by consumers of fluid-milk products.

Producers like the flexibility offered by marketing order enabling legislation. It permits them to fund advertising programs and to improve quality by enforcing grade, size, and maturity regulations. If successful in increasing sales or raising prices, marketing orders provide a relatively efficient mechanism for transferring income directly from consumers to producers. Marketing orders do not cost the taxpayer any money.

Gains to producers from marketing orders have been constrained by both economics and politics. Few commodities are likely to benefit from price discrimination, because the necessary demand conditions are not fulfilled. It may be possible to identify a market with inelastic demand, but not a secondary market that can absorb the surplus without severely depressing prices or antagonizing producers already serving that market. Without supply controls, gains are not likely to be retained for very long, but the option to limit supply is almost certain to be circumscribed by whatever government is in power. Many producers also object to limiting supply. It is not easy to get a two-thirds favorable vote for an order that contains supply management provisions.

Dairy farmers are among the strongest supporters of marketing orders. They, and the cooperatives that represent them, have benefited from legalized price discrimination. Alternative institutional arrangements for pricing milk would have to be developed if the option to adopt marketing orders were no longer available. Consumers have been protected from serious exploitation by political constraints on how much fluid milk prices can be raised and by increased supplies of milk. From the point of view of producers, the most serious criticism of marketing orders is that the successful ones have overstimulated production.

DISCUSSION QUESTIONS

7.1. Assume producers of commodity X are proposing to adopt a marketing order. What conditions must exist for producers of commodity X to gain from adopting an order that permits discriminatory pricing?

7.2. What can be done under federal marketing order enabling legislation by producers of fruits and vegetables in an attempt to enhance returns and/or stabilize prices?

7.3. Why are long-run gains to producers under federal or state marketing orders likely to be limited?

7.4. What are the principal criticisms of milk marketing orders?

7.5. What would be the economic effects on producers and consumers of: (1) reducing or eliminating the Class I price differential in milk marketing orders and (2) adopting a Class I base plan?

Appendix 7-A
Determining the Optimum Allocation
of Output between Markets with Differing
Demand Functions

The coefficients of the two linear demand functions shown in Figure 7.1 are as follows:

$$P_A = \$3.50 - 0.05 \ Q_A$$
$$P_B = \$1.50 - 0.01 \ Q_B$$

where P_A = price in market A ($/unit)
  P_B = price in market B ($/unit)
  Q_A = units sold in market A
  Q_B = units sold in market B.

The division of total output between the two markets that will maximize revenue to producers can be determined algebraically by (1) equating marginal revenue in the two markets and then solving for Q_A in terms of Q_B; and (2) substituting the result of this calculation in an equation which forces the sum of units allocated to A and B to equal 100 (that is, the total supply available).

The marginal revenue curve for each market is derived by taking the first derivative of the total revenue function (price × quantity). The marginal revenue curve is always steeper than the average revenue or demand curve. Note that the intercept on the price axis remains the same. The coefficient attached to quantity for each of the marginal revenue equations has twice the value of the corresponding coefficient in the demand equation. The marginal revenue functions for each market are as follows:

$$MR_A = \$3.50 - 0.10\,Q_A$$

$$MR_B = \$1.50 - 0.02\,Q_B$$

Equating the two functions and solving for Q_A in terms of Q_B yields the following results:

$$\$3.50 - 0.10Q_A = \$1.50 - 0.02Q_B$$
$$-0.10Q_A = -2.00 - 0.02Q_B$$

$$Q_A = \frac{-2.00 - 0.02Q_B}{-0.10}$$

$$Q_A = 20 + 0.2Q_B$$

By substituting the results from the preceding analysis in the identity equation ($Q_A + Q_B = 100$), the optimum quantity to sell in market B can be determined. The results are as follows:

$$(20 + 0.2Q_B) + Q_B = 100$$

$$1.2\,Q_B = 80$$

$$Q_B = 66.67$$

The quantity to be allocated to market A is obtained by subtracting Q_B from the total quantity available as shown below:

$$Q_A = 100 - 66.67$$

$$Q_A = 33.33$$

To determine the price that will prevail in each market, given the optimum allocation, it is necessary to substitute the optimum quantities in each of the original demand equations. With 33.33 units allocated to market A and 66.67 units allocated to market B, the price that will prevail in each market is as follows:

$$P_A = \$3.50 - 0.05(33.33) = \$1.83$$

$$P_B = \$1.50 - 0.01(66.67) = \$ .83$$

Given these prices, total revenue will be as follows:

Market A = 33.33 × \$1.83/unit =   \$60.99

Market B = 66.67 × \$.83/unit =   \$55.34

Total   Revenue   = \$116.33

Appendix 7-B
Authorized Provisions of Federal Marketing Orders for Fruits, Vegetables, and Specialty Crops in Effect, July 1, 1981[a]

Order Number[b]	Area and Commodity	Year Initiated	Grade or Size	Volume Management	Market Flow
Fruits					
904[d]	California desert grapefruit	1980	G, S	—	—
905	Florida citrus	1939	G, S	—	H
906	Texas oranges and grapefruit	1960	G, S	—	(e)
907	California–Arizona navel oranges	1953	S	—	P
908	California–Arizona valencia oranges	1954	S	—	P
910	California–Arizona lemons	1941	S	—	P
911	Florida limes	1955	G, S	—	H, P
912	Indian River (Florida) grapefruit	1962	—	—	P
913	Florida interior grapefruit	1965	—	—	P
915	Florida avocados	1954	G, S	—	H
916	California nectarines	1958	G, S	—	—
917	California pears, plums, and peaches	1939	G, S	—	—
918	Georgia peaches	1942	G, S	—	—
919	Colorado peaches	1956	G, S	—	—
921	Washington peaches	1960	G, S	—	—
922	Washington apricots	1957	G, S	—	—
923	Washington sweet cherries	1957	G, S	—	—
924	Washington–Oregon fresh prunes	1960	G, S	—	—
925[d]	California desert grapes	1980	G, S	—	H

Authorized Provisions[c]

Order Number[b]	Area and Commodity	Year Initiated	Authorized Provisions [c] Grade or Size	Authorized Provisions [c] Volume Management	Authorized Provisions [c] Market Flow
926	California Tokay grapes	1940	G, S	—	H, P
927	Pacific coast winter pears	1939	G, S	—	—
928	Hawaii papayas	1971	G, S	—	—
929	Cranberries—ten states	1960	(f)	A, M	—
930	Tart cherries—eight states	1971	(f)	R	—
931	Washington–Oregon Bartlett pears	1965	G, S	—	—
932	California olives	1965	G, S	—	—
Vegetables					
945	Idaho–E. Oregon potatoes	1949	G, S	—	—
946	Washington potatoes	1949	G, S	—	—
947	S. Oregon–N. California potatoes	1942	G, S	—	—
948	Colorado potatoes	1941	G, S	—	—
950	Maine potatoes	1954	G, S	—	—
953	Virginia–N. Carolina potatoes	1948	G, S	—	—
958	Idaho–E. Oregon onions	1957	G, S	—	H
959	South Texas onions	1961	G, S	—	H
965[d]	Rio Grande Valley (Texas) tomatoes	1959	G, S	—	—
966	Florida tomatoes	1955	G, S	—	—
967	Florida celery	1965	G, S	A	H, P
971	South Texas lettuce	1960	G, S	—	H, P
979	Texas melons	1979	G, S	—	—
Dried Fruits and Nuts					
981	California almonds	1950	G	M, R	—
982	Oregon–Washington filberts	1949	G, S	M	—
984	Pacific coast walnuts	1948	G, S	M, R	—
985[d]	Far West spearmint oil	1980	—	R, A	—
987	California dates	1955	G, S	M	—
989	California raisins	1949	G, S	M, R	—
991[d]	Idaho, Washington, Oregon, and California hops	1966	G	R, A	—
993	California prunes	1949	G, S	R	—

[a]Marketing agreements accompany all orders except those noted.

[b]Order number refers to part in the *Code of Federal Regulations* where the order is found. For example, order No. 905 is codified as 7 CFR 905.

[c]Symbols for the various provisions are defined as follows::

G = Minimum grade requirement   R = Reserve pool provision
S = Minimum size requirement   A = Producer allotment provision
M = Market allocation provision H = Shipping holiday
P = Prorate. Prorate periods are   — = indicates that the order does not
one week except for Tokay   authorize the indicated type of
grapes (three days) and Florida   provision.
celery (unspecified).

Authorized provisions are not necessarily employed every year.

[d]Order only; no marketing agreement.

[e]Restricting handler deliveries is specifically prohibited.

[f]Grade and size specifications apply only to restricted portion of crop.

SOURCE: USDA, 1981, pp. 22–24.

REFERENCES

AMERICAN AGRICULTURAL ECONOMICS ASSOCIATION, *Federal Milk Marketing Orders: A Review of Research on Their Economic Consequences,* Occasional Paper No. 3 by the Task Force on Dairy Marketing Orders, 1986.

BABB, EMERSON M., ROBERT D. BOYNTON, WILLIAM D. DOBSON and ANDREW M. NOVAKOVIC, "Milk Marketing Orders," *Federal Marketing Programs in Agriculture: Issues and Options,* edited by Walter J. Armbruster, Dennis R. Henderson, and Ronald D. Knutson. Danville, Ill.: The Interstate Printers and Publishers, 1983.

BIRNBAUM, JEFFREY H., "Crop Controversy: Farm, Budget Officials Clash on Supply Curbs by Marketing Boards," *Wall Street Journal,* Dec. 7, 1982.

BOVARD, JAMES, "Can Sunkist Wrap Up the Lemon Industry?" *Wall Street Journal,* Jan. 24, 1985.

BOYNTON, ROBERT D., and ANDREW M. NOVAKOVIC, "The Role of Milk Marketing Orders," *The Farm and Food System in Transition: Emerging Policy Issues,* FS14. East Lansing, Michigan: Cooperative Extension Service, Michigan State University, 1983.

CONGRESSIONAL RECORD, "Conference Report on H.R. 2100, Food Security Act of 1985," vol. 131, no. 175—Part II, Dec. 17. Washington, D.C.: U.S. Government Printing Office, 1985.

CRITTENDEN, ANN, "Fruit Growers' Control of Market Assailed," *New York Times,* March 25,1981.

DOBSON, W. D., and LARRY E. SALATHE, "The Effects of Federal Milk Orders on the Economic Performance of U.S. Milk Markets." *American Journal Agricultural Economics* 61(1979), 213–27.

FORKER, OLAN D., "Chronology of Agricultural Economics Research Directed Toward Evaluating Promotion Programs," in *Research on Effectiveness of Agricultural Commodity Promotion,* Chicago: Farm Foundation, 1985.

JESSE, EDWARD V., and AARON C. JOHNSON, Jr., *Effectiveness of Federal Marketing Orders for Fruits and Vegetables,* Agricultural Economic Report No. 471. Washington, D.C.: Economics and Statistics Service, 1981.

LINDSEY, ROBERT, "Citrus Farmers Hold Off Reagan Plans," *New York Times,* Dec. 13, 1983.

MANCHESTER, ALDEN C., *Dairy Price Policy: Setting-Problems-Alternatives.* Washington, D.C.: Economics, Statistics, and Cooperative Service, 1978.

NOTT, SHERRILL B., and LARRY G. HAMM, *Quotas for U.S. Dairy Farmers? A Review,* Agricultural Economics Report No. 490. East Lansing, MI: Department of Agricultural Economics, Michigan State University, 1986.

TOMEK, WILLIAM G., and KENNETH L. ROBINSON, *Agricultural Product Prices,* 2nd ed. Ithaca, N.Y.: Cornell University Press, 1981.

THOR, PETER K., and EDWARD V. JESSE, *Economic Effects of Terminating Federal Marketing Orders for California-Arizona Oranges,* Technical Bulletin No. 1664. Washington, D.C.: Economic Research Service, 1981.

U.S. DEPARTMENT OF AGRICULTURE, *A Review of Federal Marketing Orders for Fruits, Vegetables and Specialty Crops: Economic Efficiency and Welfare Implications.* Washington, D.C.: Agricultural Marketing Service, 1981.

U.S. DEPARTMENT OF AGRICULTURE, *Guidelines for Fruit, Vegetable and Specialty Crop Marketing Orders,* 1982.

WARMAN, MARC, "1985 Farm Bill OK's Growth of Farm Commodity Research and Promotion," *Choices,* Second Quarter (1986), 32–33.

8

Structural Policies

This chapter is about policies that affect the survival prospects for medium-sized and small-scale family farms, the cost and availability of credit, and the pattern of land ownership. These policies are often referred to collectively as "structural policies." The United States has never had a well-defined structural policy. Congress on many occasions has made clear its desire to preserve family farms, but no comprehensive plan has been put forward to achieve this objective. Credit and price-support programs have been the principal policy instruments adopted in an attempt to help family farms survive. Unlike many countries in Europe, the U.S. government has not imposed restrictions on entry into agriculture or limited the size of farms. Farm structure in the United States has been influenced much more by changes in technology and by market forces than by government policies. Support programs have affected directly commodities that account for less than half of U.S. agricultural income, and land owners have had almost unlimited freedom to buy, sell, or rent land.

Not everyone thinks the U.S. has a structural problem, or at least one sufficiently serious to require additional government intervention. Successful farmers, in general, do not see any need for more generous credit, changes in agricultural research priorities, or prohibitions against corporate farming. They like the "rules of the game" as it is now being played. But as pointed out in Chapter 3, many people view recent trends in agriculture with considerable apprehension. They are concerned about the disappearance of small-scale farms, the decline in rural communities, and the concentration of production on larger units (USDA, 1981).

POLICY ALTERNATIVES

As in the preceding chapters, the principal policy alternatives are first outlined. One of the alternatives, of course, is to accept the changes that have been taking place rather than to adopt new and more controversial policies. If, however, one wants to alter recent trends, the following alternatives might be considered.

- Offer more liberal credit for small-scale farmers.
- Fund special research and extension programs designed to favor small-scale farms.
- Target price-support benefits to farms below a certain size.
- Prohibit ownership of farm land by nonfamily corporations.
- Eliminate provisions in the tax laws that favor nonfarm investment in agriculture and encourage expansion by large-scale farmers.
- Impose an upper limit on farm size, or at least limit the area of land eligible for government-subsidized water for irrigation.
- Authorize the government to purchase land for resale or lease to entering farmers or small-scale operators who need to expand.
- Create local land purchase review committees with the power to prohibit land transfers that lead to concentration of production on large-scale units.

This listing is more or less in declining order of political acceptance. Those items at the top command wider support than those listed at the bottom.

EFFECTS OF PAST U.S. POLICIES

Early attempts to promote family ownership of farms in the United States are reflected in the land distribution laws that were enacted in the 19th century. These were designed to enable potential farm operators with limited capital to acquire public land (see Chapter 2). Once the frontier was settled, emphasis shifted to credit as the principal instrument to aid in preserving family farms. Ultimately, two types of credit systems were created to assist farmers. One was a government-sponsored, but privately-financed, cooperative credit system. The other was a government-subsidized system. The former, now known as the Cooperative Farm Credit Service, pioneered in offering farmers long-term amortized loans at interest rates only slightly above those prevailing on central money markets.[1] The major contributions of the cooperative credit system have been to augment the supply of loanable funds in rural areas and to offer credit on somewhat more favorable terms to farmers. In addition, the system performed an important function in the 1930s in refinancing thousands of farmers threatened with foreclosure. This was made possible by an infusion of government capital which enabled the regional Land Banks to borrow money at favorable rates of interest. Later, the capital was repaid. The federal government again came to the aid of the cooperative farm credit system in 1988, thereby enabling the system to survive despite the large losses incurred when prices and land values collapsed in the mid-1980s.

A government lending agency, originally known as the Farm Security Administration, and later reorganized and called the Farmers Home Administration (FmHA), was created in the 1930s to augment private and cooperative sources of credit. To obtain credit from the Federal Land Banks (the regional cooperative credit banks), a borrower was required to purchase stock in the cooperative. Borrowers also had to have some equity or capital of their own to qualify for loans. This was necessary to protect the Land Banks from losses and to insure that they would be able to sell their bonds or debentures on the central money markets at low rates of interest. These requirements meant that the cooperative farm credit system could not serve all farmers. The FmHA was designed to help those with little or no capital, especially tenant farmers. One of the objectives of those sponsoring legislation authorizing a government-financed lending program was to enable farm tenants to become owners. Initially, all the funds available for lending to farmers came from annual Congressional appropriations. Because the program was designed to reduce tenancy, the funds available for lending were allocated among states partly in proportion to the number of tenant farms. As a result, more funds were allocated to Southern states where tenant farming was common than to Northern states where owner-operated farms predominated. In recent years, the Farmers Home Ad-

---

[1]Amortized loans avoid the problem of having to repay a large lump sum (the principal) at the end of the loan period. Most all loans made by private lenders as well as cooperatives and government agencies are now amortized, that is, the borrower repays part of the principal each year along with interest on the unpaid balance.

ministration has been authorized to guarantee loans made by private lenders, thus indirectly augmenting the supply of loanable funds.

FmHA loans are available only to farmers who cannot qualify for private or cooperative credit. The agency is authorized to make both farm ownership and operating loans. A farmer without any capital can obtain a loan for 100 percent of the cost of a farm, but is expected to switch to a private lender or the cooperative credit system once he or she has built up sufficient equity to qualify for loans from these sources. In return for 100 percent loans, borrowers are required to develop and implement a financial plan worked out with a loan supervisor. This raises the cost of lending but presumably enables the borrower to manage a higher debt load.

Government-subsidized lending has had only a marginal effect on U.S. farm structure. The principal reason for this is that the direct lending program has been circumscribed by appropriations and the requirement that loans be made only to those who could not qualify for credit elsewhere. In the early years of the program, funds were so limited that the Farm Security Administration was able to accommodate only one out of 100 applicants (LaDue, p. 15). The proportion of farmers served by FmHA has increased since the 1940s, but it still is relatively low. In the 1970s, for example, the number of active borrowers under the FmHA farm ownership loan program amounted to less than 4 percent of all farm operators in the United States (LaDue, p. 14). More farmers have qualified for emergency loans in recent years because of Congressional pressure to ease financial stress and to help bail out other lenders. The FmHA has become the lender of last resort, but the proportion of all farm debt held or guaranteed by the Farmers Home Administration is still much less than that owed to private lenders and the Cooperative Farm Credit Service.

In contrast to many other countries where losses associated with government lending programs have been high, those in the United States have been relatively low. This is attributable to a number of factors, including the threat of foreclosure if loans are not repaid. (In some developing countries, for example, Mexico, governments have been less inclined to insist on repayment and consequently loans have turned out to be the equivalent of a government grant.) The favorable loan loss record of the Farmers Home Administration also is a function of having been restricted in its lending by the availability of funds. The agency could not serve everyone who requested a loan. They generally selected from among the applicants those most likely to succeed. If more funds had been appropriated by Congress, the number of delinquent FmHA borrowers probably would have increased. Generally rising land prices, at least until 1981, also helped to hold down losses. If a borrower failed to meet his or her repayment obligations, the agency usually was able to sell the farm for more than the outstanding debt.

Government-sponsored or government-financed credit and price-support programs have retarded only slightly the trend towards consolidation of farms in the United States and may even have contributed, at least modestly, to such consolidation. The availability of credit on favorable terms from the Cooperative Farm Credit Service, combined with the assurance of support prices and/or government payments, have made it possible and more attractive for aggressive farm operators to expand. They have done so by purchasing neighboring farms. Thus, while the FmHA has helped some small-scale commercial farm operators to survive, other programs, either directly or indirectly, have contributed to their demise.

CONSEQUENCES OF ALTERNATIVE STRUCTURAL POLICIES

Recent trends in farm structure, at least in the United States, are not likely to be reversed or even altered significantly in the absence of substantial changes in existing policies (U.S. Department of Agriculture, 1979, pp. 17 and 23). Almost all projections of farm numbers point toward further consolidation of farms with fewer units in the middle-size range and more large farms (Congressional Budget Office). Over the next fifteen years as many as 500,000 farms may disappear (Lin, Coffman, and Penn). But this would still leave the United States with about 1.5 million farms consisting of as many as a million small-scale and subsistence units, and about 500,000 commercial farms. The latter would produce most of the food sold in supermarkets.

The scenario, as just outlined, is not attractive to those who would like to preserve rural communities and agriculture as a way of life for more families. Concentration of production does result in bypassing local merchants, farm supply, and machinery dealers. A declining farm population forces communities to consolidate schools and churches. Concentration of production on larger units also is likely to lead to a higher proportion of hired labor on farms and perhaps more nonfarm ownership of land. Large-scale farm operators usually own some land but rent additional land.

Critics of recent trends in the structure of American agriculture have emphasized the problem rather than solutions. The regional hearings that were held by the secretary of agriculture during the Carter Administration provided very little guidance as to what should be done to halt or reverse recent trends, and even less information about the consequences of alternative policies (U.S. Department of Agriculture, 1980).

If Congress decides to take additional action to preserve more small-scale and medium-sized family farms, it will face the difficult task of deciding just which of the many policy options to adopt. The following analysis is designed to provide the kinds of information needed by community leaders, farmers, and legislators who are concerned about the structure of agriculture or are confronted with the task of making structural policy decisions.

More Liberal Credit for Small-Scale Farms

One of the more popular proposals to help family farms survive is to offer them more liberal credit, perhaps by expanding lending activities of the Farmers Home Administration. United States experience with FmHA programs demonstrates that a targeted lending program can help to improve the survival prospects for some but not all economically marginal farmers. Any expansion of FmHA lending will lead to higher losses and the need for larger government subsidies.[2] More money, for example, would be required to cover the management and overhead costs of FmHA farm ownership or operating loans.

Not only management services, but also interest costs, may need to be subsidized if FmHA loans are to be extended to more economically marginal farms. Unless farm prices (adjusted for changes in costs) rise above the level prevailing in the mid-1980s, even medium-sized family farms will find it difficult to repay loans if they need to borrow money for the entire cost of the farm. It is not so much a shortage of credit that has led to the demise of small-scale commercial farms as the low level of returns on such farms and, consequently, their inability to generate the cash flow needed to cover both subsistence costs and large loan repayment obligations (Lowenberg-DeBoer and Boehlje, p. 16). Part-time farms, of course, are less vulnerable because they obtain a high proportion of their income from nonfarm employment. Their off-farm earnings are usually sufficient to avoid loan defaults. Just how much credit would have to be subsidized to make small-scale commercial farms viable is difficult to determine, partly because of the great variability in costs and management skills to be found among such farms.

One of the potential negative effects of expanding credit is to reinforce upward pressure on land prices, especially during periods of infla-

---

[2]A number of states now offer special credit programs to assist beginning farmers. The administrative and tax-subsidy costs of such programs can be substantial, especially if the money loaned to farmers is obtained by selling tax-exempt securities. The present value of all subsidies and losses in tax revenue (to the state or federal government) can amount to as much as thirty-two cents per dollar invested in beginning farmers (Lowenberg-DeBoer and Boehlje, p. 14).

tion. More liberal credit, from whatever source, makes it possible for larger numbers of farmers or prospective farmers to compete for the land which comes up for sale. Subsidized credit undoubtedly would enable some of those now excluded to compete successfully for such farms, but the aggregate effect would be to bid up land prices, at least marginally, for all new entrants into agriculture.

Keeping marginal economic units in business is unlikely to have a major impact on farm surpluses, because good land will remain in production regardless of who buys the farm. Nevertheless, successful farm operators often complain about subsidizing those who might otherwise have left agriculture. For obvious reasons, farmers who do not qualify for subsidized credit object to competing with those who do.

Targeted Research and Extension Programs

A second alternative closely related to the first is to fund research and extension programs geared to small-scale farms. Critics of the existing USDA-Land Grant College system maintain that publicly supported research and extension programs now favor large-scale agriculture (Hightower and deMarco). This is particularly true of research related to farm equipment and the development of varieties of crops adapted to mechanical handling. But mandating that more of the funds appropriated for agricultural research go to projects designed to help small-scale farmers would not necessarily improve the competitive position of such farms. It is unrealistic to expect agricultural scientists to create new varieties or practices that will offer a differential advantage to small-scale farmers. Almost anything that can be done to increase yields on small-scale farms will work equally well, or even better, on farms that possess a higher quality of land resources and/or management. Nor is it realistic to expect that cutting off research funds for such activities as agricultural mechanization would improve the competitive position of small family farms. If public research were to be prohibited, there would be even more incentive for private firms, and even cooperatives supplying farm inputs, to conduct their own research. Private research is more likely than publicly-supported research to be targeted to large farms.

Consumers and early adopters have been the principal beneficiaries of past research that has led to the development of higher-yielding varieties and lower production costs. Changing the allocation of research funds to aid small-scale farms could lead to a sacrifice in gains to consumers. Society as a whole is more likely to benefit from agricultural research if the funds are invested in projects that lead to increases in output and efficiency on the larger farms that now produce the bulk of the nation's food supply (Tweeten, p. 143).

The competitive position of at least some small-scale and medium-sized farms might be improved if they had access to a targeted extension program as well as a targeted research program. Extension agents try to provide information for all types and sizes of farms; however, there is a natural tendency for them to work more closely with successful farmers who have access to credit and are eager to adopt new technology. Small-scale commercial farm operators are often reluctant to call on extension agents or may consider their recommendations inappropriate. This reluctance to participate in extension programs can be overcome by hiring special agents to work exclusively with small-scale operators. Typically, a special agent will identify from twenty to forty operators who are motivated to change. He or she will then work intensively with this group of farm operators, making personal calls and becoming actively involved in day-to-day management decisions. Where programs of this kind have been adopted, they have succeeded in helping farmers improve their incomes (Smith). Outside funding frequently is necessary, because states and counties where substantial numbers of farmers have low incomes also tend to have a limited tax base; consequently, they cannot afford to hire additional extension agents. The cost per farmer assisted tends to be higher than for conventional extension programs, because the agent works more intensively with a smaller group.

As with liberalized credit, a targeted extension program is likely to have only a modest impact on the structure of agriculture. It is reasonable to expect some improvement in the rate of survival of farms now in the middle group, but clearly not all farms in this group have the resources or the motivation to take advantage of what amounts to a subsidized management service. Even a subsidized management service cannot offset the disadvantages of poor land resources and limited access to capital.

Target Price-Support Benefits to Farms Below a Certain Size

Price-support benefits could be skewed toward smaller farms by exempting such farms from acreage cuts or set-aside requirements and/or by making payments on only the first "X" units of production. Preferential treatment of small farms has, in fact, been incorporated in price-support legislation for certain commodities. Owners of very small tobacco allotments, for example, have been treated preferentially at times, and farmers with cotton allotments of less than ten acres were given special treatment in legislation enacted in 1965. Exempting farms below a certain size from acreage reductions or limiting acreage payments on farms above a certain size requires making difficult political decisions on cutoff points, that is, just which farms should be given preferential treatment. It also is difficult to effectively administer or enforce a program discriminating against larger units. This was demonstrated in the mid-1980s when operators of units subject to payment limitations divided the farm among family members or formed separate units so as to qualify for payments.

Payments could be divorced entirely from production. But making payments to farmers based on income criteria would present formidable administrative problems not unlike those encountered in certifying families for welfare or determining the level of benefits. Families might underreport income so as to qualify for additional benefits. With any such program, there also is the "notch" problem—that is, the point at which an individual or family no longer qualifies for benefits. Those just above the notch object to being excluded or paying for the support of those just below the notch.

Withholding benefits to farms above a certain size probably would alter only slightly the competitive position of larger farms. As pointed out in Chapter 4, supply control measures would be less effective if large farms were excluded from eligibility for price-support benefits. Price-support or payment limitations would affect only part of U.S. agriculture. Those farms that produce nonsupported commodities such as beef, pork, poultry products, fruits, and vegetables obviously would not be affected by payment limitations. Decisions to enlarge farms also may be influenced very little by payment limitations if they constitute only a small proportion of total income. An increase in the relative importance of government payments would provide more leverage to discriminate against large farms.

Legislation Restricting Corporate Farming

Many individuals, both within and outside of agriculture, view corporate farming as a threat to family farms. In response to these concerns, several states have adopted measures designed to restrict farming by other than family corporations or to discriminate against corporate farms by taxing them at a different rate from individual or family-owned farms (Krause, 1963). The statutes adopted in North Dakota and Kansas are among the most restrictive, although both states have eased restrictions in recent years to accommodate the growth of family-held corporations. West Virginia and South Carolina tax farmland owned by nonfamily corporations at a higher rate than that owned by individuals, partnerships, or family corporations. Most of the states that have adopted laws designed to restrict corporate farming are located in the upper Midwest and the Great Plains. These are states where family farming prevails. In contrast, those states where corporate farming is more important, such as California, Hawaii, Arizona, and Florida have made little or no attempt to restrict the activities of nonfarm corporations.

If national legislation were to be adopted similar to the most restrictive state statutes regulating nonfarm corporations engaged in farming, it probably would affect no more than one percent of all farms.[3] The impact on agriculture would be limited to relatively few commodities, mainly fed cattle, eggs, broilers, sugar, rice, and a few vegetables such as lettuce (Farrell). The structure of the dairy industry or grain production would not be significantly altered, because so little of the total output is now produced by large-scale corporate farms.

One of the minor side effects of restricting corporate farming would be to limit still further the opportunities for individuals with limited capital to begin farming. Becoming a manager on a corporate farm is one of the few ways in which someone with management skills and a desire to farm (but no home farm) can gain entry into agriculture.

Denying corporations the opportunity to invest in agriculture would place an even greater burden on the credit system to finance the acquisition of land and improvements. Corporations are a potential source of equity capital. A higher ratio of equity capital to debt in agriculture would reduce the risk of losses to lenders and also the pressure to "bail out" farmers and credit institutions when land prices decline. Farm operators would be less likely to lose the farm in a period of falling prices or a poor harvest if stockholders rather than local banks or other credit institutions provided a larger share of the capital.

Modify or Eliminate Tax Laws Favoring Large Farms

Tax laws have reinforced incentives to enlarge farms (USDA, 1981, p.92). Successful farmers who earn enough to pay taxes prefer to invest in ways that will minimize their tax liabilities. This frequently means buying additional equipment and land. Rapid depreciation schedules and investment tax credits reduce the cost of capital for those with substantial tax liabilities. In addition, interest on borrowed funds may be deducted as a business expense. Prior to 1987, individuals in the upper income brackets also could reduce their tax liability by converting ordinary income into capital gains, for example, by investing in livestock, citrus groves or vineyards.[4]

---

[3]Individuals, families, partners, and family corporations owned 99 percent of all farms and accounted for 96 percent of the value of all farm products sold in 1982 (Krause, 1987, p. 3).

[4]The tax reform act adopted in 1986 probably has reduced incentives for outsiders to invest in agriculture, and also for successful farm operators to expand.

Critics charge that U.S. tax policies have favored the affluent and that, as a result, agriculture is in danger of being taken over by farm operators who are in a position to exploit tax advantages (Raup). The criticism may be a bit extreme, but there is no doubt that successful farmers have expanded partly in response to tax loopholes. For this reason, tax reform is frequently mentioned as one of the policy instruments that might be adopted in an attempt to discourage concentration of production on larger units, and also the substitution of capital for labor on farms. Among the reforms suggested are to eliminate or reduce investment tax credits and the opportunity to avoid taxes on nonfarm income by writing off losses on agricultural investments, and/or to raise inheritance taxes.

A change in inheritance tax laws could conceivably influence farm structure.   Higher estate or inheritance taxes would compel some families to sell land when the original owner dies. The sale of such land would provide opportunities for more individuals with limited capital to enter farming. The prospect of having to pay higher inheritance taxes also might discourage some large-scale operators from increasing the size of the farm.

Amending tax laws in an attempt to alter the structure of agriculture is not likely to be a very popular option. Farmers strongly object to any suggestion that inheritance taxes be increased.   Even small-scale farmers think it wrong to tax away what they have worked so hard to accumulate.   Investment tax credits are popular with manufacturers of equipment as well as farmers. About the only tax reform measure that can win popular support is to curb incentives for nonfarmers to invest in agriculture, that is, to restrict "tax loss" farming (Sisson).

Impose an Upper Limit on Farm Size

Governments in many countries have imposed a ceiling on the area of land that can be owned or operated by an individual or family. It is most often done in countries that have instituted land reform programs to break up large estates. The objective of acreage ceilings is to compel large land holders to subdivide holdings and/or to prevent large areas of land from falling into the hands of successful farmers or absentee landlords. One can preserve a small farm structure if agreement can be reached on ceilings and these can be enforced. Both are difficult to do. Equitable ceilings are particularly difficult to establish where land quality varies, for example, where some land is irrigated while other land is not. Enforcement problems have plagued every country which has tried to impose ceilings either on payments (as in the United States) or on the size of farms. Owners of land with excess acreage may circumvent the ceiling by dividing the land among members of the family, or by selling land to carefully selected individuals who agree in advance to let the original owners continue to farm the land.

It is not easy to achieve both equity and efficiency in establishing land ceilings.[5] An upper limit that appears to be reasonable at one time may turn out to be too low when new technology becomes available. In Denmark, for example, efficiency has been sacrificed because of ceilings imposed earlier on the size of dairy farms.

Farms of the same size, in terms of acreage, offer quite different earning opportunities in different regions or on different types of soil. A family can earn a reasonable income on a small area of land if it is planted to fruits or vegetables but not wheat. A still larger area of land is required to achieve the same income in semiarid areas where ranching is the only feasible alternative. One way to adjust farm sizes to compensate for earning opportunities is first to establish an income goal or standard. It would be difficult, however, to agree on just what this standard should be and then to translate the income standard into equivalent acreage ceilings for different types of farms.

The United States has had only limited experience with attempting to impose ceilings on how much land an individual can farm. This experience, however, illustrates the problems likely to be encountered in attempting to use acreage ceilings to curb the growth of large farms. Acreage limitations in the United States are confined to land eligible for subsidized irrigation water in projects funded by the federal government. Under the Reclamation Act of 1902, farmers could obtain water rights for a maximum of 160 acres for an individual and 320 acres for a husband and wife. If new land was brought under a federal irrigation project, landowners with excess acreage were obligated to sell the excess land at dry land prices.

Large landholders have attempted to circumvent the restrictions, first by seeking an exemption from the acreage limits; second, by lobbying with Congress to raise the acreage ceiling; and third, by creating new owners to obtain water rights and then renting the land from the new owners. Very large farms still exist in a number of areas supplied with subsidized irrigation water, because the owners of such farms succeeded in obtaining an exemption from what is commonly referred to as the "160 acre limitation." These limits, for example, do not apply to farms in the Imperial Valley in California. Owners of large farms also have been able to persuade Congress to raise the ceiling on land eligible for low-cost water. They have argued that larger acreages are necessary to achieve maximum efficiency in production. Legislation adopted by Congress in 1982 now permits individual land owners or corporations with twenty-

---

[5]Similar problems would arise in trying to reach agreement on upper limits for livestock farms, for example, the number of broilers or pigs one might be permitted to raise.

five shareholders or less (mainly family corporations) to obtain sub-sidized water on a maximum of 960 acres. Corporations with more than twenty-five shareholders can obtain low-cost water on the first 640 acres, but must pay the full cost of irrigation water on any additional acreage that is farmed. Congress did not compel the large landholders to sell the excess acreage, as supporters of the family-farm concept wanted them to do, but responded to the argument that water used on excess acreage should not be subsidized by the taxpayer.

Compelling land owners to sell their excess acreage does not neces-sarily result in more family-operated farms, which was the intent of Congress. In some cases, large landowners have sold the excess acreage to individuals who were not farmers. As owners of 160 acres (or now up to 960 acres), the new owners are eligible to receive irrigation water at the subsidized price. The new owner becomes an intermediary who receives water rights, but then rents the land to the original owner, to be farmed as it had been before the transfer of ownership occurred. Large landowners also have avoided the obligation to sell excess acreage by in-stalling pumps to irrigate the additional acreage. Water pumped direct-ly from wells or rivers is not regulated. Underground water supplies may be recharged by infiltration from farms that are eligible to receive water from canals. The foregoing examples illustrate the weakness of using acreage ceilings as an instrument to change farm structure. To be successful, legislation must be carefully drafted to counter the ingenuity of land owners in circumventing the restrictions. It also requires a strong commitment on the part of the government to enforce the regula-tions.

Authorize the Government to Purchase Land for Resale or Lease

Another way of attempting to change farm structure is to make it easier for those with limited capital to enter farming and to prevent owners of large farms from buying the neighbor's land when the farm comes up for sale. The most common way of doing this is to authorize a government agency to become an intermediary to purchase land. The government can then resell the land under favorable terms or lease it to selected applicants. Such programs are now in effect in a number of European countries and in the province of Saskatchewan in Canada. In some cases, the public agency can preempt sales (that is, they have priority in purchasing land), but must pay the going market price for such land. In other cases the purchasing agency can buy only what land is offered to it.

The Saskatchewan scheme provides an example of how such a program might operate. The Land Commission appraises land offered to it and pays for it based on the appraised value. The land is then rented to individuals or families selected by five members of a government commission (Young). Preference is given to families of former owners of the property acquired or to neighbors and, in a few cases, to nonfarmers who have demonstrated the ability to manage a farm. The leases are favorable to tenants. Rental rates charged by the government tend to be lower than those charged by owners of private land. The government, in effect, subsidizes rents for the selected participants. After five years, the tenant has the option to purchase the land (Bray, and others, p. 301).

If the government were to become a major buyer of farms, the capital outlay would be enormous. Thus far, however, costs incurred under the Saskatchewan program have been modest, because only a small proportion of the land has been acquired by the provincial government. Land purchases have been limited because farms tend to be transferred within the family and, consequently, not much land comes on the market. Net costs to the government need not be high if land is rented at a rate sufficient to pay interest on the money invested. Political pressures, however, are likely to prevent the government from charging the full cost of the land to its tenants. As a result, tenants on government land are likely to earn more than their neighbors who own their farm or rent from a landlord. That creates conflicts within agriculture. Nonparticipants object to competing against those who benefit from government-subsidized land.

The experience of the United States with government-owned land is similar to that in Canada. Those who rent grazing rights on land owned by the government in the eleven western states pay less than the going rate for similar services on private land. Ranchers with the right to graze animals on public land receive what amounts to a subsidized service. Traditionally, Federal grazing rights have been associated with certain properties. These grazing rights enhance the value of such properties. Thus, the benefits of cheap grazing tend to become capitalized into the value of ranches that have the right to graze on public land.

If the government were to purchase more land and to offer such land (for rent or sale) on favorable terms, screening applicants and deciding who should have priority in obtaining land would inevitably become a sensitive political issue. Presumably, the government would favor small operators. This, of course, is precisely why those disenchanted with recent trends in farm structure back such a proposal. Entry into agriculture or expansion of existing farms would no longer be determined mainly by market forces or access to capital but by other criteria. Age and technical qualifications undoubtedly would be considered in deciding who should be offered land. Personal relationships between individuals and, possibly, even political considerations, might also influence the selection of candidates for low-cost government land.

Create Local Land Purchase Review Committees

Results similar to those achieved by a government land purchase and lease program might be realized by giving a local committee veto power over private land transactions. Land would still be privately owned, and prices for land would be determined by competitive bidding, but each transaction would be subject to review. The sole function of a land purchase review committee would be to prohibit sales not thought to be in the public interest. For example, such a committee might veto the sale of a particular parcel of land to a speculator or a farmer with large holdings. Presumably, the committee would be willing to approve the sale of the same parcel of land to an entering farmer or a neighbor who needed additional acreage to create a more viable economic unit. As with a government land purchase and lease program, it would be difficult to establish acceptable criteria for deciding which land transfers to approve or disapprove. The composition of the review committee obviously would have a bearing on such decisions.

Several countries in Europe have adopted programs similar to the foregoing. In the case of Sweden, the legal basis for government intervention in the land market dates from 1965. Under an Act passed in that year, County Agricultural Boards have been established with the authority to prevent the resale of uneconomic farms and to give priority to buyers who need additional land in order to create a viable economic unit. Potential land buyers must apply to the board for permission to purchase a particular farm unless the seller is a relative. While the principal objective is to encourage consolidation of farms, the powers granted under the Act also may be used to prevent speculators or large landholders from acquiring additional land or converting agricultural land to nonfarm uses. If the local board refuses to approve a sale, it is obligated to take over the property at the price negotiated between the buyer and seller (Bray and others, p. 297). The land then may be resold or combined with other units to create a viable farm.

Government intervention in the land market or the power to veto land sales provides a much more direct mechanism for altering the structure of agriculture than withholding price-support benefits or offering additional credit to selected groups of farmers. Restricting land transfers, however, would alter the structure of agriculture only very slowly, because the proportion of farms transferred each year is extremely small. Furthermore, the majority of farm transfers occur within families, a type of transfer that is excluded from public intervention in Europe.[6] If similar restrictions were to be imposed on land transfers in

---

[6]Bergmann has emphasized that European land policies have had only a limited impact on the structure of agriculture, because the authorities cannot expropriate land nor

the United States, one of the effects probably would be to encourage even more transfers within families. This would reduce the number of farms available for sale to those who are not related to present owners of farms. Restrictions on farm transfers also could result in some loss in efficiency and slightly higher food costs if low-cost producers could not acquire more land or if approved transfers were based mainly on social or political criteria rather than managerial capacity.

CONCLUSIONS

In the absence of substantial changes in existing policies, the number of small-scale and medium-sized commercial farms undoubtedly will continue to decline. More of the nation's food supply will come from the larger family farms and former family farms that have expanded to become large-scale units hiring substantial labor. Part-time and subsistence farms, however, are not likely to disappear, because most of their income is derived from nonfarm sources. As long as the land market remains relatively unrestricted, the U.S. will continue to have a very heterogeneous structure, with a wide range in farm sizes and tenure arrangements. This diverse structure makes it possible to accommodate individuals with widely differing skills, motivation, preferences, and access to capital.

The principal policy issue is whether to accept the changes that have been occurring, or to attempt to halt or reverse them by adopting more controversial proposals. Advocates of what might be termed the "passive acceptance" approach argue that efforts to change existing policies may do more harm than good (Tweeten). Heterogeneity and flexibility have characterized American agriculture. These attributes have contributed to its outstanding record of performance in providing consumers with low-cost food. Risks are involved in changing the rules under which U.S. agriculture has operated.

A reversal of recent trends will require more than just liberalizing credit policies or changing tax laws. Among the policies that might be more effective in changing structure are direct subsidies divorced from output, or some form of government intervention in the land market. The trend toward concentration of production on large-scale units is not likely to be curbed without imposing restrictions on who can purchase land. But this would involve a radical departure from past policies.

can they intervene in transactions which take place within families. They have succeeded in increasing the number of medium-sized farms, but many of the farms combined, according to Bergmann, would have been absorbed by still larger units in the absence of government intervention.

Thus far, Congress has been reluctant to consider major changes in policies that affect farm structure. Instead, it has adopted measures that are politically acceptable but relatively ineffective as instruments to preserve small-scale commercial farms. Few marginally profitable farms are likely to be saved from extinction by making more credit available. Nor are successful farm operators likely to be deterred from expanding by imposing limits on price-support payments.

DISCUSSION QUESTIONS

8.1. What have been the major contributions or benefits to U.S. agriculture and public costs (if any) of: (1) the government sponsored cooperative credit system and (2) the government-subsidized FmHA farm ownership loan program?

8.2. Assume your Congressman or Congresswoman wants to do something to help preserve small-scale commercial farms, and has introduced a bill calling for more funds for research and extension targeted to small farms. He (or she) has asked for your views on how effective such a program is likely to be in achieving the desired objective. How would you respond?

8.3. Under what conditions might one expect upper limits on price-support loans or payments to curb the growth of large-scale farms?

8.4. What types of programs have been adopted in Europe and in Canada in an attempt to create more viable economic units and to curb the growth of larger than family farms? Why have similar programs not been adopted in the United States, at least thus far?

REFERENCES

BERGMANN, DENIS R., "A Critical Examination of Structural Policy in Northwest Europe," unpublished paper. Paris: Institute Nationale de la Recherche Agronomique, 1972.

BRAY, C. E., ANNE MARIE DEL CASTILLO, and ERIC BJORNLUND, "Farm Structure Policy in Other Countries," in *Structure Issues of American Agriculture,* Agricultural Economic Report 438. Washington, D.C.: U.S. Department of Agriculture, 1979.

CONGRESSIONAL BUDGET OFFICE, *Background Paper: Public Policy and the Changing Structure of American Agriculture.* Washington, D.C.: Government Printing Office, 1978.

FARRELL, KENNETH R., *Structure and Organization of American Agriculture,* testimony presented to the Subcommittee on Antitrust, Monopoly and Business Rights of the Senate Judiciary Committee, July 17, 1979.

HIGHTOWER, JIM, and SUSAN DEMARCO, "Hard Tomatoes, Hard Times," reprinted in *Food for People, Not for Profit,* edited by Catherine Lerza and Michael Jacobson. New York: Ballantine Books, 1975.

KRAUSE, KENNETH R., *Corporate Farming: Importance, Incentives, and State Restrictions,* Agricultural Economic Report No. 506. Washington, D.C.: Economic Research Service, 1983.

———, *Corporate Farming, 1969–82,* Agricultural Economic Report No. 578. Washington, D.C.: Economic Research Service, 1987.

LADUE, EDDY L., *The U.S. Experience in Providing Financial Assistance to Small Farmers,* Agricultural Economics Staff Paper No. 79-34. Ithaca, N.Y.: Department of Agricultural Economics, Cornell University, 1979.

LIN, WILLIAM, GEORGE COFFMAN, and J.B. PENN, *U.S. Farm Numbers, Sizes and Related Structural Dimensions: Projections to the Year 2000,* Technical Bulletin No. 1625. Washington, D.C.: U.S. Department of Agriculture, 1980.

LOWENBERG-DEBOER, JAMES, and MICHAEL BOEHLJE, "Evaluation of State Legislative Programs to Assist Beginning Farmers," *Agricultural Finance Review* 43(1983), 9–20.

RAUP, PHILIP M., "Some Questions of Value and Scale in American Agriculture," *American Journal Agricultural Economics* 60(1978) 303–8.

SISSON, CHARLES A., "Tax Reform Act of 1976 and Its Effects on Farm Financial Structure," *Agricultural Finance Review* 39(1979) 83–90.

SMITH, STUART F., *1976 Farm Business Summary: Chenango County Limited Resource Program,* A. E. Ext. 77-17. Ithaca, N.Y.: Department of Agricultural Economics, Cornell University, 1977.

TWEETEN, LUTHER, "Prospective Changes in U.S. Agricultural Structure," in *Food and Agricultural Policy for the 1980s,* edited by D. Gale Johnson. Washington, D.C.: The American Enterprise Institute, 1981.

U.S. DEPARTMENT OF AGRICULTURE, *A Dialogue on the Structure of American Agriculture: Summary of Regional Meetings,* November 27-December 18, 1979. Washington, D.C., 1980.

———, *A Time to Choose: Summary Report on the Structure of Agriculture,* Washington, D.C., 1981.

YOUNG, BARBARA, "Rural Redress: Saskatchewan Government Buys up Land to Help Keep Farmers Down on the Farm," *Wall Street Journal,* February 5, 1975, 32.

9

Soil Conservation

For over fifty years popular support for conservation activities has led Congress to fund a number of programs designed to protect the soil; however, conservation has appeared as a high priority item only occasionally and for brief periods. Public interest in conservation reached a peak immediately following the drought and massive dust storms in the mid-1930s. Soil conservation declined as a public issue when production rose during the 1940s and land that had been written off as "lost forever" again yielded reasonable crops, because it rained at the right time. Loss of topsoil reemerged as a priority item during the 1970s, owing to widespread concern that too much vulnerable land was being plowed up to meet rising export demands. The popular phrase at the time was that the U.S. was "trading topsoil for oil."

Nearly everyone agrees that the government has some responsibility for preserving soil, land, and water for future generations. A great deal of controversy exists, however, over the specific objectives of conservation policy and what policy instruments or combination of instruments should be used to achieve those objectives. Critics both inside and outside the government have for many years questioned the effectiveness of U.S. soil conservation programs. Soil losses are still substantial, despite an expenditure of over $15 billion on conservation programs since 1937. Erosion rates exceed levels that would sustain the productivity of soils on about a third of U.S. cropland (Crosson and Stout, p. 15).

Congress has responded to the criticisms of past conservation programs in several ways. In 1977 it enacted the Soil and Water Resource Conservation Act. A major objective of the act is to provide information needed to design more effective conservation programs (Batie, 1985, p.116). Congressional concern about soil conservation is also reflected in the Food Security Act of 1985. The conservation provisions of the Act are, in part, a response to the charge that price support-programs have contributed to soil erosion by encouraging production of "soil depleting" crops and by making it profitable for farmers to cultivate marginal land. The probable effectiveness of the newer legislation, as well as earlier programs, is assessed in this chapter. The success of any program in achieving conservation objectives will be limited, however, unless the program deals with the constraints that make conservation practices uneconomic. For this reason, the factors responsible for the failure of farmers to adopt conservation plans are reviewed first.

WHY FARMERS FAIL TO ADOPT CONSERVATION PRACTICES

Farmers fail to plant soil-conserving crops or adopt practices that would minimize soil losses for a number of reasons, but the principal one is that conservation does not pay, at least in the short run. In many cases, the cost of conservation practices exceeds what farm operators can expect to gain from adopting such practices. Cheap fertilizer and improved technology have also made conservation practices uneconomic on many farms. Losses in yields resulting from soil erosion can be offset more cheaply by purchasing additional fertilizer than by constructing erosion-control devices. There is little economic incentive to save soil for future generations unless losses in productivity are reflected in the value of the farm. Potential losses in land values are too remote for most farmers to consider such losses as a major issue in deciding what to plant or what conservation practices to adopt.

Conservation will not pay on many farms if it necessitates a major shift in land use toward less intensive farming or the construction of relatively expensive erosion-control devices. Shifting from soil-depleting to soil-conserving crops often results in a significant loss in income. For example, the difference in net return from planting alfalfa (a deep-rooted legume) in place of corn or soybeans can amount to as much as $30 per acre (Ogg and Johnson, p. 9). There are indirect as well as direct costs associated with the adoption of farming practices that conserve soil. These indirect costs include the loss of efficiency that results from farming odd-shaped fields created by strip cropping, contour farming, or the construction of terraces. Farmers find it awkward and more costly to operate machinery where fields are small and not rectangular.

Farmers may recognize the need to conserve soil, but cannot make the changes required to reduce soil erosion because of debt repayment obligations. Short-run considerations often dictate their farm management decisions. Landowners with limited incomes and high debts cannot afford to invest in the fences, buildings, and equipment that would be required to shift from crop farming to some combination of crops and livestock. In general, conservation farming in areas of rolling terrain means that more of the land must be devoted to hay and pasture and less to crops like corn, soybeans, and wheat. Farmers may need to increase the number of forage-consuming livestock in order to utilize the crops grown on the more vulnerable land.

Landlords who want to maximize short-term income may be equally uninterested in encouraging tenants to adopt conservation practices or to invest in facilities that pay off only over a long period. An operator who plans to sell his or her farm may take a similar view towards conservation practices (Batie, 1984, p.3). This also is true of tenants who rent land only for a year at a time. Long-term contracts between tenants and landlords would give both parties more incentive to invest in good conservation practices, but such contracts are the exception rather than the rule.

Farmers may not be aware of the long-term losses in productivity that are occurring on their farms, because such losses are being masked by rising yields made possible by improvements in technology. Society has also had little information until recently about the off-farm costs of soil erosion. These are now estimated to be as high as $13 billion per year, far more than the annual cost to farmers of lost productivity (Crosson, 1986, p. 36). Thus, lack of knowledge in some instances may lead to ignoring the conservation problem.

CONSERVATION POLICY OBJECTIVES

Policy debates related to soil conservation have, until recently, focused mainly on what kinds of action should be taken rather than on policy objectives. For most of the past fifty years, conservation programs have been based on the objective of reducing erosion to "acceptable" levels. These levels have been defined as so many tons of soil lost per acre per year. The tolerance level, or "T" value, for soil erosion is the "maximum annual number of tons of soil an acre of land can lose indefinitely without impairing the agricultural productivity of the soil" (Crosson,

1986, p. 34). This figure ranges from as low as one ton on thin soils to more than five tons on deeper soils.

Economists and environmentalists are now challenging the use of T values to define the objectives of conservation policies. They argue that it is not the physical loss that is most important, but the cost of compensating for losses in topsoil or siltation of streams and reservoirs resulting from excess runoff from farms. Moderate rates of erosion can occur on some types of soil without having very much effect on future productivity.[1] This is particularly true where soils are deep as in the Palouse area of Eastern Washington. The next layer down may be almost as productive as the top layer. Furthermore, much of the soil "lost" due to erosion is simply moved further down the slope. No one likes to see sheet or gully erosion, but it is uneconomic to attempt to hold every particle of soil in place. Moderate rates of erosion can be tolerated, because it costs more to curb erosion than the long-term benefits are worth. Using physical standards such as T values to guide conservation policy leads to inefficient use of technical personnel and funds.

A shift away from emphasizing physical targets to the use of economic criteria (or some combination of the two) probably would lead to greater returns to society from the dollars currently invested in conservation activities.[2] The regional allocation of funds undoubtedly would be somewhat different. More funds would go to areas and on farms where erosion results in significant long-term losses in productivity or where runoff damages highways, bridges, and reservoirs. Off-farm damage may be more costly to correct than on-farm damage.

[1]Larson and others concluded that erosion rates of as high as 7.3 tons per acre per year on some types of Corn Belt soils would result in a loss of productivity of only about 2 percent in 100 years (Larson and others, p. 463). A loss of this magnitude could be easily offset (and probably at lower cost) by adopting water conservation measures, planting improved varieties, and more careful timing and placement of fertilizer applications than by constructing and maintaining terraces, grass waterways, etc.

[2]Based on economic criteria, soil conservation activities should be undertaken as long as the additional benefits equal or exceed the incremental costs. The benefits include improvements in water quality, reduction in losses due to siltation of streams and reservoirs or other effects of excessive runoff, and higher productivity of soils in the future or reduced costs of food and fiber. The latter benefits are especially difficult to measure and may be quite small if discount rates higher than zero are applied to future output. As Eleveld and Halcrow point out, "the value of increased food supplies in the future may not be very substantial compared with the immediate effects of conservation on environmental quality" (p. 233).

In estimating incremental costs, one must take account not only of the direct cost of conservation measures but also the indirect effects of reduced current output which can lead to higher prices. Thus, there is a trade-off between higher prices now and in the future. For a more complete discussion of the technical aspects of attempting to derive an optimum conservation policy see Eleveld and Halcrow.

POLICY OPTIONS

The activities or programs most frequently suggested to achieve soil conservation objectives are as follows:

- education
- technical assistance
- cost-sharing subsidies for adopting approved practices
- tax benefits or favorable tax treatment for constructing erosion-control devices
- requirements to adopt conservation plans to remain eligible for price supports, government payments or credit (cross-compliance)
- regulations to prohibit cultivating vulnerable land or to require certain practices on such land.

From the 1930s through the 1970s, the United States relied mainly on education, technical assistance, and cost-sharing conservation subsidies to limit soil losses. Conservation objectives also have been incorporated in programs designed to reduce farm output such as the Soil Bank and the Conservation Reserve. Cross-compliance provisions (that is, tying price-support eligibility to conservation objectives) were incorporated in legislation for the first time in 1985. The Food Security Act adopted in that year requires farmers to implement approved conservation plans (within a certain time period) to remain eligible for price-support benefits.

Education

For the most part, the U.S. has opted for voluntary programs in efforts to achieve soil conservation objectives. If this approach is to be successful, approximately two million farmers and other landowners must be persuaded to adopt practices that will limit erosion. Clearly this is a formidable task. It is necessary to make landowners aware of the problem and to induce them to invest in practices that will be consistent with maintaining long-run productivity and limiting off-farm damage. The principal government-supported agencies charged with the responsibility of educating farmers about how to conserve soil are the Extension Service and the Soil Conservation Service. The mission of the Extension Service is so broad, however, that extension personnel cannot devote a great deal of time and effort to conservation, although farm management specialists and agronomists routinely incorporate soil conservation practices into their recommendations. The Soil Conservation Service was created in part to overcome this limitation. Dr. Hugh Hammond Bennett, the USDA scientist who had most to do with creating the Soil Conservation Service, was convinced that the soil-erosion problem could be solved only by forming a new agency with a more targeted approach. This agency has made a major contribution to educating farmers and the public regarding the seriousness of the conservation problem. But calling attention to the problem and to what must be done to conserve soil does not necessarily lead to action. There is no legal authority to compel farmers to adopt the recommendations made by either the Extension Service or the Soil Conservation Service.

Technical Assistance

In addition to educating farmers and the public about conservation measures, the Soil Conservation Service (SCS) provides farmers with technical assistance. This takes the form of mapping farms to determine the appropriate practices to adopt on each field and advising land owners about the location and kinds of erosion-control devices to construct. SCS pays the salaries of technicians, but generally has not paid farmers to adopt the practices they recommend. The Great Plains Conservation Program, which the SCS administers, is an exception. The agency also has sought funds to encourage land treatment under small watershed planning programs.

Typically, the SCS technician will classify each acre or field on the farm into one of eight land classes, based on its susceptibility to erosion or other crop production hazards. Level land requiring few erosion-control practices is called Class I land. Land classes II through VIII have increasingly severe hazards to crop production, including wetness and stoniness as well as susceptibility to erosion. Different practices are recommended for each class of land. Fields in land class VIII, for example, may require changes in land use. Land in this class is not suitable for crop production and, therefore, should be devoted to grazing or forestry.

Critics of the Soil Conservation Service maintain that making individual farm plans is not a cost-effective way to prevent erosion, because the plans frequently are filed in a desk drawer and ignored. A survey conducted in the 1970s revealed that as much as a third of the time of SCS technicians was spent in preparing plans that were not being followed by farmers (General Accounting Office, p. 12). Recommended practices were not being adopted, because they were believed to be unprofitable. In general, land was cropped more intensively than recommended by the SCS technicians.

Like staff members of the Extension Service, local SCS personnel tend to work with landowners who come to the office voluntarily seeking advice. Those who do so are likely to operate farms on the better land with less severe erosion problems. For this reason, the General Account-ing Office (GAO), in its report submitted to Congress in 1977, recom-mended that more time be devoted to seeking out farmers with the most severe erosion problems. The GAO report also recommended that SCS personnel provide more technical help and follow-up calls to encourage farmers to carry out the practices recommended (General Accounting Of-fice , p. 26).

SCS technicians must now devote more time to implementing the "sodbuster," "swampbuster," and cross-compliance provisions incor-porated in the Food Security Act of 1985.[3] Under this Act, farmers producing crops on erodible land are required to implement a conserva-tion plan if they are to remain eligible for price-support loans, deficiency payments, crop insurance, and other government programs. Farmers also may lose benefits if they plow up grassland or drain swamps. The Soil Conservation Service is responsible for checking compliance as well as conducting soil surveys and preparing soil maps to identify areas eligible for inclusion in the Conservation Reserve.

Farm planning may not be very cost-effective as an erosion-control measure, but farmers generally like the SCS and the assistance it offers. A local technician who can assist in identifying where a farm pond should be located or where best to install drains is an asset to farmers. In recent years, the agency has promoted minimum or zero-tillage, a practice that conserves soil. It has proved to be a popular option with farmers, although the practice is not profitable on all types of soil.

Subsidies or Tax Benefits

A major reason for the failure of farmers to adopt conservation practices, as pointed out in the introductory section, is that the changes in land use or investments in erosion-control practices recommended by the SCS are not profitable. In some cases, land now planted to row crops would have to be devoted to hay and pasture. This would require adding a livestock enterprise to use the additional forage. In other cases, farmers would have to construct terraces and plant in strips on contours. In areas of rolling terrain these practices could result in less efficient use of labor and equipment. Resistance to making these changes could be overcome by offering subsidies or tax benefits to compensate for lower returns, higher direct costs, or losses in efficiency.

The U.S. has made only limited use of subsidies to encourage soil conservation. Cost-sharing subsidies to farmers have been provided

---

[3]The term "sodbuster" refers to plowing up grassland to convert it into cropland; "swampbusting" is the common phrase used to describe draining wetlands (often used by birds as nesting areas) so that the land can be cropped.

under the Agricultural Conservation Program (ACP) and the Great Plains Conservation Program, but the amount of money appropriated for this purpose has been quite small. In the early 1980s, ACP appropriations averaged around $200 million annually. If divided equally among commercial farms, the subsidy would amount only to about $200 per farm.

The ACP program is a legacy of the 1930s. It was introduced partly to encourage conservation and partly to raise farm incomes. Subsidizing conservation practices was considered to be more politically acceptable than making price-support and income payments to farmers. Now, however, the latter far exceed the amounts available to subsidize conservation practices. Successive presidents beginning with Eisenhower have recommended that the program be terminated. It has survived, despite these recommendations, because it is popular with key members of Congress, particularly Jamie Whitten, the longtime chairman of the committee that controls ACP appropriations. The ACP program brings federal money into rural communities and gives the appearance of doing something to reduce soil erosion, although the major effect of the program has been to increase output rather than to conserve soil.

ACP subsidies cover only part of the cost of adopting approved conservation practices. Farmers bear roughly half of the cost, most often in the form of providing their own labor and equipment. State and local committees compile a list of practices available for cost-sharing subsidies (within the guidelines established by the supervising agency in Washington). In the past, many practices on the list contributed relatively little to conserving soil. The GAO study referred to earlier found that funds were being used to subsidize practices that increased yields but contributed relatively little to reducing erosion (General Accounting Office. pp. 28–41). Among the practices falling into this category were subsidies for applying lime and fertilizer and installing tile drains or irrigation systems.

Selective participation by farmers also limits the effectiveness of the ACP program. Farmers on the better land where erosion is less serious tend to be more aggressive in seeking assistance; those on the more vulnerable land may not know that assistance is available or cannot afford to adopt the practices eligible for cost-sharing subsidies. A study conducted in the 1970s revealed that nearly half of ACP subsidies at that time went to those farming land on which erosion averaged less than five tons per acre per year (Crosson and Stout, p. 17). That is below the tolerance level or T value for most farms. Only about one-fifth of the money was used to subsidize conservation practices on farms where erosion was high (exceeding fourteen tons per acre per year).

Since 1980, efforts have been made to target more of the funds to areas and farms where erosion is a serious problem. The list of practices eligible for cost-sharing subsidies has been cut back, and more emphasis has been given to paying for ones that result in reducing erosion rather than simply increasing yields. Targeting of funds, however, has en-. countered political resistance. Senators and Representatives do not want to see a reduction in the funds made available for their state or district. To minimize the impact, farmers and those representing areas that might suffer from the diversion of funds to other areas have succeeded in broadening the definition of targeting, so that few areas are excluded. Congressman Whitten has insisted that no state's allocation of ACP funds be reduced by more than 1 percent (Batie, 1985, p. 120). This leaves little money to reallocate to other areas. Thus, while targeting makes sense from the standpoint of increasing the amount of conservation achieved per dollar spent, it has proved difficult to implement the concept. Political pressures dictate that the funds be spread broadly. Furthermore, as long as participation is voluntary and the allocation of funds remains under local control, the more aggressive and successful farmers, often with the better land, will tend to benefit disproportionately.

United States experience with the ACP program illustrates the dilemmas faced in designing conservation programs. Efficiency and political acceptability are often at odds. More erosion control per dollar spent probably could be obtained if the allocation of funds were more tightly controlled from Washington. But this would reduce local support for the program. Farmers and their representatives in Congress prefer to maintain a substantial degree of local control. As noted, this often leads to subsidizing practices that increase output rather than conserve soil and benefits those who least need help.

Favorable tax treatment could be used as an alternative to subsidies (or as a supplement) to encourage the use of good conservation practices. The most compelling argument for this approach is that tax avoidance is a highly motivating factor on the more successful commercial farms. On several occasions, provisions designed to encourage farmers to invest in soil conservation have been written into the tax code. In the early 1950s, for example, the federal tax code was modified to make certain conservation expenditures deductible as ordinary business expenses. Writing off an investment in one year is preferable to depreciating the same investment over several years, particularly for a farmer who wants to avoid paying taxes in a high-income year. That, among other fast write-off provisions, was dropped in the tax reform act passed in 1986.

The principal limitation of using tax benefits as an inducement to invest in conservation (aside from the loss in tax revenue) is that the conservation effects are likely to be highly selective among farms. Tax avoidance is of interest mainly to the more affluent farmers with substantial tax liabilities. Farmers in this position usually own the better land. Those who farm more vulnerable land have less incentive to make use of favorable tax provisions, because they earn lower incomes and, therefore, pay less in taxes or none at all. Tax benefits are likely to be cost-effective as a conservation measure only on farms where erosion is potentially serious and tax avoidance is a major consideration in making farm management decisions. Relatively few farms satisfy both criteria for cost-effectiveness.

Cross-Compliance

Denying the benefits of price-support and other government programs to farmers who fail to conserve soil has enormous political appeal. For many years conservationists have argued that it makes no sense to subsidize farmers who plow up vulnerable land or ignore good conservation practices. Much of the pressure to use eligibility for government programs as leverage to achieve conservation objectives has come not from traditional farm organizations but from a coalition of conservation and environmental interest groups including the Sierra Club, the Audubon Society, the Natural Resources Defense Council, and the National Wildlife Federation (McCullough and Weiss).

Conservationists were particularly upset by reports that farmers in the Great Plains were converting large areas of range land to wheat production in the late 1970s. Price guarantees and the availability of disaster payments encouraged these changes in land use. Farmers were eligible for compensation for reduced yields even if they plowed up vulnerable land. The shift from grassland to wheat, however, was influenced more by market forces than by government programs (Huszar and Young). The price of wheat rose relative to the price of beef during the 1970s, thus encouraging farmers to plant wheat rather than to graze livestock. Creditors also encouraged shifts in land use because cropland could be sold for a much higher price than range land.

Congress responded to the concerns of conservationists by holding hearings on a number of bills designed to discourage plowing up grassland. These were referred to as "sodbuster" bills. None of the sodbuster bills became law, but equivalent provisions were incorporated in the Food Security Act of 1985. Title XII of that Act denies eligibility for government credit as well as price-support programs to farmers who plow up vulnerable land or convert wetlands to cropland. Program benefits also may be denied to farmers who fail to implement appropriate conservation practices on land susceptible to erosion that is being used to produce supported commodities. These "cross-compliance" provisions represent a significant departure from previous conservation efforts, which relied mainly on voluntary action by participating farmers.

The authorizing legislation falls short of direct regulation but provides the secretary of agriculture with much more leverage to induce farmers to implement conservation plans.

Cross-compliance has two major limitations as an instrument to achieve conservation objectives. First, withholding benefits will not necessarily lead to conservation measures on the most vulnerable land; second, enforcement will be difficult. Farmers with the least erosive land will find it relatively easy to qualify for benefits. Those with high potential soil losses may not produce commodities that are supported or may find compliance too costly. If they elect to forego benefits, the legislation will not have achieved the objective of reducing soil losses. The farms that can least afford the loss in income may be penalized the most.

Only about one-third of all U.S. cropland will be directly affected by the cross-compliance provisions incorporated in the 1985 Act (Reilly, p. 15). Conservation practices on some of the most vulnerable land will not be significantly altered, because farmers do not produce crops that are supported, or such crops account for only a small proportion of their income. Those farmers who use most of the grain they produce to feed livestock will have little incentive to change existing practices unless deficiency payments are very large. Soybean producers, likewise, may have little incentive to implement conservation plans if market prices remain close to or above price-support loan rates and they are not offered deficiency payments. The potential gains from remaining eligible for price-support loans must exceed the costs of implementing conservation plans in order for the program to have a significant effect on soil losses. The less farmers depend on government payments or price-support loans, the less effective the program will be in reducing erosion. If market prices for supported commodities rise or payments decline because target prices are reduced, cross-compliance will become a relatively ineffective instrument for achieving soil conservation objectives. Using price-support benefits as leverage to achieve conservation objectives will inevitably produce selective effects among regions. The impact of the 1985 legislation, for example, will be greatest in the Corn Belt, the Great Plains, and parts of the South where cotton, rice, and peanuts are important commodities. It will not lead to significant changes in conservation practices in the Appalachian region or the Northeast. Income disparities among farms also could widen if cross-compliance provisions are fully implemented. Those farmers with only a small proportion of erodible land, or those who already are using conservation practices on such land, will find it relatively easy to remain eligible for benefits. Those with more erodible land will have to accept a lower income because of foregone payments or higher costs associated with implementing approved conservation plans.

The 1985 Act imposes a large administrative burden on the Soil Conservation Service, which must complete soil maps to determine land capability classes and then must develop conservation plans for all land on farms classified as highly erodible. Disagreements will inevitably arise in deciding what criteria to use in defining "highly erodible land." Farmers can be expected to challenge the classification on their farm if it leads to the denial of program benefits. What constitutes an "appropriate" conservation practice also may become a controversial issue. Finally, the SCS will have to decide at what point the farmer has failed to implement the approved conservation plan. Ultimately, the courts may be asked to decide some of these issues.

Past experience suggests that no matter how carefully the guidelines are drawn up, farmers will be able to find loopholes and take advantage of them. If the program is administered so rigidly that a large number of farmers are denied eligibility, Congress will be under considerable pressure to amend the legislation.

Government Rental or Purchase of Vulnerable Land

An alternative to requiring farmers to adopt approved conservation practices on vulnerable land is to retire such land from cultivation under long-term contracts. This may be done either by purchasing or renting erosion-prone land. Such a program is especially attractive if surpluses are a problem. Both Republican and Democratic administrations have found it politically expedient to adopt long-term land retirement schemes as a method of attempting to reduce surpluses. The Soil Bank program adopted in the 1950s, and the Conservation Reserve program which replaced it in the 1960s, were designed mainly to restrain production, but they did succeed in keeping idle several million acres of cropland, some of which, especially in the Great Plains and the fringes of the Corn Belt, was highly susceptible to erosion. Congress has recognized that there is more political appeal to a program linked to conservation objectives than one which simply pays farmers to idle cropland. For this reason a long term land retirement program designed to retire vulnerable cropland was incorporated in the Food Security Act of 1985. The Conservation Reserve program revived by that Act is targeted to retire forty to fifty million acres of erodible cropland by 1990.

Land rental is more acceptable politically than a government land-purchase program. Under a land-rental program such as the Conservation Reserve, landowners agree to idle vulnerable land for a specified period (ten years under Conservation Reserve contracts). During the period land is under contract to the government, the owner cannot harvest any crop from the land (nor under the Conservation Reserve can a farmer graze livestock on the acreage rented to the government). A cover crop of grass or trees must be maintained to prevent erosion. In return, the owner of the retired acreage receives annual payments equivalent to the rental value of the land. The owner continues to pay real estate taxes as before. If the land is sold, the new owner must comply with the terms of the contract or pay a penalty.

Government purchase of vulnerable land is a less attractive option than renting land, partly because the initial cost would be much higher (assuming the land is purchased at prevailing market prices).[4] Local communities also object to taking land off the tax rolls. Presumably, the government would be obligated to make payments to local units of government or to school districts in lieu of taxes, but the amount paid is likely to be a sensitive issue. Government ownership of land is not popular in the eleven western states where large areas of relatively poor land are already owned by the federal government. In some states, there is considerable pressure to convert government land to private holdings. Any attempt to increase the amount of land held by the government would meet with strong local opposition, particularly if the land acquired were held off the market and could not be used for grazing.

The effectiveness of either a government land-rental or purchase program as a conservation measure (as well as the cost of the program) will be strongly influenced by the rules established for eligibility. The Conservation Reserve program authorized in the 1985 Food Security Act limits eligibility to land which is "highly erodible." This term can be interpreted in several ways. Eligibility for admission to the Conservation Reserve has been based on SCS land-capability classes and T values.[5]

The area of land eligible, as well as its location, will depend on whether eligibility is based on an estimate of the current rate of erosion or on potential erosion. More land is potentially "highly erodible" than is currently eroding at some multiple of the T value, for example, three times the tolerance limit. According to a study conducted in the early 1980s, the area of land eligible for the Conservation Reserve would rise from 69 million acres to 118 million acres if potential rather than actual erosion were to be used as the criterion for eligibility (Dicks and Reichelderfer, p. 2). Where and how much land is to be retired also will depend on whether priority is to be given to output reduction or soil con-

[4]The U.S. has had only limited experience with a land-purchase program aimed at retiring vulnerable cropland. Some severely damaged farms located in the dust bowl were purchased by the Resettlement Administration in the 1930s. These farms were sold in the 1940s when more production was needed.

[5]Under interim rules established for the first four sign-up periods, eligibility for participation in the Conservation Reserve was limited to land in SCS land capability classes VI, VII, and VIII, *or* to land that was eroding at more than three times the T value for that land.

servation. The optimum pattern of land retirement will differ depending on whether one is seeking to minimize the cost of achieving the desired reduction in output or to maximize the amount of soil saved per dollar of government cost (Jagger and Robinson).

There is no assurance under a voluntary land-retirement program that the most vulnerable land will be offered to the government. Landowners decide whether or not to submit a bid and name the rental rate they are prepared to accept. Under the Conservation Reserve Program, the government has the option of accepting or refusing land at the price offered by the landowner. The government may decide not to accept some of the land offered if it believes the rental rate is too high.

Ceilings imposed on the proportion of acreage that can be retired in a county or state also may limit the effectiveness of a land-rental program as a conservation measure. Congress generally has imposed upper limits on the area of cropland that can be retired under supply-management programs. A similar restriction was written into the Conservation Reserve legislation. Under the 1985 Act, no more than 25 percent of the cropland in any one county can be accepted unless it can be shown that increasing the proportion idled would have little adverse effect on the local economy. This provision reflects the political resistance to retiring large areas of cropland even if it is potentially highly erodible. No elected representative wants to see farming disappear from his or her district.

Renting or purchasing vulnerable land is an expensive solution to the nation's soil-erosion problem. Costs will be especially high if crop prices are favorable and/or price-support payments make it attractive for farmers to keep land in production. The higher the level of support, the more expensive it will be to induce farmers to retire land under long-term contracts. Costs would be somewhat less if payments were made to compensate only for the loss of cropping rights. If the government were to purchase crop easements (that is, the right to produce annual crops), landowners would be free to use the land for other purposes, such as grazing, forestry, water conservation, or recreation. Under such a program, the government would need to pay landowners only for the difference in returns between planting the land to annual crops, such as wheat, sorghum, or corn, and the next most profitable use.[6]

From an economic perspective, it makes sense to rent cropping rights on vulnerable land and to permit such land to be grazed or used to produce forest products; however, the politics of renting cropping rights is less favorable. Livestock producers object to any program that in-

---

[6]Research conducted in the 1960s indicated that a crop-limiting easement might be purchased for 80 percent or less of the average market value of cropland than prevailing in the lower-yielding counties in the Great Plains (Griffing and Fischer, pp. 64–66).

directly subsidizes shifts in land use from crops to grass. They view induced changes in land use as unfair competition for existing cattlemen although some might, in fact, benefit from being able to rent additional grazing land at lower cost.

Regulation

The principal alternative to subsidizing conservation practices or paying farmers to change land use or retire erodible land from cultivation is to enforce regulations that would achieve the same objectives. Thus far, Congress has resisted the regulatory approach, although a number of states have adopted erosion and sediment control legislation which includes mandatory provisions (Crosson, 1986, p. 37). The most compelling argument for this approach is to achieve better control over soil losses at reduced public cost.

Environmentalists question whether voluntary programs will ever be able to reduce off-farm losses to acceptable levels, particularly where there is little visible loss in productivity of the land. Owners of erosion-prone land will have little incentive to participate in voluntary conservation programs if productivity losses are small or can be offset at modest cost by purchasing additional inputs. Landowners, of course, could be paid to adopt conservation practices that yield few benefits to them but major benefits to society as a whole. It would be difficult, however, to decide on levels of compensation. Regulating those who contribute to off-farm "soil-pollution" would be a lower-cost alternative. This has been the approach used to improve air and water quality. Regulating runoff would be similar to imposing restrictions on the use of high-sulphur coal or the discharge of toxic chemicals into lakes or streams. Crosson suggests that opposition to the regulatory approach may diminish as the public becomes more aware of the off-farm costs of soil erosion (Crosson, 1984, p.225).

Runoff regulations would be extremely difficult to administer. One would need to trace the source of runoff and decide on tolerance limits. Farmers are not the only source of sediment. Much of the siltation of streams and reservoirs is attributable to runoff from construction sites or land that is not used for agriculture. Tracing the source of sediment damage or water pollution is technically difficult. It would be even more difficult to prove that runoff from a particular farm was "excessive." Some of those charged with producing excess runoff could be expected to take their case to the courts. Political acceptance of runoff regulations is likely to be limited by potential administrative problems and the prospect of endless litigation.

Land-use regulations are much more easily enforced and have been found by the courts to be legal, at least in some states. Zoning ordinances are common in urban areas and could be used in rural areas to prohibit plowing up vulnerable land or to regulate land use. An Iowa court has ruled that police power may be used by a conservation district to restrict the freedom of farmers to plant certain crops on erodible land. A conservation district or some other public agency also might compel farmers to adopt certain conservation practices. Compliance with land-use regulations or conservation requirements is relatively easy to check because land use can be observed any time during the growing season. This obviously is not true of runoff, which can be checked only during certain times and can be measured only with the aid of special equipment. As with any regulatory program, acceptance will depend on the costs imposed on those who are regulated. Local communities will be reluctant to use the police power to regulate land use if this results in substantial income losses to significant numbers of farmers.

CONCLUSIONS

The combination of policies that the United States has implemented in recent years probably is sufficient to maintain the productive capacity of most farms within tolerable limits. Soil losses will continue to exceed T values in some areas and on some farms, but the overall effect on the capacity to produce food over the next 50 to 100 years is likely to be quite small. Targeting more of the effort to those areas and farms missed or inadequately served by current programs would reduce the amount of soil loss.

Public funds could be used more efficiently if greater emphasis were given to economic objectives and less to physical losses. Even a moderately high rate of erosion on some soil types may not lead to a significant long-term loss in productivity. Society would gain more from a given appropriation for soil conservation activities if a higher proportion of the funds were targeted to areas where the combined farm and off-farm costs of compensating for damage are relatively high.

Conservation programs will continue to have selective effects among farms and regions because they are voluntary. Some farm operators cannot afford to adopt soil-conserving measures because of the economic pressure to maintain marginal land in production and to use the land more intensively than conservationists would recommend.

The cross-compliance provisions included in the Food Security Act of 1985 provide additional leverage to get soil conservation plans adopted, but the added inducement applies only to farms highly dependent on government payments or price-support loans. These inducements may become less effective if budgetary pressures force Congress to reduce the level of support for grains and cotton.

Future conservation policies may be shaped more by the influence of environmentalists than by traditional agricultural interest groups, especially if the public is persuaded that off-farm costs associated with erosion are substantial. This could result in placing less reliance on voluntary programs to achieve conservation objectives, and more on compulsory regulations relating to land use and cropping practices.

DISCUSSION QUESTIONS

9.1. What are the principal criticisms of using T values to guide conservation policies? What changes in policies might one expect if economic criteria rather than T values (physical losses) were given higher priority?

9.2. Why have farmers in many cases failed to adopt appropriate conservation measures despite fifty years of soil conservation programs?

9.3. How might existing conservation programs be modified in the United States to increase their effectiveness in reducing soil erosion and runoff? Why have the proposed changes been resisted by Congress?

9.4. Are the "cross-compliance" provisions incorporated in the Food Security Act of 1985 likely to bring about a significant reduction in soil loss?

REFERENCES

BATIE, SANDRA S., "Soil Conservation Policy for the Future," *The Farm and Food System in Transition,* Leaflet No. 23. East Lansing, MI: Cooperative Extension Service, Michigan State University, 1984.

———, "Soil Conservation in the 1980s: A Historical Perspective," *Agricultural History* 59, no. 2 (1985), 107–23.

CROSSON, PIERRE R., with ANTHONY T. STOUT, *Productivity Effects of Cropland Erosion in the United States.* Washington, D.C.: Resources for the Future, 1983.

CROSSON, PIERRE, "New Perspectives on Soil Conservation Policy," *Journal of Soil and Water Conservation* 39 (1984), 222–25.

———, "Soil Conservation: It's Not the Farmers Who Are Most Affected by Erosion," *Choices,* 1, no. 1 (1986), 33–38.

DICKS, MICHAEL R., and KATHERINE REICHELDERFER, *Choices for Implementing the Conservation Reserve,* Agriculture Information Bulletin 507. Washington, D.C.: Economic Research Service, 1987.

ELEVELD, BARTELT, and HAROLD G. HALCROW, "How Much Soil Conservation is Optimum for Society?" *Soil Conservation Policies, Institutions and Incentives,* edited by Harold G. Halcrow, Earl O. Heady and Melvin L. Cotner. Ankeny, Iowa: Soil Conservation Society of America, 1982.

GENERAL ACCOUNTING OFFICE, *To Protect Tomorrow's Food Supply, Soil Conservation Needs Priority Attention,* CED-77-30. Washington, D.C.: Congress of the United States, 1977.

GRIFFING, MILTON E., and LOYD K. FISCHER, "Government Purchase of Crop Limiting Easements as a Means of Reducing Production," *Journal of Farm Economics,* 47 (1965), 60–73.

HUSZAR, PAUL C., and JOHN E. YOUNG, "Why the Great Colorado Plowout?," *Journal of Soil and Water Conservation* 39 (1984), 232–34.

JAGGER, CRAIG, and KENNETH L. ROBINSON, *Long-Range Land Retirement as a Solution to the Wheat Surplus Problem,* A.E. Res. 86-31. Ithaca, N.Y.: Department of Agricultural Economics, Cornell University, 1986.

LARSON, W.E., F.J. PIERCE, and R.H. DOWDY, "The Threat of Soil Erosion to Long-Term Crop Production," *Science* 219, no. 4584 (1983), 458–65.

MCCULLOUGH, ROSE, and DANIEL WEISS, "An Environmental Look at the 1985 Farm Bill," *Journal of Soil and Water Conservation* 40 (1985), 267–70.

OGG, CLAYTON, and JAMES JOHNSON, "Policy Options for Targeting Conservation Expenditures," NCR-111 Symposium on Policy Incentives for Soil Conservation, 1981.

REILLY, WILLIAM K., "Agriculture and Conservation: A New Alliance," *Journal of Soil and Water Conservation,* 42 (1987), 14–17.

U.S. DEPARTMENT OF AGRICULTURE, *An Economic Analysis of USDA Erosion Control Programs: A New Perspective,* Agricultural Economic Report Number 560. Washington, D.C.: Economic Research Service, 1986.

10

Assisting Human Resource Adjustments

Declining employment in agriculture has been a fact of life for over fifty years. With one or two minor exceptions, there have been fewer farms each year and a smaller farm population; however, the rate of exodus from agriculture has not been constant. It has varied with conditions both within and outside of agriculture. The major factors contributing to high rates of exodus have been rapid changes in technology, low farm prices, and readily available off-farm job opportunities.

Congress has been concerned mainly with trying to keep people in agriculture by supporting farm prices and augmenting private credit facilities, not in aiding those displaced from agriculture. Public sentiment favors keeping people on the land; the programs adopted, however, have not prevented adjustments from taking place in response to changes in technology and the availability of off-farm jobs. Economists have tried to persuade policymakers to devote more attention to programs designed to assist individuals and families displaced from agriculture, or at least to alleviate some of the consequences of rapid technological advances, but without much success. Congress has paid more attention to idling land than to retiring farmers.

Policies or programs that might be adopted to assist adjustments, not prevent them from taking place, are reviewed in this chapter. The broader issue addressed is what to do about rural poverty. Only part of the rural poverty problem is the result of changes that have occurred within agriculture during the past two decades. Some of the rural poor are the legacy of an earlier generation of families displaced from agriculture. Others are low-paid or temporary agricultural workers, or those displaced from resource-based industries such as mining, forestry, or fishing.

Adjustment problems obviously are not confined to agriculture or unique to rural areas, but the measures proposed to alleviate rural poverty or to make life a bit more comfortable for the "people left behind" by changes in agricultural technology are somewhat different from those proposed for urban areas. The politics of rural poverty also differs somewhat from the politics of urban poverty; proposals are likely to be handled by different committees in Congress and to involve different coalitions of interest groups.

Nearly 40 percent of all the families with incomes below the poverty line in the mid-1980s lived in rural areas. Since less than 25 percent of the total U.S. population reside outside metropolitan areas, this means that the incidence of poverty, that is, the proportion of the population falling in the poverty group, is higher in rural than in urban areas. In 1983, 14.8 percent of the nonmetropolitan population fell below the poverty line; the comparable figure for urban areas was 11.1 percent (Statistical Abstract, 1985, p. 458).

TRENDS IN FARM NUMBERS AND EMPLOYMENT

Much publicity was given to farm stress and the forced exodus of families from agriculture during the mid-1980s; however, the number of families who left agriculture during that period in response to low prices and unmanageable debts was much smaller than the number who left earlier. The rate of exodus from agriculture was especially high during the 1950s and 1960s. In the decade between 1950 and 1960, for example, the number of units defined by the census as farms dropped from 5.6 million to 4.0 million, a decline of nearly 1.6 million (Figure 10.1). This is more than five times the number of farms that disappeared between 1975 and 1985. Changes in farm employment also were much greater during the 1950s and 1960s than those that occurred in the 1970s and early 1980s. The trend line in Figure 10.1 showing changes in total farm employment (including hired as well as family workers) flattened and then declined less steeply after 1970.

Fewer individuals and families will be leaving agriculture over the next two decades than during the past two decades simply because the

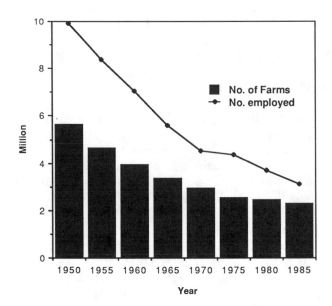

Figure 10.1   Number of farms and total employment on farms, 1950-1985. (Source: U.S. Bureau of the Census. 1985, pp. 631–32 and 1987, pp. 619 and 621.)

population base is now much smaller. Less than 3 percent of the total U.S. population remains on farms. But adjustments are not over. Farm labor requirements will continue to decline, especially if research results based on biotechnology accelerate the trend towards higher yields and more efficient conversion of grain and forage into milk and meat production.

One should not assume that all those who leave agriculture are in need of assistance. The majority of those who left farming between 1940 and 1980 did so voluntarily. Not everyone wants to work long hours for low returns. Many of those displaced from agriculture retired or remained in the community and found other jobs. Ex-farmers can be found driving school buses, operating construction equipment, selling real estate, or working for agribusiness firms. Some migrated to areas where jobs were more readily available. Only a minority of those who once farmed or were employed as hired farm workers have failed to find reasonable employment. But there are areas where substantial numbers were unable to migrate or to find jobs paying much more than minimum wages. Those trapped in rural areas are referred to in the 1967 Report of the President's National Advisory Commission on Rural Poverty as the "people left behind."

GEOGRAPHICAL CONCENTRATION OF THE RURAL POOR

Rural poverty, like the conservation problem, is concentrated in certain areas of the United States. Over 90 percent of persistent low-income rural counties are to be found in Appalachia, the Mississippi Delta, and the Ozark-Ouachita Plateau region (Long and others, p. 10). Pockets of rural poverty also exist in the Southwest, especially among Indian and Hispanic communities. Rural poverty is much less pervasive in the Northeast and Midwest, because nonfarm jobs are available within commuting distance of many rural communities. Out-migration has helped to minimize the rural poverty problem in the Great Plains and the Intermountain region, but the exodus has left in its wake a much smaller population and derelict communities. Part-time farming has eased the transition out of agriculture for many families, particularly in the Piedmont region and in the Northeast.

REASONS FOR THE PERSISTENCE OF RURAL POVERTY

Low incomes tend to persist because the adjustment process works imperfectly. Racial discrimination, limited education, physical and mental handicaps, and what often is referred to as a "culture of poverty" are among the factors that contribute to keeping successive generations poor. The loss of self-esteem is both a cause and an effect of poverty. Children growing up in families where the older members are demoralized and discouraged often do not do well in school and eventually drop out. With limited education, they find it difficult to move to other areas or to qualify for higher-paying jobs; thus poverty extends into the next generation. Case studies of families with limited incomes have shown that such families often are confronted with multiple problems, including poor health, marital conflicts, alcoholism, and teenage pregnancy (Crosswhite). Incomes are never quite adequate to cope with emergencies, and these occur frequently. Families are likely to live in dilapidated housing or in mobile homes that are fireprone. The old car needed for transportation to a job may fail at a critical time, or the well runs dry. One of the consequences of trying to meet a succession of crises is emotional exhaustion or paralysis (Fitchen p. 193). Under such conditions problems often accumulate, making it even more difficult for a family to lift itself out of poverty.

Low wages and intermittent employment also contribute to the perpetuation of rural poverty. A high proportion of poor rural families have at least one member who is employed; however, the jobs available to them often pay only minimum wages. Even if fully employed, an individual with a spouse and two children cannot earn enough at minimum wages to rise above the poverty level.[1]

The low-income problem is often associated with seasonal employment. Jobs simply are not available during certain periods of the year. This is true of forestry, fishing, and resort communities as well as agriculture. Farmers need 1.0 to 1.5 million more workers in July and August than in January. The earnings of seasonal farm workers tend to be low (even where hourly or piece-rate wages are relatively high) because they are idle many days. Some may work only a few hours a day. As more and more tasks are mechanized, the number of hours a seasonal worker is typically employed during the year becomes less and less. Peaks in labor demand for the remaining nonmechanized crops remain the same, but there are fewer jobs in total. Seasonal workers find it more difficult to put together a sequence of jobs to keep fully employed when some crops are mechanized. This is illustrated by what happened in Michigan and New York. In the 1950s it was common for seasonal workers to begin harvesting cherries in July, then move on to green beans, sweet corn, tomatoes, and finally to apples, grapes, and potatoes. Harvesting of most of these crops has been mechanized, except for apples sold for fresh use. Thus, recruitment of labor to harvest the late-season crops has become more difficult for employers because seasonal workers are no longer in the area. Seasonal workers are reluctant to leave other areas for such a short period of employment. The shortage of workers leads farmers to push for additional research that would make it possible to mechanize the remaining tasks or to import temporary workers.

A combination of characteristics—many older people, low education levels and a high proportion of individuals with disabilities—reinforces the poverty problem in rural counties. In 1980 nearly 15 percent of persons aged sixteen to sixty-four in persistent low-income counties reported a work-limiting disability, and over 50 percent of the population over age twenty-five had not completed high school (Long and others, p. 11). In addition, racial or ethnic minorities constitute a high proportion of those living in poor rural counties in the South and Southwest. The lack of resources, limited formal education and, in some cases, racial prejudice make it difficult for families with low incomes to improve their economic situation. Migration to other areas is not a realistic alterna-

---

[1]An individual employed at the 1987 minimum wage of $3.35 per hour working 40 hours per week for 50 weeks (2,000 hours per year) would earn less than $7,000. The officially designated poverty line for a family of four was approximately $11,000 in 1987. This is about $4,000 more than one could earn if paid the minimum wage prevailing at that time.

tive for many of those now locked in poverty because of their age and/or limited education.

Migration compounds the problems of poor counties. Those individuals that remain are often unmotivated, the least educated, or disabled. Innovative citizens who might provide community leadership to reverse the downward trend are among the first to leave (Tweeten, p. 394). The tax base often declines along with the population. Consequently, there is less money to maintain water and sewer facilities, schools, hospitals, and highways. Industries are reluctant to move into areas where services are poor and the tax base is weak. This tends to perpetuate poverty in areas where it already exists.

POLICY ALTERNATIVES

The kinds of programs that might help those left behind are as follows:

- in-place assistance in cash or in kind (medicaid, food stamps, etc.)
- additional funds for education and training programs
- expanded employment services
- inducements in the form of tax benefits or subsidized credit to encourage industries to locate in poor areas.

The first alternative simply tries to make life a bit easier for those who are left behind; cash grants or in-kind assistance, however, do little to help people escape from poverty. The next two alternatives are designed to help individuals qualify for better-paying jobs and to find out where such jobs might be available. The last alternative is politically attractive because it reduces the need for out-migration. An additional set of policies might be considered if the objective is to improve the economic position of seasonal farm workers who remain in agriculture.

Most of the foregoing list of alternative policies would require additional appropriations, although of varying amounts, depending on the program. An expanding economy obviously would make it easier to finance such programs. The success of all but the first alternative in alleviating poverty also will depend on how rapidly the economy expands. There is little point in offering training programs if jobs are not available to those who complete the program. Adding jobs in one area will have little merit if there is an offsetting decline in job opportunities in other areas. For this reason, macroeconomic policies that accelerate economic growth are as important as microeconomic policies in eliminating rural poverty or assisting those displaced from agriculture.

In-Place Assistance

In-place assistance may take many forms. The rural as well as the urban poor are eligible for such cash benefits as social security, supplemental security income (SSI), and aid to families with dependent children (AFDC). In addition, poor families qualify for in-kind benefits including medicaid, food stamps, and school lunches. More liberal in-place assistance probably did more to relieve poverty in the 1960s and 1970s, especially among older persons, than all the other antipoverty programs adopted during the Kennedy-Johnson years in the White House. The rural poor, as well as the urban poor, obviously benefited from these programs. In some poor rural counties, a high proportion of the income obtained by those who remain now comes in the form of transfer payments from the federal government. The people left behind qualify for assistance because they are old or disabled.

Opponents of welfare programs argue that they are too costly and fail to address the underlying causes of poverty. Expenditures on such programs did indeed rise enormously during the 1960s and 1970s. Federal expenditures on social welfare programs more than quadrupled in real terms (that is, when adjusted for inflation) between 1960 and 1980 (Statistical Abstract, 1987, p. 340). As a proportion of the total federal budget, such expenditures rose from less than 40 percent in the early 1960s to nearly 60 percent in the late 1970s and early 1980s. Resistance to paying for such programs undoubtedly contributed to the election of a more conservative president in 1980.

While more generous welfare programs helped to reduce the proportion of families with incomes below the official poverty line during the 1970s, such programs (aside from food stamps) did relatively little for the working poor. Few of those who are under 65 and not disabled qualify for public assistance, partly because they are employed, at least part-time. One must fall in a particular category (for example, blind, over sixty-five, or a single parent) to be eligible for welfare payments. Single parent families, which make up the bulk of urban welfare recipients, are less likely to be found in rural communities, although the proportion of poor rural families in this category probably is rising.

Even when eligible for some form of public assistance, rural families may not seek help.[2] In some cases this is due to pride or an aversion to having anything to do with the government. Participation also may be inhibited by lack of knowledge, administrative barriers, and inadequate transportation facilities. Poor rural families may not be able to get to the county seat where the welfare office is located because they

[2]The participation rate in welfare programs among potentially eligible families tends to be lower in rural areas than in urban areas (Bryant, and others, pp.36–37).

do not own a car and bus service is unavailable. Low-income counties tend to be poorly served by public transportation. Furthermore, the local welfare office may not be open at times convenient for the working poor. In some rural counties officials have been known to discourage participation in welfare programs by instituting complex procedures or bureaucratic delays. Unsympathetic administrators are partly responsible for the low participation rate among the rural poor in the Food Stamp Program.

A substantial part of the rural poverty problem could be eliminated simply by raising the level of benefits under current programs. In-place assistance is about the only feasible way to improve the incomes of the elderly and even those who are between fifty-five and sixty five. As many as a third of the rural poor may fall in these age groups. It is too late in life for most of them to move and because of limited education and the lack of salable skills, they probably could not compete successfully for better-paying jobs even if they did move.

The danger in liberalizing welfare programs, of course, is that providing more generous grants will further reduce incentives to work or even to participate in other types of programs that might enable the poor to earn more money. There is already a strong disincentive to work more hours if, in doing so, one becomes ineligible for Medicaid, subsidized housing, food stamps, and free school lunches for the children. It is not easy to design a welfare program that helps those who are incapable of earning much more money and still preserve incentives for others to get off welfare. Proponents of welfare reform have struggled with this issue for years without arriving at an acceptable solution.

Education and Training

Education and training programs designed to help individuals escape from poverty have much greater popular appeal than welfare programs. A convincing case can be made for federal subsidies to strengthen education (and health services) in low-income counties. The argument for doing so is that it will be cheaper in the long run to remove some of the underlying causes of poverty than to bear the burden of higher welfare costs later. Federal subsidies for primary and secondary education would help low-income communities compensate for a weak tax base. School taxes in relation to average incomes are higher in many low-income counties than in high-income counties. But the amount of money spent per pupil is lower simply because less money is raised from local taxes. This means that poor communities cannot afford to pay salaries competitive with other areas or to maintain more expensive science and computer literacy programs. Schools located in poor areas also may be unable to finance special education programs to help the disadvantaged. These deficiencies handicap young people from low-income areas in competing for jobs.

Congress has been unwilling to subsidize local education except for districts severely impacted by government projects such as military bases. High-income states object to paying the additional taxes required to subsidize other areas. Even some of the states that might benefit from federal grants for primary and secondary education have opposed federal subsidies because they fear that accepting federal money would lead to federal control.

Special training programs can help to compensate for deficiencies in basic education and to provide the skills needed to qualify for better-paying jobs. Success in achieving these objectives depends on the willingness of low-income families to participate in such programs, and on the availability of jobs. While many of those who are unemployed or are working at low-paying jobs might benefit from further training, they are not always eager to participate in job-training programs. This was demonstrated in the 1960s. A retraining program in Huntington, West Virginia, for example, interested only 640 of an estimated 7,000 to 8,000 unemployed, even though each was offered a subsistence allowance of $23 per week (McPherson, pp. 1369–70). Only 200 of those seeking information about the program completed the forms and hence were certified for training. Unemployed individuals who declined to participate were asked why they decided not to do so. They generally gave one of the following answers:

- I'm not interested.
- I expect to be called back to work soon.
- I'm too old to be starting all over again.

Clearly the factor of motivation is an important one and needs to be considered in designing antipoverty programs.

Lack of motivation is only one of the factors limiting the success of training programs. The availability of jobs is another. Many of those trained in the 1960s remained unemployed after the training period ended. In some cases, individuals were trained for jobs that did not exist. Success was greatest where training was closely linked to employer demands for a particular skill, such as a telephone operator or typist. Job placement was easier for women than for men because there were unfilled demands for jobs traditionally held by women.

Job training programs work best when there is a shortage of skilled workers. This was demonstrated during World War II. Large numbers of unskilled workers were trained at that time to become welders. Tweeten argues that the most cost-effective way to operate a training program is to subsidize private industry to conduct such programs. They have an incentive to train individuals for the skills they need; however, employers tend to "cream" the applicants, that is, to select the best of those who apply. As a result, the poorest of the poor who often are deficient in basic education or even language skills fail to benefit.

At best, training programs can help only a minority of the poor, but clearly there are some who would benefit from the opportunity to acquire a marketable skill. Even when trained, workers face barriers in finding jobs and in migrating to new areas. A successful training program may require auxiliary services. For example, an expanded employment information service may be needed to enable those from poor rural communities to identify areas where jobs are available. Without some guarantee of employment, families may be reluctant to risk moving to a new area. Migration assistance would help families relocate, but there is little support for such assistance. Politicians don't want to lose constituents and local firms want to keep as many customers in the area as possible.

Inducements to Encourage Industries to Locate in Poor Areas

Most senators and representatives prefer to encourage economic expansion in poor rural areas rather than migration to other areas. Even urban congressional representatives may vote for programs designed to keep people in rural areas, because they fear additional migration might raise unemployment and welfare costs in their community. Thus, there is a broad basis of support for what is commonly referred to as "rural development" or "rural revitalization." Typically, a rural development program authorizes additional credit or grants for rural housing, water and sewer facilities, highway construction, and the development of industrial parks. Tax benefits also may be offered to firms that locate in depressed areas. A major objective is to increase local employment opportunities.

Rural development programs have, in many instances, turned out to be little more than public works projects. Money appropriated for rural development goes to communities to finance sewer and water projects or, in some cases, even to build major highways. Such projects are always popular with politicians because they bring money into their district. Local contractors also benefit from public works projects. But such projects usually offer only temporary employment and do not necessarily lead to development. A new or improved highway may even accelerate movement out of the area rather than bring in new industries.

Few communities have been rescued from poverty by the availability of low-cost credit or other inducements to locate manufacturing plants in low-income areas. The array of benefits typically offered under rural development programs is not sufficient to compensate for poor location with respect to markets, inadequate transportation facilities, and a shortage of skilled labor (Long and others, pp. 15–16). The types of businesses that respond to tax incentives and subsidized credit are often economically marginal firms or those associated with depressed industries. In many instances, they are looking for low-cost, nonunionized labor. Resource-based firms such as those associated with fishing, forestry, or recreation frequently locate in depressed areas, but they seldom pay high wages and may not offer steady employment throughout the year.

The principal weakness of rural development programs is that they promise more than they can deliver. Only a few rural counties or depressed regions can expect to attract the high-wage growth industries that every state or community would like to have. A low-income county located far from markets or raw-material supplies and without convenient air service has little to offer a company looking for a place to expand (Bryant, p. 232). Executives also are interested in amenities. They want good schools, an attractive place to live, and nearby recreational facilities.

The counties most likely to succeed in competition for new plants or service facilities are those well above the poverty line. Not only do these counties have more resources, but they also are more likely to have individuals knowledgeable about grant proposals and how to take advantage of federal programs. Persistent low-income areas which have few natural resources and a high proportion of individuals with low levels of education are least likely to benefit from such programs.

The potential negative effects on other communities of successful efforts to attract industries into poor rural counties are often overlooked. Total manufacturing output in the United States was relatively stagnant between 1980 and 1986. When this situation prevails, plant relocation becomes a zero-sum game, that is, the benefits of one area are offset by losses in another area. The individual firm may benefit from lower taxes, subsidized facilities, and cheap labor, but if relocation results in shifting unemployment from one region to another, society gains very little. These negative effects can be avoided only if the economy is expanding.

Assisting the Transition Out of Agriculture

The policy alternatives that have just been reviewed encompass most of the things that might be done to help those just leaving agriculture. The children of existing farmers would benefit most from good education. Middle-aged displaced farmers could be helped by training programs, an expanded employment service, and more local jobs. About the only way to help those of retirement age is to offer in-place assistance. The immediate problem confronting many families leaving agriculture is little or no cash income. They may, however, have too many assets to qualify for welfare. Even if eligible, farm families often are reluctant to accept welfare payments. Food stamps may be the only form of assistance available to those with little or no cash income. An automatic entitlement program similar to unemployment insurance for which displaced farm families might quality would provide a more acceptable alternative than going on welfare. Farmers do not qualify for unemployment compensation unless they worked off the farm for an employer who contributed to the unemployment compensation fund. There is no equivalent compensation program for unemployed farm operators. Some form of transition payment might be offered to displaced farmers based on rules similar to those that apply to unemployed workers, that is, eligible families would receive a modest amount of cash income for a limited period. A transition payment program for farmers, however, would be more difficult to finance and to administer than the existing unemployment compensation scheme. Taxing farmers to create a transition assistance fund would be less feasible than taxing employers of workers covered by unemployment compensation. It would be difficult to decide just who should be taxed and how much each should contribute. Equally difficult problems would arise in deciding who would qualify for transition payments.

The principle of compensating individuals adversely affected by imports has already been accepted in legislation. These payments are financed from general tax revenue, not a special fund to which employers contribute. Transition payments to farmers might be financed in a similar fashion. Implementing the compensation program for those unemployed because of changes in import policies has not been easy or entirely satisfactory to displaced workers, but the administrative problems encountered in extending the compensation principle to agriculture should be no more difficult to solve than those confronting administrators of the program designed to aid those displaced by imports.

Assisting Seasonal Farm Workers

Seasonal farm workers constitute an important subgroup of the low-income rural population. The public tends to think of seasonal farm workers as mainly migrants, but this is not accurate. In the mid-1980s, interstate migratory farm workers accounted for less than 6 percent of the total hired farm work force (U.S. Department of Agriculture, 1985. p. 386). The majority of hired farm workers, even seasonal laborers, now live in areas near where they are employed. Because seasonal labor requirements are closely linked to the major horticultural crops, high concentrations of seasonal farm labor are to be found in California, Arizona, the Rio Grande Valley, Florida, and Hawaii. A less hostile attitude toward "staygrants" (those who remain in the area where they are employed as seasonal workers) has reduced the pressure for workers to move out of the area when the harvest season is over (Fuller, xii).

A number of special programs have been adopted or proposed to assist low-income seasonal farm workers. Some of these have been directed toward migrants, particularly regulations that apply to housing and crew leaders.[3] Other policy alternatives include extending unemployment benefits to a larger percentage of those employed in seasonal farm work; raising minimum wages for farm workers; and guaranteeing the rights of farm workers to organize and bargain collectively for better wages and working conditions.

Prior to 1960, employers of farm labor and farm workers were excluded from most of the legislation designed to protect labor and enhance the incomes of workers (Holt, p. 29). Farmers, for example, were exempt from minimum wage regulations, and agricultural workers were not eligible for unemployment compensation. The trend since 1960 has been to eliminate these exemptions and to narrow the gap in protective legislation between farm and nonfarm workers (Erven, p. 377). Farms employing mainly family labor or only one or two hired workers, however, are still generally exempt from regulations relating to minimum wages, unemployment compensation, and the employment of minors. Current regulations apply only to those employing farm workers for more than a minimum number of hours during a calendar quarter.[4] For example, provisions relating to unemployment compensation apply to those hiring ten or more workers (or the equivalent in number of hours worked or wages paid) in a three-month period. While the regulations apply to relatively few farms, they cover a substantial proportion of seasonal workers.

One way of adding to the incomes of seasonal workers would be to extend and liberalize unemployment compensation. Not all seasonal workers are eligible for unemployment benefits. Eligibility depends on whether or not the employer contributed to the insurance fund, and only

---

[3]The irresponsible and sometimes unscrupulous activities of crew leaders or labor contractors led Congress to enact legislation in 1965 (and to strengthen the legislation in 1974), compelling crew leaders to register and to adhere to certain standards in recruiting and providing services to migrant workers. According to Erven, the emphasis has been on registration of labor contractors rather than on finding illegal activities and bringing action against leaders who engage in unscrupulous behavior (Erven, p.405).

[4]For a succinct summary of labor laws and regulations which apply to farmers and farm workers, see Erven, pp. 381–88.

employers with substantial numbers of hired workers do so. A farm operator who hires only four or five workers does not have to contribute to the fund; consequently, workers on that farm are not covered. Payment of unemployment compensation to farm workers is further complicated because an individual may work for more than one operator, not all of whom contribute to the fund. This leads to discrimination among workers.

Extending benefits to more workers would require a corresponding increase in contributions from employers. Farmers object to the burden of record keeping and to the cost that an unemployment compensation program entails. In the past, some farm operators have successfully avoided the cost and administrative burden by hiring illegal aliens, but the 1986 Immigration Reform and Control Act forecloses this option. In the short run, farmers have to bear most of the added cost of unemployment compensation, because they have no way of forcing buyers to pay more for their product.[5] In the longer run, higher labor costs may lead to further mechanization or reduced output of crops that require large amounts of labor.

Another alternative course of action is to raise the minimum wage. This, however, is not likely to have a major impact on the earnings of seasonal workers unless the increase is substantial. Most employers of seasonal labor, at least those operating the larger farms, now pay more than the minimum wage. Seasonal workers are commonly paid on a piece-rate basis (so much per container or per unit of weight). The skilled workers that employers prefer to hire generally earn much more than the minimum hourly wage when they are employed; however, in any given week or for the year as a whole, they may earn less than someone who is employed full time at minimum wages. The low earnings of seasonal workers are due more to the limited time they are employed than to substandard wage rates. Those most likely to benefit from higher minimum hourly wage rates are young people, the elderly, and part-time workers. Many of these individuals enter the farm labor force temporarily, and frequently find it difficult to earn minimum wages at piece rates offered by their employers.

Agricultural workers are not covered by provisions of the National Labor Relations Act, the basic legislation that compels employers to bargain in good faith with unions once they have been certified.[6] Unioniza-

---

[5]It is possible that in the 1990s, labor shortages owing to restricted immigration and a smaller number of entrants into the labor force will force employers to raise real wages and offer farm workers more benefits, such as health insurance. Market forces may then result in a reduction in output (or a slower rate of increase in production), which could lead to higher farm prices as well as higher real wages.

[6]State legislation, however, gives farm workers the right to organize and to bargain collectively in California and Hawaii (Paarlberg, p.226).

tion of agricultural workers has been strongly opposed by farmers and representatives of food processing firms because of the vulnerability of farmers to strikes when crops are being harvested. Timing is so critical for many horticultural crops that a delay of even a day or two in harvesting and processing the crop can be disastrous.

Extending provisions of the National Labor Relations Act to agriculture probably would affect only a small proportion of seasonal farm workers. Union organizers are likely to be successful only in areas where there is a high concentration of seasonal workers (for example, in Florida and California). Industries in which workers are scattered and firms are small, as is the case with agriculture, are notoriously difficult to organize. The seasonal nature of farm work and the high rate of turnover among workers adds to the problem of attracting support for a union.

If unions were successful in organizing farm workers and becoming certified as the bargaining agent, employers would be compelled to enter into wage negotiations. The ability of unions to raise wages and improve working conditions depends on competitive conditions within the industry. Those industries facing import competition are likely to be constrained in granting wage increases. Large-scale farm operators may shift production to Mexico or threaten to do so if wages are increased unduly. Processors of fruits and vegetables already are buying more of their produce south of the border. The threat of job losses due to further mechanization also may constrain unions in negotiating wage increases.

Unionization of farm workers is likely to benefit mainly those who work for the larger firms that grow fruits and vegetables.[7] Workers employed by these firms are generally paid more than those who work for small firms. Unionization could lead to widening income differences among farm workers—those now receiving somewhat higher incomes probably would gain more than those at the lower end of the income distribution. In practice, extending the collective bargaining option to agricultural workers is not likely to be a very effective policy to reduce rural poverty (Coffey, p. 374).

THE POLITICS OF RURAL POVERTY PROGRAMS

Congress has been willing to provide more money for rural credit programs, subsidies for rural housing and public works projects, but not for programs that might yield significant long-run benefits, such as better schools and health facilities. The latter programs are less attractive than those that offer immediate benefits, such as construction projects.

[7]Some of these are already members of unions and now work under union contracts.

Programs specifically directed towards helping the rural poor are not likely to win widespread support in Congress, because the constituency is too small and scattered. The rural poor are a minority in nearly every congressional district. Furthermore, they are geographically dispersed, seldom organized, and often do not vote. Consequently, programs designed to aid the rural poor generally have a low priority among members of Congress. The urban poor are better represented, and for this reason it is easier to form a coalition in support of aid to the urban poor than the rural poor.

Targeting benefits to the poorest of the poor areas has proved to be especially difficult. Every elected official wants a development project in his or her district. As a result, eligibility criteria for federal assistance tend to be modified so that more areas can qualify. This results in spreading the funds over a wide area rather than concentrating them in a few severely impoverished counties.

The evolution of the Appalachia regional development program illustrates how difficult it is to restrict benefits to a small area. President Kennedy, in his election campaign in 1960, promised to do something for West Virginia. He proposed a regional development program limited to a relatively small number of counties in the Appalachian region. Congress readily accepted his proposal to channel funds for public works projects into the region, but diluted the impact of the program by enlarging the area eligible for assistance. Counties as far away as New York eventually became part of Appalachia. The result, as one Congressman quipped, was a "wall to wall Appalachia program."

Congress has been criticized for not doing enough to help the rural poor. The lack of response is partly due to the complexity of the problem. No one program will eliminate poverty. This means that a package of programs or activities must be put together, involving not one but several congressional committees. A proposal to subsidize education in low-income counties, for example, would have to go to one committee; a proposal to aid seasonal farm workers would have to go to another committee; a bill to liberalize food stamp benefits would be assigned to still a third committee; and so on. The committee system makes it difficult for Congress to deal with poverty in a comprehensive way.

CONCLUSIONS

Rural poverty is the result of a complex set of factors including technical change in agriculture, declining nonfarm industries, physical disabilities, advanced age, lack of motivation, and the inability or unwillingness of families to migrate. Clearly no one program can be expected to deal effectively with the multiple causes of rural poverty. The problems of those left behind can be alleviated, however, by providing better education for the young, training programs and more jobs for those of working age, and in-place assistance for the old, poorly educated, and handicapped.

Political support for rural poverty programs is limited because the rural poor are a minority and are geographically dispersed and unorganized. The poor simply do not have enough votes to elect representatives who would give priority to alleviating rural poverty. Congress has also been reluctant to fund programs that might accelerate the exodus from rural areas. Appropriations for rural development programs have been limited and the funds dispersed widely rather than concentrated in a few areas of greatest need.

Monetary and fiscal policies that encourage economic growth are an essential ingredient of a successful antipoverty program. Creating more jobs makes all adjustments easier. But training programs and more jobs alone will not eliminate rural poverty. The poorest of the poor may be unable or unwilling to take advantage of the programs offered. Rural development programs, as with other public subsidies, tend to benefit disproportionately those already somewhat better off. Even with expanded employment opportunities, there is likely to be a legacy of poverty that can be alleviated in the short run only by transfer payments and in the long run by better education and health services.

DISCUSSION QUESTIONS

10.1. What factors have contributed to the perpetuation of rural poverty in certain geographical areas? Why has it been difficult to concentrate programs designed to alleviate poverty in such areas?

10.2. Are subsidies or special credit facilities designed to encourage industries to locate in low-income rural areas likely to be effective in reducing rural poverty? Who or what groups are most likely to benefit from rural development programs of this type?

10.3. What factors are likely to limit the effectiveness of education and training programs as policy instruments to alleviate or reduce rural poverty?

10.4. What kinds of policy initiatives are most likely to benefit low-income farm workers? Why have the policy initiatives you suggest not been adopted?

REFERENCES

BRYANT, W. KEITH, "Rural Poverty," *Agricultural Policy in an Affluent Society,* edited by Vernon W. Ruttan, Arley D. Waldo, and James P. Houck. New York: W.W. Norton & Company, Inc., 1969.

BRYANT, W. KEITH, D.L. BAWDEN, and W.E. SAUPE, "The Economics of Rural Poverty—A Review of the Post-World War II United States and Canadian Literature," *A Survey of Agricultural Economics Literature,* vol. 3, edited by Lee R. Martin. Minneapolis: University of Minnesota Press, 1981.

COFFEY, JAMES D., "The California Agricultural Labor Relations Act and National Agricultural Labor Relations Legislation: Comments," in *Seasonal Agricultural Labor Markets in the United States,* edited by Robert D. Emerson. Ames: Iowa State University Press, 1984.

CROSSWHITE, WILLIAM M., ed., *People in Poverty: Selected Case Studies.* Raleigh: The Agricultural Policy Institute, North Carolina State University, 1970.

ERVEN, BERNARD L., "Impact of Labor Laws and Regulations on Agricultural Labor Markets," in *Seasonal Agricultural Labor Markets in the United States,* edited by Robert D. Emerson. Ames: Iowa State University Press, 1984.

FITCHEN, JANET M., *Poverty in Rural America: A Case Study.* Boulder: Westview Press, 1981.

FULLER, VARDEN, "Foreword" in *Seasonal Agricultural Labor Markets in the United States,* edited by Robert D. Emerson. Ames: Iowa State University Press, 1984.

HOLT, JAMES S., "Introduction to the Seasonal Farm Labor Problem," in *Seasonal Agricultural Labor Markets in the United States,* edited by Robert D. Emerson. Ames: Iowa State University Press, 1984.

LONG, RICHARD W., J. NORMAN REID, and KENNETH L. DEAVERS, *Rural Policy Formulation in the United States,* ERS Staff Report No. AGES870203. Washington, D.C.: Economic Research Service, 1987.

McPHERSON, W.W., "An Economic Critique of the National Advisory Commission Report on Rural Poverty," *American Journal of Agricultural Economics,* 50 (1968), 1362–71.

PAARLBERG, DON, "People on the Fringe," *Farm and Food Policy Issues of the Nineteen Eighties.* Lincoln: University of Nebraska Press, 1979, 221–226.

REPORT BY THE PRESIDENT'S NATIONAL ADVISORY COMMISSION ON RURAL POVERTY, *The People Left Behind.* Washington, D.C.; U.S. Government Printing Office, 1967.

TWEETEN, LUTHER, "Rural Poverty: Prospective Programs," *Foundations of Farm Policy.* Lincoln: University of Nebraska Press, 1970, 361–459.

U.S. BUREAU OF THE CENSUS, *Statistical Abstract of the United States.* Washington, D.C.: U.S. Government Printing Office, 1987.

U.S. DEPARTMENT OF AGRICULTURE, *Agricultural Statistics.* Washington, D.C.: U.S. Government Printing Office, 1985.

11

Domestic Food Subsidy Programs

Domestic food subsidy programs have been an integral part of every major farm bill enacted during the past fifteen years. Such programs, unlike other welfare programs, are administered mainly by the U.S. Department of Agriculture, and are controlled and funded by the agricultural committees of Congress. This somewhat anomalous situation is a by-product of history and politics. Food subsidy programs were initiated during the 1930s by the Department of Agriculture (with support from the agricultural committees), in an attempt to help dispose of surplus commodities and to increase the total demand for farm products. They have remained under the control of agriculture for the past fifty years, despite objections from some welfare activists and even agricultural organizations who argue that the Department of Agriculture should not be in the business of funding and administering what have become mainly nonfarm welfare programs. In a number of recent years, expenditures on food subsidy programs have equalled or exceeded those on traditional agricultural programs. In fact, if not in name, the U.S. Department of Agriculture has become a department of food and agriculture.

The agricultural committees of Congress have been reluctant to relinquish control over such programs for very practical political reasons. They argue that keeping such programs in the Department of Agriculture is preferable because it insures that they will be administered in a way that benefits farmers. Furthermore, by keeping food subsidy programs in the Department of Agriculture, the agricultural committees of Congress retain control over legislation relating to such programs. If administration and funding were to shift to the Department of Health and Human Services, control of eligibility requirements and other regulations would fall under the jurisdiction of different congressional committees. While food subsidy programs inflate the USDA budget and give the Department a somewhat different focus, they provide the agricultural committees with leverage to gain support from urban congressmen for comprehensive farm bills. Agricultural support programs could well have been rejected in 1981 and 1985 without the votes of those representing urban areas. The needed votes have been won by combining food subsidy and price support provisions in one bill.

POLICY ISSUES

The initial question that must be addressed in dealing with food and nutrition policy is to decide whether or not domestic food subsidy programs are necessary. If deemed necessary, the next question is what form should such subsidies take; for example, should they be in the form of food stamps, surplus commodities, free school lunches, or vouchers to enable nutritionally vulnerable groups to purchase specific foods? The third set of questions relates to eligibility standards and how the program (or programs) should be administered. Each of these issues is addressed in turn. In the final section, an attempt is made to assess the relative effectiveness of alternative types of food subsidy programs in meeting different objectives, including the elimination of hunger, improved nutrition, a reduction in agricultural surpluses, and improved welfare of program participants.

Are Food Subsidies Necessary?

Hunger, whether at home or abroad, is first and foremost an income problem. Families and individuals could avoid hunger if they had sufficient income to purchase whatever quantities of food are required for a minimum adequate diet. For this reason it has been suggested that the solution to the "hunger problem" is simply to raise the level of benefits under existing welfare programs and to extend coverage to those who are now missed because of holes in the safety net. Clearly, there are individuals and families who are inadequately served by existing welfare programs, most notably some of the working poor, those temporarily unemployed, elderly women living alone, and the homeless. Benefit levels in some states are extremely low.

No one knows how many individuals are hungry or seriously mal-nourished in the United States, first because it is difficult to define hunger precisely and, second, because data on caloric deficiencies are fragmentary and incomplete. If one defines hunger as the inability to purchase as much food as one would like to have, there are obviously substantial numbers of hungry people. Newspaper stories and anecdotal evidence from doctors and those involved in emergency feeding programs confirm this fact. Soup kitchens and food pantries report increased num-bers of individuals seeking help. On the other hand, if one defines hunger in clinical terms based, for example, on the weight-for-age of children or other evidence of persistent caloric deficits, the evidence sup-porting the contention that hunger is widespread and a serious problem in the United States is extremely weak.[1] Food consumption surveys in-dicate that relatively few families are seriously short of calories or even protein. Many more, however, are consuming foods that are deficient in calcium, iron, and vitamin A. Poor nutrition is not confined to families with low incomes, although the incidence of nutritional deficiencies tends to be somewhat higher among low-income groups. The absence of clinical evidence of widespread caloric deficiencies can be attributed in part to the existing array of food subsidy and volunteer feeding programs.

Poor nutrition is a much more serious problem in the United States than undernutrition. More people are overweight than underweight. Moreover, the medical costs of coping with the consequences of excess consumption of sugar, fats, and alcohol undoubtedly are greater than those associated with the lack of calories and protein. But the conse-quences of overnutrition are less likely to be featured in newspaper stories and TV documentaries. Reports of mothers running out of food and pictures of the homeless queuing up at food kitchens have had a dramatic impact on the American public. No one wants to see people go hungry. Consequently, there is a broad basis of support for food subsidy programs.

What Types of Food Programs Should Be Funded?

The U.S. government has funded four major types of food subsidy programs in recent years:

---

[1]The 1984 report of the President's Task Force on Food Assistance, after reviewing the evidence on hunger, concluded as follows: If hunger is defined in clinical terms (that is, a "weakened, disordered condition brought about by prolonged lack of food"), "there is no evidence that widespread undernutrition is a major health problem in the United States" (pp. 34–35).

- food stamps, which enable recipients to purchase almost any food product in local grocery stores
- child nutrition programs, which provide free or reduced-price meals, mainly to school children
- the Women, Infants and Children (WIC) program, which provides specific foods or nutrient supplements to individuals identified as malnourished or potentially malnourished
- direct distribution of commodities to schools, public institutions, Indian Reservations and, sometimes, directly to low-income families.

The Food Stamp Program is by far the largest, both in terms of government cost and the number of participants. In the mid-1980s this program accounted for about 60 percent of the total annual cost of all domestic food subsidy programs (Figure 11.1). At that time an average of close to twenty million people were participating in the Food Stamp

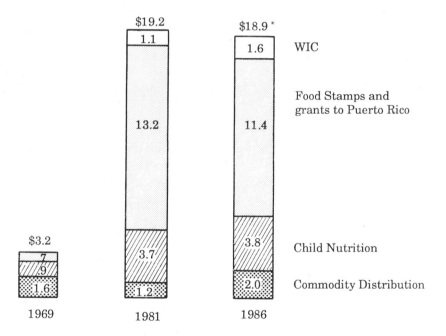

* Figures do not add to total due to rounding

Figure 11.1 Expenditures on USDA food subsidy programs, 1969, 1981, and 1986 (figures in billions of 1986 dollars [converted from nominal values using the Consumer Price Index]). Source: Boehm and Gallo, p. 23 and Matsumoto, 1987a, p. 24.)

Program.[2] This is equivalent to slightly more than 8 percent of the total U.S. population.

The second most important component of U.S. domestic food subsidy programs is the collection of activities referred to as Child Nutrition Programs. Approximately twelve million children were served free or reduced-price meals in the mid-1980s. Other children not eligible for free or reduced-price meals also benefit from slightly lower costs for full-priced meals served in schools.

The WIC program was not introduced until 1972. While the percentage rate of growth of the WIC program was very high between 1972 and 1986, the program accounted for less than a fifth of total food subsidy costs in the latter year. The number of participants in that program in 1986 was about three million.

The cost of donated food, the other major component of domestic food subsidy programs, has varied from year to year depending on the availability of surplus commodities and policy decisions made by the administration in power. At one time, surplus commodities accounted for a much higher proportion of the total cost of food subsidy programs than they have in recent years. In addition to free food, the government also provides small amounts of money for feeding programs for the elderly.

The large increase in federal government expenditures on domestic food subsidy programs which occurred between 1969 and 1981 (even after adjusting for inflation) is illustrated in Figure 11.1. Annual expenditures in constant (1986) dollars rose from just over $3 billion in 1969 to about $19 billion in 1981. Between 1981 and 1986, the aggregate cost (in constant dollars) declined slightly. Conservative members of Congress, partly in response to leadership from the White House and the Office of Management and Budget (OMB), were able to slow the growth of expenditures on domestic food subsidy programs during this period, but were unable to reduce them as much as they would have liked.

Supplemental food programs began in the 1930s with the distribution of commodities acquired by the government as a result of price-support operations or purchases made under provisions of Section 32 of the Agricultural Adjustment Act of 1935.[3] Particularly during the Depression, there was widespread support for using surplus commodities to

---

[2]This does not include the number of people receiving benefits from an equivalent cash subsidy program in Puerto Rico.

[3]Section 32 of the 1935 Act makes available to the Secretary of Agriculture 30 percent of the revenue from customs receipts (Benedict and Stine, p. 377). This money, commonly referred to as Section 32 funds, may be used to subsidize exports and to acquire surplus commodities. Such funds have been used in recent years mainly to purchase non-supported perishable commodities such as turkeys, pork, beef, citrus fruit, and eggs.

feed hungry people. The program is popular with farmers and farm organizations because it helps reduce surpluses.

Schools and public institutions are now the major outlets for surplus commodities although, at one time, surpluses were made available to families on relief.[4] Participation in the surplus distribution program is entirely voluntary. Schools and other institutions that elect to make use of surplus commodities pay nothing for the farm products they decide to use but must cover the cost of transporting such commodities from central warehouses or distribution points. The program is unattractive to some potential users, not only because they incur costs in using the commodities, but also because the commodities offered are not necessarily those desired.

The Food Stamp Program gradually replaced the commodity-distribution program in the late 1960s and early 1970s as the principal policy instrument to relieve hunger among low-income families. The commodity-distribution program was widely criticized at that time because it failed to reach many of those who were at risk of being hungry. It also cut into the sales of local merchants in counties where free food was made available to families on welfare. Many potential recipients failed to receive free food because local officials decided against participation in the program. Each county had the option of deciding whether or not to participate. Some elected not to do so because they did not want to incur the additional costs associated with transporting and distributing government surpluses. Others refused to participate because they thought offering free food would encourage more families or individuals to seek welfare or remain unemployed. Nutritionists criticized the direct distribution program because the commodities offered were not necessarily those most needed to improve diets. Even when surplus commodities were made available by the county (usually in the town or city where the county seat was located), many families in rural areas or those without transportation found it difficult to take advantage of the program.

The Food Stamp Program was adopted partly in response to criticisms of the commodity-distribution program. It gives participants much greater freedom in choosing foods and, because it operates through stores, is far more popular with local merchants. Under the Food Stamp Program, participants are given stamps which are the equivalent of cash but can be used only to purchase food. They are not restricted to certain commodities as was done initially when the Food Stamp Program was

---

[4]Direct distribution of surplus commodities to low-income families almost disappeared during the 1970s, but the program was revived for a brief period in the mid-1980s, mainly to dispose of surplus dairy products.

introduced on a trial basis in the early 1940s. Participating stores exchange the stamps for cash at local banks.

Eligibility for participation in the Food Stamp Program is limited to families or individuals with incomes that do not exceed a given percentage of the official poverty line.[5] The subsidy in the form of stamps that one actually receives is determined by a complex set of factors including:

- the value of the food stamp allotment which is determined by the cost of USDA's thrifty food plan
- the size of the family
- total family income, including welfare payments
- allowable deductions for such items as earned income, child care payments, and excess housing costs
- the benefit reduction rate, that is, the percentage of adjusted income that is deducted from the value of the allotment.

The following example illustrates the calculations that must be made to determine the value of stamps an eligible individual or family receives. Assume the value of the food allotment for a family of four is $280 per month.[6] This is based on the average retail cost of the list of foods that make up the "thrifty food plan," a low-cost food plan designed by USDA nutritionists. Families are not compelled to purchase these foods. The list is important, however, because it establishes the maximum value of stamps that can be given to a family or an individual. If a person has no income, this is the value of stamps he or she receives. For those with some cash income, either earned or from welfare payments, food stamp benefits are reduced thirty cents for each additional dollar of adjusted net income. This is called the benefit reduction rate. It is equivalent to a marginal tax rate of 30 percent, that is, for each additional dollar earned, benefits are reduced by thirty cents. An eligible individual or family receives stamps equal in value to the food stamp allotment less 30 percent of adjusted net income. Obviously, the higher the adjusted net income, the greater the reduction and, hence, the less one receives in food stamps.

Complex calculations are required to determine the adjusted net income. Assume the monthly income of family X (a family of four) is $500, about the amount one would earn if employed at minimum wages. The

---

[5]In 1986, the maximum income one could receive and still remain eligible was 130 percent of the poverty income level, a figure which is calculated each year by the Office of Management and Budget. Poverty income levels vary by family size. Asset restrictions and work requirements also limit eligibility.

[6]The monthly allotment varies by family size; in 1987 it was $81.00 for a single individual, $271.00 for a family of four, and $489.00 for a family of eight.

adjusted net income is calculated by subtracting a standard deduction, an earned income deduction (specified as 20 percent of earned income in the 1985 Act) and any special deductions for dependent care, excess housing costs, etc. Assume these amount to $200 per month. Based on these assumptions, the adjusted net income and the value of food stamps issued to family X would be as follows:[7]

Monthly income	$500
Less deductions	200
Adjusted income	300 × 30% (benefit reduction rate) = $90
Food stamp allotment	280
Less 30% of adjusted income	90
Value of stamps given to family X	$190

The family would receive stamps valued at $190 per month, $90 less than the full value of the allotment. Families with lower incomes and/or higher allowable deductions obviously would receive more stamps. A lower benefit reduction rate also would raise the value of stamps issued to family X.

Child nutrition programs, the second most important component of U.S. food subsidy programs, provide funds for school breakfasts and lunches, the school milk program, food for child care centers, and summer youth programs. Funding for these programs is widely supported in Congress. Throughout the 1970s annual appropriations consistently rose, even when school enrollments began to decline. A break came in 1981 when the Reagan Administration succeeded in reducing appropriations for the school milk program and for subsidized lunches for those not eligible for free meals. Administration officials argued that such subsidies were unnecessary because they benefited mainly middle and upper-income families. Eligibility rules also were changed by reducing the percentage above the poverty income level that families could earn and still remain eligible for reduced-price meals. The lower level of funding compelled schools to raise meal prices. This led to a reduction in the number of students participating in the school lunch program, primarily among those who paid the full cost of such meals (including those who no longer qualified for reduced-price meals because of the change in eligibility standards).

The WIC program targets benefits to women and children who are deemed to be at "nutritional risk." In order to be eligible, participants

[7]Actual calculations are likely to be even more complex. Those seeking benefits must itemize earnings, including social security and veterans payments. The amount of time and effort required to fill out the application form for Food Stamp benefits is nearly equivalent to what one must devote to preparing an income tax return (Guyon).

must be certified by a doctor, a welfare office, or a clinic as falling within this category (Shaffer and Stallmann, p.2).   Participation also is restricted to those with limited incomes and assets.

Unlike the Food Stamp Program, which allows participants to purchase whatever foods they desire, the WIC program provides specific foods or vouchers that can be exchanged at stores or supermarkets only for designated foods such as infant formula, baby cereal, fruit juice, or iron-fortified products (Longen, p.9). The average value of benefits per individual is quite modest. In 1986, for example, it amounted to about $40 per person per month.

Some of the funds appropriated for the WIC program are used to cover the cost of nutrition education. Congress has mandated that WIC recipients be provided with information and counseling services to help them select appropriate foods and, thus, improve their diet.

ASSESSING THE EFFECTS OF U.S. FOOD SUBSIDY PROGRAMS

Domestic food subsidy programs are supported by members of Congress because they help dispose of agricultural surpluses, increase the demand for farm products, and reduce hunger and malnutrition. In practice, they also have proved to be a politically acceptable alternative to raising welfare benefits. Congress has been more willing to fund food subsidy programs, for example, than to liberalize benefits for single-parent families. In-kind benefits in the form of free lunches and food stamps incur less political resistance than other forms of assistance to the poor.

Programs vary in their effectiveness as instruments to reduce surpluses, increase the demand for farm products, and reduce hunger and malnutrition. The differential effects of the domestic food subsidy programs that the U.S. government has offered in recent years are highlighted in the sections which follow.

Effect on Farm Surpluses

Only the commodity-distribution program enables the government to dispose of physical surpluses. The other programs, insofar as they increase the total demand for food, may help to reduce carryover stocks, but the effect is indirect. Families receiving food stamps and schools offering free or reduced-price meals may purchase more food but not necessarily surplus commodities. Producers of fruits, vegetables, milk, beef, and broilers probably have benefited from the Food Stamp and Child Nutrition programs because these are the foods commonly purchased when incomes rise. Indirectly, the producers of livestock feed ingredients gain when the demand for livestock products increases.

Effect on Total Food Demand and Farm Sales

Food subsidy programs which result in freeing an equivalent amount of cash for the purchase of other goods and services are not an efficient way to increase the demand for farm products or to aid farmers. Free meals for children and food stamps are almost as good as a cash grant to participants. The money that otherwise would have been spent on food can now be used to purchase other things. It also could be used to purchase more food.

The degree to which normal food purchases are displaced by free food or by food stamps is called the substitution rate. If the value of food purchased by an individual from his or her income is reduced by an amount equal to the value of free food or food stamps given to that individual, the substitution rate is 100 percent. The substitution rate would be only 50 percent if the individual reduced his or her food expenditures by an amount equal to only half of the value of the free food. For most U.S. food subsidy programs, the substitution rate probably lies somewhere between 50 and 100 percent. Families participating in the Food Stamp or Child Nutrition programs are likely to spend less of their cash income on food but the reduction in their cash food purchases may be smaller than the value of the free food given to their children or the value of bonus stamps. The free food or bonus stamps are equivalent to an income supplement. Some of the increase in real income will be used to buy additional food. The greater the propensity to purchase food out of additional income, the more effective an income supplement will be as an instrument to increase the demand for food.

The income elasticity of demand for food, that is, the percentage change in food purchases associated with a 1 percent change in income, is almost invariably positive and likely to be higher for low-income families that participate in food subsidy programs than for others.[8] It could be as high as 0.25. If so, this would mean that for each additional dollar received in the form of free food or food stamps, total food purchases would increase by twenty-five cents. A positive income elasticity will lead to an increase in total food expenditures, but not for all types of

---

[8]Income elasticities are likely to be higher for expenditures on food than for physical quantities consumed. For the U.S. population as a whole, the aggregate income elasticity of food expenditures is quite low. Based on the 1977-1978 National Food Consumption Survey, it was estimated to be 0.8 for expenditures on food consumed away from home, but only 0.15 for food purchased for preparation at home (Smallwood and Blaylock, p. 1).

foods. The substitution rate for surplus commodities such as corn meal, rice, and skim-milk powder, for example, is likely to be 100 percent. Families may, however, use the income formerly spent on these commodities to purchase other foods or more expensive types of foods, such as TV dinners or steaks rather than hamburger.

The degree of substitution varies among programs. Free school breakfasts, for example, are more likely than an equivalent value of food stamps to result in a net increase in demand because those who benefit from free breakfasts would not otherwise have eaten anything before going to school. Surplus commodities given to schools, on the other hand, are likely to displace on a one-for-one basis foods that otherwise would have been purchased locally. Free or bonus food stamps, likewise, can be expected to result in only a small net increase in total demand because food stamps are used to buy the same foods that otherwise would have been purchased with cash.

Hypothetical differences among programs in the substitution rate and, hence, in the effect on total food demand are shown in Table 11.1. The figures in the first column are the assumed substitution rates. Those in the third column indicate how much an expenditure of $1 billion on each of the four alternative programs might be expected to increase total food demand. The last column shows the effect on farm-level demand. The calculations are based on the assumption that farmers receive only 30 percent of the retail value of commodities sold through

TABLE 11.1 Hypothetical Effects on Total Food Demand and Farm-Level Demand of a One Billion Dollar Expenditure on Each of Four Types of Domestic Food Subsidy Programs

			Net addition	
			To Total	To Farm-
	Assumed	Assumed	Food	Level
	Substitution	Government	Demand[c]	Demand[d]
Type of Program	Rate[a] (percent)	Expenditure[b]	(billions of dollars)	
Food stamps[e]	70	1.0	0.3	0.1
Child nutrition	60	1.0	0.4	0.1
Commodity distribution	80	1.0	0.2	0.2
WIC (vouchers)	50	1.0	0.5	0.1
Total		4.0	1.4	0.5

[a]The percentage of the subsidy or the free food which substitutes for what otherwise would have been purchased or consumed by participants in the program.

[b]Excluding administration costs.

[c]Calculated by multiplying one minus the substitution rate by $1.0 billion.

[d]The net addition to total demand multiplied by the percent of the retail value or cost which customarily goes to farmers; for meals away from home or food supplements it is assumed to be only 20 percent; for surplus commodities donated to schools and individuals, it is close to 100 percent.

[e]Assuming there is no cash purchase requirement.

stores and an even smaller percentage of the value of meals provided under child nutrition programs and food supplements made available to participants in the WIC program.[9]

Gains to farmers from food subsidies depend on what types of foods are purchased with the added income. If food stamp participants purchase foods with a high service component, such as TV dinners, farmers will gain relatively little from the program. They will gain much more if participants elect to spend their additional income on commodities such as eggs, milk and meat.

While the figures shown in Table 11.1 are not precise, they illustrate how little farmers are likely to gain from increased spending on domestic food subsidy programs. The net increase in total food demand from an additional expenditure of $4 billion dollars per year on domestic food subsidy programs probably would not exceed $1.4 billion. Farmers would receive only about $0.5 billion. The foregoing figure suggests that only about 12 percent of what the government spends on domestic food subsidy program trickles down to farmers. Clearly, this is an inefficient way to subsidize agriculture. The principal beneficiaries of such subsidies are the participants who gain from free stamps, free commodities, and free or low-cost meals. This gives them the opportunity to spend more money on food and also on other goods and services. Food stores and food manufacturers also gain from increased sales, especially of higher-valued products.

Effects on Hunger and Malnutrition

The combination of food subsidy programs offered in recent years undoubtedly has helped to reduced the incidence of hunger and malnutrition, but underconsumption has by no means been eliminated. As pointed out earlier, firm conclusions regarding the incidence of hunger cannot be drawn from the available data. The evidence does suggest, however, that the number of seriously malnourished or hungry individuals declined during the 1970s. The downward trend was halted and possibly even reversed between 1981 and 1985 because of changes in eligibility requirements, higher levels of unemployment, more homeless individuals (partly the result of sending former mental patients back to the community), an increase in the number of single-parent families and

---

[9]The farmers share of the retail food dollar, that is, the percentage of what the consumer spends on food that goes to pay for the raw product, averages around 25 percent. It is higher for commodities like eggs and milk than for highly processed foods or TV dinners. The farmers share also is higher for food purchased at supermarkets than for meals consumed in restaurants (USDA, 1987, p. 6).

reduced appropriations, at least in real terms (Ranney, p. 1258–9).[10] In 1979, a group of doctors concluded that most of the gross malnutrition that they had observed in the rural South and in Appalachia a decade earlier had been eliminated (King). A similar group of physicians issued a less optimistic report six years later. According to a study group led by the head of the Harvard School of Public Health, as many as twenty million U.S. citizens may be hungry at least during some period each month (Physician Task Force on Hunger in America, p. 8). The study group blamed much of the increase in hunger on changes in government policies that occurred during the early 1980s.

Not all the increase in reported cases of hunger can be attributed to tightening up on eligibility standards or reduced appropriations. Some of the increase in the number of individuals seeking free meals or additional supplies from food pantries observed in the early 1980s was the result of Congressional action designed to liberalize the Food Stamp Program. Congress adopted an amendment in 1978 which eliminated the requirement that participants give up a certain amount of cash in return for stamps (the so-called "cash purchase requirement"). Prior to 1979, participants were compelled to purchase stamps equal to 30 percent of their income. In addition, they were given bonus stamps equal to what they now receive. By compelling participants to buy stamps equal to their assumed normal food expenditures (the "cash purchase requirement"), the program forced families to set aside in advance a certain amount of income for food purchases. For example, a family eligible for $280 in stamps with an adjusted income of $300 per month would have been required to purchase stamps valued at $90 per month. Thus, each month, family X (the example cited earlier) would have been given stamps worth $280, not $190 as under the program in effect after 1979.

Without the cash-purchase requirement, families must budget their income carefully to make sure they do not run out of food toward the end of the month. Typically, food stamps cover only part of the family's food bill. Participants are expected to spend out of their cash income as much for food as someone in their income bracket normally does; however, not every family accepts this principle or budgets accordingly (Morentz). Families complain that they do not receive enough stamps to last through the month. This is true for most families, because they receive stamps worth less than the full value of USDA's "thrifty food plan." The program is designed to supplement food purchases, not to provide 100 percent of each family's needs in the form of bonus stamps. By eliminat-

---

[10]Ranney adjusted total food subsidy expenditures for both inflation and the number of individuals falling below the poverty line in 1981 and 1985. The result was a decline in real expenditures (in 1985 dollars) per poor person from approximately $629 in 1981 to $602 in 1985 (p. 1259).

ing the cash-purchase requirement, Congress gave families the option to spend the money no longer required to purchase additional stamps for other purposes.   But in giving families greater freedom of choice, Congress also made it more likely that they would run out of food before the end of the month.

The increase since 1980 in the number of families and individuals who show up at soup kitchens and food pantries because they have run out of food is partly the result of having eliminated the cash-purchase requirement.   Participants may be "hungry by choice" because they have elected to spend their money in other ways (Giertz and Sullivan).   The availability of food from churches and other groups that offer emergency food services permits some families to act irresponsibly.   If they fail to set aside enough cash to buy food after their supply of food stamps has run out, families, at least in some communities, can avoid the consequences of their action by obtaining free food.

The Food Stamp Program makes it possible for families to spend more on food but does not compel them to do so. Furthermore, there is no control over what kinds of foods they purchase. Food intake among participating families probably is slightly greater, but it is difficult to show a significant improvement in diets except among the elderly and blacks (Allen and Newton, p. 1249).   Spending more on food does not necessarily lead to a better diet.   Studies based on biochemical analysis show only a weak relationship between food expenditures and nutritional status (Davis, p.1023).   Food consumption surveys indicate that food stamp participants allocate their income among commodities in a manner similar to nonparticipants.   Participants generally purchase more of the foods they are accustomed to eating, not necessarily those that are more nutritious.

The school lunch and school breakfast programs and the WIC program are probably more cost effective in reducing underconsumption and improving diets than the Food Stamp Program. Research has indicated that the school lunch program has improved the nutrient intake of children coming from low-income households (Akin, Guilkey and Popkin, p.483). Similar positive results have been reported for the WIC program (Shaffer and Stallmann). It has helped to reduce iron anemia among children, raised growth rates and reduced infant mortality.

Relative Cost-Effectiveness of Alternative Food Subsidy Programs

The attractiveness of one type of food subsidy program relative to another depends on what one wants to accomplish. Some programs are more effective in reducing hunger and malnutrition while others offer greater benefits to farmers or to participants. Table 11.2 illustrates how

TABLE 11.2 Ranking of Four Types of Food Subsidy Programs on the Basis of Cost Effectiveness in Achieving Alternative Objectives

Type of Program	Ranking Based on Alternative Objectives[a]		
	Increase Total Food Demand	Increase Welfare of Participants	Improve Nutrition
Free stamps	3	1	4
Free commodities[b]	4	3	3
Free meals	1	2	2
Free vouchers[c]	2	4	1

[a]Most cost-effective program is ranked 1; the least effective is ranked 4.
[b]Assumed to be mainly whole grains, surplus dairy products, and foods purchased with Section 32 funds.
[c]Assumed to be given to "at risk" groups and usable only for purchasing specific nutritious foods; vouchers would be more attractive to participants if they could be used to buy any food.

one might rank four alternative types of food subsidy programs on the basis of their cost effectiveness in achieving three different objectives, that is, increasing the total demand for food, increasing the welfare of participants, and reducing hunger and malnutrition. One may disagree with the suggested ranking, but the exercise helps to explain why the U.S. has chosen to maintain a combination of programs rather than a single program.

Free meals in schools and vouchers rank high in terms of cost effectiveness in reducing hunger and malnutrition; free food stamps rank much lower because families are not compelled to purchase additional food or even more nutritious food. Bonus stamps are the equivalent of an income supplement. For this reason, participants like the program, although they probably would prefer a cash grant which would not identify them as being poor or subsidized by the taxpayer. The bonus stamp plan without a cash purchase requirement comes as close as any in-kind welfare program to offering participants freedom of choice.

Farmers and farm organizations presumably want to get rid of surpluses and, therefore, prefer a program that does not allow participants to substitute free food or bonus stamps for normal food purchases. Free meals, whether offered to school children, the elderly, or the homeless, rank much higher as a way of increasing the total demand for food than food stamps, partly because some of the food will be wasted. Free commodities, while they may help to dispose of surpluses, are likely to displace normal purchases and, therefore, may add little to the total demand for food.

Clearly, one cannot argue that a particular type of food subsidy program is "best" without specifying the objectives. When one wants to achieve several objectives simultaneously, it is appropriate to make use of a combination of programs. By authorizing and funding different types of programs, Congress has been able to respond to the multiple interests of farmers, welfare activists, and nutritionists. This has helped to maintain a broad basis of support for food subsidy programs.

POLICY ISSUES RELATED TO THE FOOD STAMP PROGRAM

The Food Stamp Program is not only the largest but also the most controversial of all the domestic food subsidy programs. It has been the target of criticism from both the right and the left. Conservatives charge that the program subsidizes idleness and benefits some who do not need help. Representatives of farmers object to converting a program originally designed to help increase the demand for farm products to what now has become a general welfare program. Critics from the left argue that too many people are being missed by the current program and that the level of benefits is too low.

The response of Congress to pressure from the right has been to eliminate benefits for most college students and striking workers. In addition, Congress has incorporated work requirements for those capable of being employed and has instituted more administrative controls in an attempt to reduce fraud and misuse of funds. The result of these restrictions has been to add substantially to the administrative burden imposed on welfare offices and to discourage participation.[11]

Some members of the agricultural committees of Congress would like to restore the cash-purchase requirement. While this would force families to spend more for food, it probably would reduce participation in the program. One of the principal arguments for eliminating the cash-purchase requirement in the late 1970s was to make it easier for families short of cash to obtain stamps.

Proponents of liberalizing the Food Stamp Program would like to make it simpler, not more difficult, for individuals to qualify for assistance. Clearly, many who might benefit from the program either do not know they are eligible for assistance or elect not to participate. In the mid-1980s, less than two-thirds of those classified as poor (that is, those having incomes below the poverty line) participated in the Food Stamp Program. Participation rates are especially low among the elderly, the homeless, and the working poor. Some of those not participating are technically ineligible, despite low incomes, because they have more

[11]The Physicians Task Force on Hunger in America reported that the changes mandated by Congress in the early 1980s compelled the Department of Agriculture to initiate ninety regulatory changes in a period of thirty months. In one state, the regulatory manual increased in length from 20 pages to 1965 to 978 pages in 1983 (p. 164).

savings or other assets, such as a home, than the law allows. This is most likely to be true of the elderly and the "new poor," that is, those who have recently exhausted their unemployment benefits. Others are too proud to seek help or consider the benefits not worth the hassle of filling out forms and confronting the bureaucracy in the local welfare office. A simpler sign-up procedure and a less adversarial attitude on the part of welfare offices might lead to greater participation by those who are eligible for food stamp benefits.

In addition to eligibility requirements and administrative procedures, controversy surrounds the level of benefits offered under the Food Stamp Program. Benefits could be increased in several ways, for example, by basing the food stamp allotment on a higher-cost diet; by allowing participants greater deductions for such items as child care, housing, and excess medical expenses; and by lowering the benefit reduction percentage, say from 30 percent to 25 percent.

Those seeking to liberalize benefits have concentrated their attack on use of the thrifty food plan as a basis for calculating the value of the food stamp allotment.[12] While it is technically possible to purchase a nutritionally adequate diet with stamps equal in value to the cost of the thrifty food plan, it requires careful management to do so. The level of benefits could be increased very simply by shifting from the thrifty food plan to the Department of Agriculture's low-cost food plan as a basis for calculating the value of an allotment. The low-cost plan contains slightly more higher-valued foods and offers more variety. Therefore, it costs more. Basing the value of allotments on this plan in the mid-1980s would have raised the value of benefits to participants by as much as 25 percent. It would not, of course, have required that participants purchase foods included in the low-cost plan; it would, however, have given them more food stamps.

Critics point out that food prices in low-income urban areas are often higher than the national average prices used to calculate the value of the allotment. If higher prices or a higher-cost diet were used to calcu-

---

[12]The thrifty food plan also has been criticized because it does not quite meet all the nutritional requirements for a minimum adequate diet. It provides 100 percent of the recommended dietary allowances for energy, protein, most all vitamins and minerals, but it does not quite meet the minimum requirements for iron for young children, zinc, folacin, and Vitamin E. The plan allows for wastage of about 5 percent (Allen and Newton, p.1250). While the diet used to calculate the level of benefits is slightly deficient in some items, one can, by purchasing a somewhat different combination of low-cost foods, meet all the minimum requirements. Low-income families frequently do so, but confining one's diet mainly to starchy-staples, carrots, cabbage, liver, and other low-cost sources of nutrients is not very attractive. The thrifty food plan is viewed by USDA nutritionists as a guide to purchases in emergency situations, not as a recommended diet for use over a long period of time.

late the value of the food stamp allotment, fewer families would find it necessary to visit food pantries or to show up at soup kitchens toward the end of the month. Liberalizing welfare programs or simply offering more cash to eligible families would achieve the same objective. Obviously, either of these alternatives would raise the cost of welfare programs.

The frequency of adjusting the value of the food allotment to reflect changes in food prices is also an issue. Earlier, the value was recalculated semiannually using prices prevailing at the time. More recently, it has been adjusted only once a year. In periods of rapidly rising prices, this means that the purchasing power of the allotment diminishes substantially during the course of a year. The longer the interval between adjustments, the less likely that families will be able to purchase an adequate diet with the stamps offered to them.

One can, of course, rely on private initiatives to ease the hunger problem rather than liberalizing benefits or encouraging greater participation in the Food Stamp Program. During the mid-1980s, this was the solution adopted by many communities. The number of soup kitchens and food pantries grew rapidly between 1981 and 1986 (Davis and Senauer, p. 1255).[13] While voluntary programs have achieved significant results in reducing hunger, they are unlikely to provide an adequate long-term alternative to government-funded programs. Not all communities are in a position to provide such services or have accepted the responsibility of doing so. It also may be difficult to sustain programs offered by churches and other community groups. Donors lose interest and volunteers become tired and want to do other things. As a result, staffing becomes a problem. Some of the limitations might be overcome if funds were made available from public sources for hiring workers. It probably would be cheaper to pay volunteer agencies to offer supplemental feeding programs than to raise the level of food stamp benefits.

CONCLUSIONS

Domestic food subsidy programs now contribute relatively little to disposing of surpluses or increasing the total demand for farm products. Their primary function is to supplement welfare programs and to reduce hunger and malnutrition. Programs that provide meals or vouchers for specific foods to targeted groups are more efficient instruments for

---

[13]Between 1980 and 1987, the number of soup kitchens and food pantries in New York City grew from 30 to nearly 500. In 1987, over a million meals were being served each month in New York City by nonprofit groups. The principal sponsoring groups were churches (Daley).

reducing hunger and improving nutrition than the Food Stamp Program. The latter helps to ease the income constraint that prevents individuals and families from purchasing all the food they need (or desire), but it has not proved adequate for this task. Not all low-income families or individuals elect to participate and those that do frequently run out of stamps and money to purchase food before the end of the month. Hunger persists partly because of ignorance, but mainly because of holes in the safety net and not enough money to pay for housing and other necessities besides food.

Domestic food subsidy programs are likely to be continued because they serve multiple functions, including vote trading for farm price-support programs. Congress has demonstrated a willingness to fund domestic food subsidy programs on a much larger scale in recent years; however, the Food Stamp Program remains controversial. One can expect conflicts to persist over such issues as eligibility standards, the benefit reduction rate, the use of the thrifty food plan in calculating benefits, and the frequency of adjustments in the value of allotments.

The cost of food subsidy programs also may come under attack. Treasury costs are dictated principally by eligibility standards and the level of benefits offered. As with other entitlement programs, Congress has little alternative but to pick up the check for food subsidy programs once the eligibility standards and level of benefits have been established. Thus, eligibility standards will always be a critical issue.

DISCUSSION QUESTIONS

11.1. Why was the Food Stamp Program adopted and then expanded in the 1960s and 1970s rather than increasing the scope of the commodity distribution program as a way of reducing hunger and malnutrition in the United States?

11.2. Why did Congress resist efforts by the White House and the OMB to reduce appropriations for domestic food subsidy programs in the early 1980s?

11.3. Assume Congress is considering a 10 percent reduction in the appropriation for the Food Stamp Program. Is this likely to have a significant impact on: (1) the aggregate net income of farmers, (2) the welfare of food stamp participants, and (3) the incidence of hunger and malnutrition in the United States?

11.4. Assume alternatively, that Congress and the Administration have agreed to add $1 billion to the total budget for domestic food subsidy programs. The issue still to be decided is the allocation among programs. Which of the existing domestic food subsidy programs do you think the following groups would prefer to expand: (1) farmers and farm organizations, (2) nutritionists, (3) representatives of welfare rights organizations?

11.5. Why was the cash purchase requirement eliminated by Congress in the food stamp legislation adopted in 1977, and why are some members of the agricultural committees of Congress advocating its reinstatement?

REFERENCES

AKIN, JOHN S., DAVID K GUILKEY, and BARRY M. POPKIN, "The School Lunch Program and Nutrient Intake: A Switching Regression Analysis,." *American Journal of Agricultural Economics* 65 (1983), 477–85.

ALLEN, JOYCE E., and DORIS EPSON NEWTON, "Existing Food Policies and Their Relationship to Hunger and Nutrition," *American Journal of Agricultural Economics* 68 (1986), 1247–52.

BENEDICT, MURRAY R., and OSCAR C. STINE, *The Agricultural Commodity Programs*. New York: The Twentieth Century Fund, 1956.

BOEHM, WILLIAM T., and ANTHONY E. GALLO, "Has Food Assistance Helped?," *National Food Review* 3 (1978), 23–26.

DALEY, SUZANNE, "Soup Kitchens Rise Sharply, Report Finds," *New York Times,* June 25, 1987.

DAVIS, CARLTON G., "Linkages between Socioeconomic Characteristics, Food Expenditure Patterns, and Nutritional Status of Low-income Households: A Critical Review," *American Journal of Agricultural Economics* 64 (1982), 1017–25.

DAVIS, CARLTON G., and BENJAMIN SENAUER, "Needed Directions in Domestic Food Assistance Policies and Programs," *American Journal of Agricultural Economics* 68 (1986), 1253–57.

GIERTZ, J. FRED, and DENNIS H. SULLIVAN, "Giving Recipients a Choice Lets Some Go Hungry," *Wall Street Journal,* Jan. 11, 1984.

GUYON, JANET, "Doleful Problem: Food-Stamp Red Tape Raises Tension Levels in Understaffed Offices," *Wall Street Journal,* June 27, 1984.

KING, SETH S., "Doctors Say Federal Food Plans Have Slashed Gross Malnutrition," *New York Times,* May 1, 1979.

LONGEN, KATHRYN, *Domestic Food Programs: An Overview,* ESCS-81. Washington, D.C.: U. S. Department of Agriculture, 1980.

MATSUMOTO, MASAO, "Recent Trends in Domestic Food Programs," *National Food Review* 36 (1987), 24–27.

——— "Domestic Food Programs: An Update," *National Food Review* 37 (1987), 24–25.

MORENTZ, DEBORAH S., *Effects of Recent Changes in the Food Stamp Program on Participation and Food Consumption of Participating Households in Tompkins County, New York,* A.E. Research 80-30. Ithaca, N.Y.: Department of Agricultural Economics, Cornell University, 1980.

PHYSICIAN TASK FORCE ON HUNGER IN AMERICA, *Hunger in America: The Growing Epidemic.* Middletown, C.T.: Wesleyan University Press, 1985.

PRESIDENT'S TASK FORCE ON FOOD ASSISTANCE, *Report of the President's Task Force on Food Assistance.* Washington, D.C., 1984.

RANNEY, CHRISTINE K., "Hunger and Nutrition in America: Discussion," *American Journal of Agricultural Economics* 68 (1986), 1258–60.

SHAFFER, JAMES D., and JUDITH I. STALLMANN, "Domestic Food and Nutrition Programs: Sorting Out the Policy Issues," no. 13 in *The Farm and Food System in Transition: Emerging Policy Issues.* East Lansing, MI: Cooperative Extension Service, Michigan State University, 1983.

SMALLWOOD, DAVID, and JAMES BLAYLOCK, *Impact of Household Size and Income on Food Spending Patterns,* Tech. Bul. No. 1650. Washington, D.C.: U.S. Department of Agriculture, 1981.

U.S. DEPARTMENT OF AGRICULTURE, *Food Costs From Farm to Retail.* Washington, D.C.: Economic Research Service, 1987.

12

Agricultural Protection

Some form of agricultural protection exists in nearly all countries, although the level of protection varies widely among nations, and frequently differs among commodities within countries as well. In general, political pressure from producer organizations leads elected representatives to seek trade liberalization for those commodities that they are able to produce at low cost and protection for those that cannot compete with imports. The United States, for example, seeks to liberalize trade in grains, soybeans, and poultry products but, at the same time, continues to restrict imports of dairy products, beef and sugar. Similar inconsistencies are to be found in most other countries.

Producers may be protected against lower-cost imports in a number of ways. Tariffs, variable levies, and quotas are the most common instruments employed to raise the cost of imported items. Imports also may be restricted by enforcing pesticide residue or health regulations. In a few countries, imports are limited indirectly by requiring processors to utilize domestically produced rather than imported commodities. For example, an artificial market for grain can be maintained by compelling flour millers to use a minimum percentage of domestically produced wheat.

Quantitative import restrictions such as quotas play a much greater role in inhibiting trade in agricultural commodities than industrial products (Hillman). Nonfarm products are more likely to be protected by tariffs, although voluntary quotas (for example, on steel and automobiles) have become an important form of protection for some industrial products in recent years. In general, it has proved to be easier to negotiate reductions in tariffs than non-tariff trade barriers.

In this chapter, the theoretical consequences of alternative forms of protection are first described. This provides a basis for assessing the economic effects of U.S. protectionist policies. The consequences of measures adopted by the European Community to protect its own producers are then described. The final section deals with trade negotiations and the attempts that have been made over the past twenty years to liberalize trade in farm products.

ALTERNATIVE FORMS OF PROTECTION AND THEIR ECONOMIC CONSEQUENCES

The economic impact of protection differs depending on which method is used to restrict imports. All forms of protection share one thing in common: They raise prices to producers and, except for deficiency payments, place the burden of supporting agriculture directly on consumers. Higher prices encourage domestic production and reduce consumption, thereby leading either to a larger export surplus or a smaller volume of imports. The slopes or elasticities of demand and supply schedules in the country imposing tariffs (or import restrictions) determine how much trade will be affected by protectionist policies. These effects are illustrated for tariffs, variable levies, deficiency payments, and quotas.

Tariffs

Tariffs must be paid by importers (not the exporting country) before customs officials will permit commodities arriving from abroad to be removed from the dock or a bonded warehouse. There are two types of tariffs: fixed and ad valorem. A fixed rate is specified as so many cents (or other units of currency) per physical unit of product (pound, kilogram, etc.). An ad valorem duty is a percentage of the value of the imported product. Thus, the absolute magnitude of the import duty rises with the value of the imported product if ad valorem rates are in effect. In contrast, with fixed rates the tariff remains the same regardless of the value of the product. It becomes a smaller proportion of the import price as the price of the product rises and, therefore, affords less protection. This is illustrated by the fixed tariff on beef which has not been raised despite an increase in beef prices. In the 1930s, when beef prices averaged around ten cents per pound, a duty of three cents per pound afforded producers a 30 percent level of protection. More recently, with wholesale beef prices averaging seventy cents or more per pound, the same three-cent duty provides producers with a level of protection of less than 5 percent.

The effects of a tariff on internal prices, domestic production, consumption, and imports are illustrated in Figure 12.1. Domestic production is assumed to be less than consumption and, hence, some quantity must be imported. The absolute value of the tariff or import duty (whether fixed or ad valorem) is represented by the vertical distance between P_2 and P_1. The import price is P_1; after paying the duty, importing firms sell the product for P_2. Raising the internal price from P_1 to P_2 leads to an increase in domestic production from Q_1 to Q_2. The amount of the increase is determined by the size of the tariff and the slope of the supply schedule; with a flatter slope, production will respond even more to a given increase in the domestic price.

The consumption effect of a tariff is determined by the slope of the demand schedule. In Figure 12.1 this effect is represented by the decline in total use from Q_4 to Q_3. With higher internal production and reduced consumption, imports decline from Q_4 less Q_1 (the volume that would be

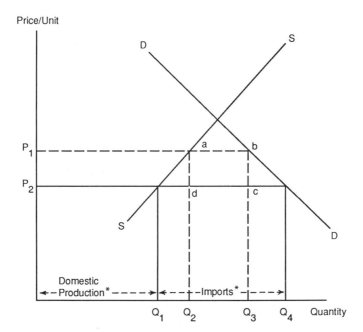

* Without protection

Figure 12.1   Effects of agricultural protection on domestic production, consumption, and the volume of imports.

imported in the absence of a tariff) to Q_3 minus Q_2. Clearly, the flatter the slopes of the supply and demand schedules, the greater the impact on imports.[1] If both supply and demand schedules are price inelastic, even a substantial tariff will not seriously distort production or trade from the levels that would prevail under free market conditions.

The foregoing illustration assumes the import price (P_1) is unaffected by the decrease in trade. To put it another way, the import supply schedule is assumed to be flat or perfectly elastic at P_1. This assumption is not always correct. If the export-supply schedule slopes upward, a decrease in import demand will depress the world or import price (P_1 in Figure 12.1). A significant price reduction is most likely to occur if the country imposing a tariff is a major importer. Under such circumstances, import demand would shift to the left. This shift in demand, combined with an inelastic supply schedule, would result in lower world prices. If the world price declines, at least a part of the price effects resulting from protection will fall on producers in exporting nations.

The incidence of a tariff (that is, who bears the burden of the import duty) will depend on the relative elasticities of demand and supply in the exporting and importing nations.[2] The more inelastic the supply and demand schedules confronting exporting nations relative to those in the importing country, the greater the impact on prices in exporting nations. Consumers in the importing country will bear most of the added cost if domestic demand and supply are more inelastic than world demand and supply. Support programs in exporting countries may prevent world prices from falling when export demand shifts to the left. If this situation prevails, the principal effect of protection in importing countries will be to raise the cost of imports and to increase surplus stocks in exporting nations.

Tariffs or import duties are a source of government revenue provided the country continues to import some of its requirements. The total tax revenue is a function of the amount of the tariff (P_2 minus P_1) multiplied by the quantity imported (Q_3 minus Q_2). This is represented by the area *abcd* in Figure 12.1. If the demand and supply curves are relatively flat, raising the tariff will lead to a substantial decline in imports and, consequently, in tariff revenue.

---

[1] The effect on imports of a given tariff (or level of protection) can be calculated as a percentage change as well as an absolute change. The elasticity of import demand (percentage change in imports for a 1 percent increase in the internal or domestic price) is a function of the weighted average of the supply and demand elasticities (which also are percentage relationships). If imports represent only a small percentage of total supply, even a modest change in the level of protection can result in a large percentage change in imports (Tomek and Robinson, p. 285).

[2] The technical relationships that determine the price and volume of trade effects of a tariff are illustrated in an appendix to this chapter.

Variable Levies

A variable levy provides a more effective means of protecting domestic producers than either a fixed or an ad valorem tariff because it is adjusted up or down to compensate for any changes in import prices. A variable levy is simply the difference between a guaranteed internal price (represented by P_2 in Figure 12.1) and the import price (P_1). If the import price falls for any reason, the variable levy is raised by a corresponding amount, thus completely insulating domestic prices from changes in international prices. For example, if the guaranteed price for grain (P_2) is $200 per ton and the world price (P_1) falls from $120 to $100 per ton, the importing country would counter the potential adverse effects on domestic producers of lower world prices by raising the variable levy from $80 to $100 per ton.

As with a tariff, the revenue which the importing country's government obtains from a variable levy depends on the volume of imports multiplied by the size of the levy. Thus, if the world price declines the government obtains more revenue, assuming the volume of imports remains the same. With a variable levy system, agricultural exporting nations gain nothing by cutting prices. In fact, as Martin Abel has suggested, variable levies are an open invitation for exporting nations to collude in raising prices to countries which impose such levies (Abel, p. 206).[3] If exporting nations could form a cartel and raise the world price to P_2, consumers in the importing country would be no worse off than with the variable levy; the government, however, would lose the revenue which would now go to the exporting nations. Under a variable levy system, increases or decreases in world prices determine how the total revenue obtained from the sale of imported commodities will be shared between the government of the importing country and producers in the exporting country.

The effect of a variable levy on the quantity of imports depends on the level of prices guaranteed in the importing country (P_2 in Figure 12.1) and the slopes of the demand and supply schedules. With relatively flat slopes and/or a high guaranteed price, it is possible for a country to become a net exporter of agricultural commodities rather than an importer.

---

[3]The opportunity obviously exists for the United States and other exporting countries to do so vis-a-vis the European Community; however, enforcement of an international two-price plan (with EC countries being compelled to pay higher prices) would be difficult. Other countries that might buy at lower prices would tend to undercut sales by the colluding exporters. Deciding how the higher-priced market would be shared among exporters also would present formidable negotiating problems.

Deficiency Payments

Deficiency payments are not strictly a method of protection al-though they may produce the same effect, that is, by inducing domestic producers to increase output they result in reduced imports. With deficiency payments, however, the impact on imports is less than with a tariff or a variable levy because there is no consumption effect. The con-sumer pays the import price rather than the price guaranteed to producers. Thus, consumption does not decline as it would with higher prices induced by a tariff. Imports decline, however, because home production rises in response to the higher guaranteed price. The produc-tion effect is identical to that resulting from a tariff. The quantitative ef-fects can be illustrated by referring again to Figure 12.1. Assume the guaranteed price is P_2. To maintain that price to farmers, the govern-ment will have to make a deficiency payment per unit of product equal to the difference between the import price and the guaranteed price (P_2 minus P_1). The amount the government will have to pay producers is represented by the rectangle P_2adP_1. Production rises from Q_1 to Q_2; im-ports are reduced by a corresponding amount. But consumption remains at Q_4 because consumers still pay prices dictated by the cost of imports (P_1).

Under a deficiency payment scheme, consumers benefit if world prices decline; the government, however, has to spend more on deficiency payments because the gap between P_2 and P_1 increases. This is an im-portant difference between using variable levies to protect agriculture and deficiency payments. A lower world price increases revenue for the importing country under a variable levy support system; the same price reduction will increase government costs under a deficiency payment scheme. Under the latter system, imports will rise because consumers purchase more in response to lower world prices. Exporters can win larger markets by cutting prices if producers are protected by deficiency payments in importing countries; they cannot do so if producers are protected by variable levies.

Quotas

An alternative method of protecting domestic producers is to restrict imports by imposing an import quota or by authorizing im-porters to bring in only certain quantities. The effects of quantitative restrictions on imports also can be illustrated by referring to Figure 12.1. Assume imports are restricted to the quantity represented by Q_3 minus Q_2. The effect on internal prices will be the same as imposing a tariff equal to P_2 minus P_1. Consumers pay the higher price (P_2), but the government no longer collects any revenue. This now goes to those countries possessing a quota (or to licensed importers if they are granted the right to import certain quantities). Exporting nations fortunate enough to obtain the right to sell in the importing country will receive the prevailing internal price for whatever quantity they are permitted to market. Thus, under an import quota system the benefits of protection are shared by selected overseas suppliers as well as domestic producers.

A bilateral agreement may achieve the same degree of protection as an import quota. Such agreements are usually negotiated between an importing country and a particular supplier. The United Kingdom negotiated a number of such agreements during the 1960s. One such agreement was called the "Bacon Market Sharing Understanding" (Ritson, p. 368). Under this agreement, the British government undertook to limit home production of bacon in return for commitments on the part of selected suppliers to restrict bacon imports. This kept prices higher than otherwise would have prevailed and enabled the selected suppliers to share in the benefits of the higher prices paid by U.K. consumers.

Importers may be licensed to bring in certain quantities as an alternative to issuing quotas to foreign suppliers. If this is done the importer, not the foreign supplier, receives the additional revenue, that is, the difference between the import price and the higher internal prices. Buying at world prices and selling in a protected market can be extremely profitable as importers of foreign cars have discovered. It is for this reason that licensing importers frequently leads to fraud and corruption. Every importer seeks a larger share of the protected market and may be willing to pay for the privilege of obtaining a permit to import a larger quantity.

The price-enhancing benefits of quotas can be retained by the government of the importing country rather than passed along to foreign suppliers or licensed importers. This can be done by selling the right to import rather than allocating quotas on the basis of political favors or foreign policy considerations. Under perfectly competitive market conditions, potential exporters to a country that restricts imports would be willing to pay a premium equal to something less than the price advantage (P_2 minus P_1 in Figure 12.1) for each unit they could sell in that market. By auctioning quotas the government should be able to obtain revenue approximately equal to abcd in Figure 12.1. Import quotas could be sold either to foreign suppliers or to domestic importers.

Other Methods of Restricting Imports

Complex customs procedures, grading and labeling requirements and sanitary regulations are among the other methods used by some importing countries, particularly Japan, to restrict imports of farm products. The production, consumption, and price effects of such regulations are similar to a quota. In some cases sanitary regulations (for example those pertaining to pesticide residues) are so strict that imports are effectively prohibited.

Compulsory mixing requirements or other measures designed to create an artificial market for domestically produced agricultural commodities also have the effect of reducing imports. In Finland, for example, millers are required to use a certain amount of domestic wheat in manufacturing flour. The European Community has at times required feed manufacturers to use surplus skim-milk powder as a protein supplement in animal feed, thus displacing soybean meal which otherwise might have been imported for this purpose.

AGRICULTURAL PROTECTION IN THE UNITED STATES

The United States, like most other countries, uses a variety of devices in an attempt to protect producers and to enhance prices. Tariffs are imposed on a number of agricultural commodities, but they generally are low in relation to current market prices and, therefore, afford only a modest degree of protection. Inflation over the past fifty years has made fixed tariffs established during the 1930s much less effective in protecting producers. Successive rounds of international trade negotiations also have reduced or eliminated tariffs on many commodities. Unlike many other countries, the United States does not tax imports of tropical products such as coffee, tea, cocoa, and palm oil. Among tropical products sugar is an exception.

Quantitative restrictions are much more important than tariffs as a method of protecting farmers in the United States. Import quotas and/or negotiated agreements with foreign suppliers have been employed since the 1930s to limit imports of such commodities as wheat, cotton, peanuts, dairy products, beef, and sugar. Under Section 22 of the Agricultural Adjustment Act of 1933 (which is still in effect), the President may impose import duties or quotas on any commodity if imports threaten to undermine the effectiveness of price-support programs. In the absence of import restrictions, the government would be compelled to buy or store whatever quantities of supported commodities were displaced by imports. Thus, to hold down government costs practically all supported commodities are protected by import quotas.

Over the past thirty years, policy debates related to the level of protection in the United States have centered around a very small group of commodities, principally sugar, wool, dairy products, and beef. The United States obviously is not alone in protecting these commodities, but other governments often use U.S. import restrictions on such commodities as beef and dairy products to justify their own high levels of protection. This has been particularly true of Japan.

The Consequences of U.S. Sugar Policies

In most years, the U.S. price for sugar has been maintained above the "world" or import price.[4] Imports have been restricted by allocating quotas to selected suppliers. The Philippines, Brazil, Australia, Taiwan, Fiji, Haiti, the Dominican Republic, Mauritius, Thailand, and South Africa are among the countries that have been granted quotas in the past. These countries have been able to earn more from sugar sold in the United States than they could have earned by selling sugar at world market prices. Thus, the U.S. sugar program has been a vehicle for selectively aiding certain countries.

The total import quota as well as the allocation among suppliers has been strongly influenced by political considerations. Domestic producers of both sugar beets and sugar cane want to restrict imports and gain a larger share of the total market. In return for protection U.S. producers have had to accept acreage restrictions. Production rights have been allocated to certain states. When sugar production is profitable, members of Congress and senators vie with each other to obtain an allotment for their district or state (or to obtain a larger allotment). One way the domestic allotment can be increased is to reduce the import quota. When Cuba was cut off as a major U.S. supplier following the Castro-led revolution, Congress reallocated part of the Cuban quota to domestic producers. Lobbyists for the U.S. sugar industry have continually sought to maintain or increase the domestic quota at the expense of foreign suppliers.

Congress has dictated the allocation of quotas among external suppliers as well as among states. Competition among potential suppliers for a quota or the enlargement of a quota has been intense. Countries seeking a quota or a larger share of the U.S. market have been known to hire lobbyists and offer payments or free vacations to members of Congress who were in a position to influence the allocation of import quotas. Much of the lobbying in the 1960s was directed toward members of the House Committee on Agriculture (Berman and Heineman). Charges that the chairman of the House agricultural committee accepted favors

[4]Protection for sugar is so widespread that there is only a limited residual market for sugar not committed to particular countries under bilateral agreements. As a result, small changes in residual supplies or the demand for additional non-quota sugar can lead to large changes in the so-called "world" price of sugar. This price applies to only a small proportion of world sugar production.

from foreign governments seeking to enlarge their quota contributed to his defeat in the election of 1966.

Foreign policy considerations have inevitably played a role in determining who gets a quota and how large it will be. The Philippines, for example, were guaranteed a quota as part of the treaty granting independence. The Irish lobby in the United States succeeded at one time in getting a small quota for Ireland. Australia retains a quota partly because it has been a reliable ally. Some members of Congress have tried to use sugar quotas as leverage to achieve other objectives. Members of the "Black Caucus," for example, have on several occasions attempted to reduce or eliminate the sugar quota given to South Africa.

Producers of sugar substitutes have been the principal beneficiaries of U.S. sugar policies, not foreign suppliers. The high internal prices maintained in recent years (at least relative to world prices) have provided a golden opportunity for producers of corn sweeteners to capture a larger share of the market. Soft drink manufacturers have almost entirely switched from sugar to high fructose corn syrup or to non-caloric sweeteners. As a result, sugar now accounts for less than half of the total U.S. market for caloric sweeteners (USDA, SSRV 12N2, 1987). The impact of declining sugar consumption has fallen entirely on foreign suppliers. Between 1976 and 1986 total U.S. sugar consumption declined from around eleven million tons (raw value) to just over eight million tons. Foreign suppliers provided nearly five million tons of the eleven million tons consumed in 1976. By 1986, imports (excluding the quantities imported and processed for reexport) had declined to about 1.7 million tons.[5] During this same ten-year period, U.S. sugar production remained relatively stable at around six million tons.

World sugar prices have been depressed in recent years, not only by the reduction in U.S. import quotas, but also by the protectionist policies of other major industrial countries. The European Community and Japan continue to support domestic producers of sugar beets by maintaining internal prices well above world prices. All the major industrial countries including the Soviet Union share responsibility for limiting the potential market for sugar produced by developing countries.

The Impact of Beef Quotas

Beef producers in the United States also have been protected by quotas or the threat of imposing quotas.[6] Under legislation enacted in

[5]Because of excess stocks and higher domestic production, the total import quota was reduced to 1.0 million tons in 1987 and to 750,000 tons in 1988.

[6]Legislation adopted in 1964 authorized the Secretary of Agriculture to impose quotas whenever beef imports threatened to exceed prescribed levels. In most years, it has

1979, import quotas vary inversely with the level of U.S. beef production; that is, the amount that can be imported rises as domestic production declines and vice versa. By varying the level of permissible imports, Congress hoped to stabilize consumer supplies of beef and to avoid extreme price fluctuations. The effect of this policy is to shift part of the U.S. instability problem to foreign suppliers. Prices in world markets may become even more unstable if the principal exporters are asked to compensate for changes in U.S. beef production.

The price effects of U.S. protectionist policies have been much less for beef than for sugar. In most years, beef quotas have enhanced producer prices, but probably by no more than 5 percent. Eliminating beef quotas would not result in a flood of imports, because the supply of beef that meets U.S. health and sanitary regulations is limited. The United States is by far the world's largest importer of beef, although beef imports typically add only 7 to 8 percent to total supplies available to U.S. consumers. An increase in beef imports of as much as 50 percent (say, from 7 to 10 or 11 percent of total U.S. beef supplies) would add only 3 to 4 percent to the per capita availability of beef (Jackson, p. 2). The price effect of this change in quantity can be estimated by dividing the percentage increase in per capita availability by the price elasticity of demand for beef. If one assumes a price elasticity of -0.9, a 4 percent increase in total supply would reduce the average U.S. wholesale price for beef by approximately 4.5 percent. In the long run, the magnitude of price changes might be somewhat greater, because beef production would increase in exporting nations. But there would be less incentive to maintain production in the United States. Under free trade, U.S. beef prices would fall and import prices would rise, but the changes probably would not be very large (Jackson; Freebairn and Rausser).

U.S. import restrictions have had mixed effects on beef exporters. Countries such as Australia and New Zealand, with substantial import quotas, have benefited from selling part of their output to the United States at higher prices. It is not clear, however, whether they have been net winners or losers. The loss in sales may have more than offset the price advantage. Residual exporters are the principal losers. Those without a quota cannot sell beef in the United States and receive lower prices because they must compete with larger residual supplies from quota countries.

not been necessary to do so because the principal suppliers (Australia, New Zealand, Ireland, and several small Central American countries) have "voluntarily" agreed to restrict shipments. Thus, the threat of quotas has been sufficient to hold imports below the critical level.

AGRICULTURAL PROTECTION IN THE EUROPEAN COMMUNITY [7]

The protectionist policies of the European Community (EC) have had equally serious consequences for agricultural exporting nations. High levels of protection combined with rapid improvements in technology have overstimulated production. As a result, the European Community has become a substantial net exporter of many temperate-zone agricultural commodities. Surpluses of wheat, beef, dairy products, sugar, wine, and olive oil have been dumped on world markets. The shift from a net importer to a net exporter of farm products has reduced sales for traditional agricultural exporting nations and depressed world prices.

Variable levies and quantitative import restrictions are the principal devices used to protect EC producers from lower-priced imports. Almost all commodities produced in large volume in the European Community are protected. Grains and livestock products are protected by variable levies, while fruits and vegetables are protected by quantitative import restrictions (at least during certain periods of the year) and by health regulations. The prices of durum wheat, olive oil, and some oilseed crops such as rapeseed and sunflowers are supported by deficiency payments.

Traditional exporters of temperate-zone agricultural commodities have been highly critical of the Common Agricultural Policy (CAP) of the European Community, not so much because of the methods of protection employed, but because of the high level of support maintained. Prices have been established well above world or import prices for grains and most livestock products. Support prices for grain largely determine the level of guaranteed prices for livestock products because the cost of producing livestock products is closely related to the prices of grain and other feed ingredients.

The level of support prices is determined by negotiation, not by a formula. Last year's prices always serve as a starting point for establishing prices for the current year. Civil servants (the EC Commission) make recommendations for price changes based on increases or decreases in costs of production, the size of surplus stocks and budgetary constraints. Their recommendations, however, are not always accepted by the Council of Ministers, the group that makes the final decisions. The Council of Ministers consists of the cabinet member or whoever rep-

---

[7]Originally, the European Community consisted of the Netherlands, Belgium, Luxembourg, Germany, France, and Italy. Three members, the United Kingdom, Ireland, and Denmark, were added in 1973. Greece became a full member in 1981 and Spain and Portugal in 1986.

resents agriculture in the government of each member country. Their decisions inevitably are influenced by political considerations.

The two critical prices the EC Commission establishes for cereals are the target price and the intervention price. The target price ultimately determines the size of the variable levy while the intervention price puts a floor under internal farm prices much the same way as the price-support loan rate does in the United States. The relationship between these two prices is shown schematically in Figure 12.2.

The variable levy is the difference between the threshold price and the cif import price (that is, the price paid for imported grain, including the cost of the grain, insurance, and transport or freight costs to the port of entry). The threshold price is linked to the target price. It is equal to the target price at Duisburg, Germany (or some other major grain deficit region) less the cost of moving grain from the port to that location. The variable levy when paid by the importer brings the total cost of imported grain (including transport and handling costs) up to the target price if it is shipped to Duisburg. The relationship between the target price, the threshold price, and the import price is illustrated in Figure 12.2.

A numerical example may help to make clear the relationship between these prices. Assume the target price for wheat is $200 per ton, and that the cost of transporting grain from Rotterdam to Duisburg is $20 per ton. The threshold price is then $180 per ton ($200 less $20). If the cif price of imported grain at Rotterdam is $120 per ton, the variable levy will be $60 per ton (the threshold price of $180 per ton less the import price of $120 per ton). The variable levy is adjusted weekly to com-

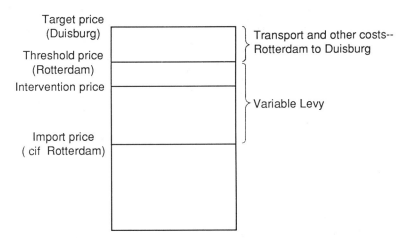

Figure 12.2 Schematic representation of EC support prices and the variable levy for grains. (Source: Roberts and Tie, p. 297.)

pensate for changes in import prices. For example, if the import price falls, the variable levy will be raised by a corresponding amount.

The intervention price is the support level or floor price; it is the price at which the EC is prepared to purchase commodities whenever local supply exceeds demand. In recent years, substantial quantities of soft wheat, dairy products, and beef have been purchased at intervention prices.[8] Export subsidies (usually referred to in the EC as "export restitution") are necessary to make EC prices on world markets competitive with those offered by other countries. Such subsidies are paid to exporting firms which buy at the higher internal price and sell at the prevailing world price.

Economic Consequences of the CAP

The European Community has maintained support prices for grains and other agricultural commodities at levels which have encouraged farmers to produce more than enough to meet internal requirements. EC support prices have declined in real terms (that is, when adjusted for inflation) since the late 1970s, but not enough to curb production. Surpluses of wheat, dairy products, beef, wine, and olive oil have created an enormous financial burden for the Community. Disposing of these surpluses also has led to strained relations with the United States and other agricultural exporting nations.

In a period of less than ten years, the EC shifted from a major net importer to the second or third largest exporter of wheat. The change in position from a net importer to a major net exporter was due entirely to higher levels of production, not a reduction in consumption. Between 1977-1978 and 1984-1985, a period of seven years, average production of all cereal grains combined rose from 129 million tons to 166 million tons, an increase of approximately 29 percent (Table 12.1). Domestic use of grain during this same period remained static at around 144 million tons. Thus, in the earlier period, production fell short of domestic use by 15 million tons; in the latter period, production exceeded use by 22 million tons. This is equivalent to a decline in the export market for other suppliers of 37 million tons or about 18 percent of world grain trade. The appearance of EC wheat surpluses on world markets occurred at a time when the demand for grain imports was stagnant or growing only very slowly. If the change had occurred in the 1970s when demand was growing much more rapidly, the impact on other suppliers would have been much less.

[8]High quality wheat more desirable for breadmaking is still imported by the EC despite a wheat surplus. Lower quality wheat including some usable only for animal feed is purchased by EC authorities at intervention prices.

Table 12.1   Production and Domestic Use of Wheat and Coarse Grains Combined, European Community,[a] 1977-1978 and 1984-1985

	1977-78[b]	1984-85[b]
	(million tons)	
Production	129	166
Domestic Use	144	144
Difference	−15	22

[a]Combined production for the twelve nations that made up EC in 1986.
[b]Average production and use for two marketing years.
SOURCE: U.S. Department of Agriculture, FG 8-87, 1987.

cultural exporting nations have had to contend with EC exports of surplus dairy products and beef as well as wheat. Australia, New Zealand, Canada, and the United States have been among the principal losers from EC support policies and, hence, have been the most vocal critics. The Soviet Union and countries in North Africa and the Middle East have been the principal winners. They have benefited from subsidized exports of wheat, beef, butter, and skim-milk powder. Butter, for example, has been sold to the Soviet Union at prices far below those prevailing in the European Community. Understandably, this has irritated EC consumers.

The EC maintains, with some justification, that other countries subsidize agricultural exports and, therefore, they should not be singled out for criticism. In some instances, the United States has countered EC export subsidies with subsidies of its own. They did so to sell wheat to Egypt in 1983 and to the Soviet Union in 1986. Nearly all U.S. exports of butter and skim-milk powder are subsidized. Australia and New Zealand are on firmer moral ground in criticizing EC export restitution payments. In general, these countries do not subsidize exports, or do so to a much smaller extent than either the European Community or the United States.

Not all exporters, however, have been net losers from EC policies. Selective application of the variable levy system has helped exporters of nongrain feed ingredients such as corn gluten, cassava (manioc), and soybean meal. Imports of these commodities have risen because they are cheaper sources of energy and protein than homegrown cereals and oilseed meals. At the time the CAP was first put together, it was not considered necessary to tax imports of commodities other than cereals and livestock products, because they were not being produced in significant volume within the Community. For this reason variable levies have not been assessed against imports of corn gluten, citrus pulp, cassava chips, and other substitutes for whole grain in animal feed. A tariff is imposed on some products, but it is much lower than the variable levy which applies to corn, wheat and other cereals. Manufacturers of animal feed have taken advantage of this loophole by importing noncereal ingredients. The cheaper ingredients have displaced grain that otherwise might have been imported or purchased from local suppliers.

Thailand has earned additional foreign exchange by selling dried cassava chips to EC feed manufacturers. Producers of corn gluten (a by-product of converting grain into alcohol) have also benefited from the Community's discriminatory pricing system for feed ingredients. The United States found a ready market in the late 1970s for by-products of its expanding wet corn milling industry. Soybean producers gained as well because of the need for additional high-protein ingredients to compensate for the use of more low-protein sources of energy such as cassava chips.

EC policies have altered the relative economic position of producers in exporting nations. The shift from importing grain to importing non-grain feed ingredients has hurt grain exporters but helped soybean producers. U.S corn producers have sold less corn to the EC but have benefited indirectly from increased sales of products derived from corn milling.

The benefits of cheaper feed ingredients have been unevenly distributed within the European Community. Livestock feeders near major ports (for example, dairymen and pig feeders in the Netherlands) have been the principal beneficiaries of lower-cost feed ingredients. They have gained relative to farmers who must purchase feed made from higher-cost homegrown cereals.

The Common Agricultural Policy is widely criticized by many within the Community as well as by outsiders. The principal internal criticisms are that it costs too much and overprices food, although there has been less organized opposition to high food prices than one might have expected based on U.S. experience. European farmers also have been unhappy with some of the pricing decisions. Price increases in recent years have failed to keep pace with rising costs (Roberts and Tie, p. 298). As a result, the real earnings of farmers were lower in the early 1980s than they had been in the 1970s.

The rising cost of acquiring and disposing of surpluses in the mid-1980s occurred at a time when less revenue was available from variable levies. This was an inevitable consequence of the shift from deficit to surplus. When imports decline, the income from variable levies also declines. EC support costs are now paid principally out of revenue obtained from a Community-wide, value added tax (equivalent to a sales tax). Even this fund has not been sufficient in some years to cover losses. Member states have been asked for additional contributions. Governments do not respond favorably to such requests. The United Kingdom has been especially critical of the EC support costs and the way they have been allocated among member states. More hours probably have been spent by heads of member states in trying to resolve conflicts over funding agricultural support costs than any other single issue.

The principal measures that have been proposed or adopted to reduce surpluses and lower the cost of the CAP are as follows:

- lower support prices
- institute supply-control measures
- tax or restrict imports of non-grain feed ingredients and vegetable oils.

Pressure for reform has led to very modest reductions in support prices and to the adoption of measures designed to curb growth in production of surplus commodities. Intervention prices for cereals were lowered slightly in the mid-1980s, but the Council of Ministers was reluctant to reduce target prices as much as technocrats in Brussels suggested because of objections from farmers. European producers, like their counterparts elsewhere, were being squeezed by rising costs and declining farm prices. As production rose, more grain was being sold at the lower intervention price. This resulted in a decline in average farm prices for grain that exceeded the reduction in announced support prices.

Beginning in 1984, the Community sought to curb increases in milk production by introducing a quota scheme. Each country was assigned a quota. These, in turn, were divided among milk cooperatives in some countries and individual producers in others. The quota scheme prevented production from rising but did not result in as much reduction in output as planned. Apparently, the penalties imposed on excess production were not sufficient or were not administered in such a way as to insure compliance by all producers. Changes have been made since the program was first introduced in an attempt to make the scheme more effective.

A discriminatory pricing scheme has been adopted in an attempt to curb overproduction of sugar. Farmers receive a higher price for a limited quantity and a lower price for over-quota production. A similar type of overquota pricing scheme has been proposed for wheat.

In an attempt to create a larger market for home-grown grain, proposals have been made to restrict imports of non-grain feed ingredients. Thailand agreed to limit exports of cassava chips voluntarily but this was done in response to the threat of imposing quotas. The U.S. government has objected strongly to any suggestion that imports of corn gluten be restricted or subjected to variable levies. A proposal to tax imported vegetable oils met with an equally hostile reception. The EC would like to tax soybean oil and palm oil, partly to raise revenue and partly to reduce the cost of supporting domestically produced oilseed crops such as rapeseed and sunflowers. A further switch in land use from wheat to these crops would help to reduce the wheat surplus. These measures illustrate the important secondary effects of attempting to solve a surplus problem created by protectionist measures designed originally to achieve self-sufficiency in food production.

TRADE NEGOTIATIONS

Several attempts have been made during the past two decades to reduce the level of agricultural protection through trade negotiations. The results thus far have been disappointing. Negotiating reductions in nontariff barriers is much more difficult than simply cutting tariffs. As pointed out earlier, nontariff barriers play a much greater role in restricting trade in farm commodities than in industrial products. The failure to achieve significant reductions in trade barriers also can be attributed to political resistance to altering current support programs. A general move toward trade liberalization would necessitate subjecting the support programs of the United States, Japan, and the European Community to international review and negotiation. Neither the U.S. Congress nor the representatives of other countries are likely to relinquish control over their domestic farm policies.

Experience with two rounds of trade talks, the Kennedy round which began in 1964 and the Tokyo round which began in 1975, illustrates the difficulties encountered in trying to liberalize trade in farm products. The primary emphasis in both rounds of negotiations was on reducing industrial tariffs; however, the United States wanted to use the trade talks as a vehicle for relaxing import restrictions on farm products as well. The strategy adopted by the United States was to offer concessions on industrial products in return for reduced barriers to the entry of U.S. farm products in Europe and Japan. But this strategy turned out to be unsuccessful. Negotiations became stalled over the issue of agricultural concessions and remained deadlocked for many months. The European Community was unwilling to alter the level of support for agriculture or to guarantee entry for a minimum quantity of U.S. farm products. Finally, in July 1967, the United States was forced to capitulate in order to salvage what progress had been made in negotiating reductions in industrial tariffs, because the five-year grant of authority to carry on the negotiations was about to expire. The compromises ultimately adopted did relatively little to reduce agricultural trade barriers. Tariffs were reduced on only a small group of commodities, mainly tobacco, fruits, and vegetables.

A decade later, the United States again made an effort to link concessions on industrial products to trade liberalization for farm products. Success in the Tokyo round of trade talks was no greater than in the previous round of negotiations. The United States obtained a few concessions from Japan on imported tobacco, fruit, and beef. The European Community also agreed to retain (bind) the zero duty on soybeans and soybean products. In return, the United States agreed to a very modest liberalization of import restrictions on cheese.

Both Democratic and Republican presidents in recent decades have supported trade liberalization. Farmers and farm organizations have been divided on the issue. Producers of most cereal crops, soybeans, and perhaps broilers and turkeys would benefit from international negotiations that succeeded in reducing trade barriers for farm products. Gains for these producers, however, would be offset in part by lower returns to producers of such commodities as milk, wool, and sugar. A number of studies have concluded that U.S. farmers as a group would benefit from trade liberalization provided U.S. concessions were matched by those of other countries (Johnson; Vermeer et al.). Consumers also would gain from cheaper dairy products, wool, and sugar. Those who might benefit, however, are less well organized to present their case than producers who might lose from trade liberalization. This makes it difficult to win majority support for reducing the level of protection. Measures to liberalize trade are even less likely to win approval if the principal winners are producers in another country. This clearly would be the case if the United States were to relax import restrictions on sugar. About the only way trade in farm products can be liberalized is to reduce the power of the agricultural committees in Congress to dictate legislation. In the case of industrial products, success in reducing tariffs was achieved by giving negotiators freedom (within certain limits) to work out reciprocal trade agreements.

The United States proposed in 1987 that all agricultural support measures of the industrial countries (principally those of the United States, the European Community, and Japan) be placed on the negotiating table during the round of trade talks that began with a conference in Uruguay in 1986. The objective of the U.S. proposal was to bring about a phased reduction in support levels or the degree of protection over some prescribed period, perhaps extending for as long as a decade. To carry out this plan, it would first be necessary to achieve some measure of agreement on the level of protection afforded producers in different countries. This might be done by making use of a study conducted by the Organization for Economic Cooperation and Development (OECD). Economists associated with OECD developed a technique for measuring the margin of support which they called the "producer subsidy equivalent." Once agreement on support levels had been achieved, negotiators would then need to decide how much the level of protection would be reduced, on which commodities, and over what time period. Judging from the earlier experience with trade negotiations, one cannot be very optimistic about the prospects for success. Nevertheless, the proposal is an important development because it explicitly recognizes that agricultural protection can be reduced only if there is mutual acceptance of changes in national support programs.

CONCLUSIONS

The costs of protecting agriculture are borne mainly by consumers, and to a lesser extent by low-cost producers foreclosed from markets by trade barriers. If barriers were reduced, these two groups would gain at the expense of producers who are now protected. Costs to consumers from attempts to maintain farm incomes could be minimized by permitting imports to come in at world prices and compensating producers for their losses by making deficiency payments. Distortions in production resulting from overpricing farm products in protected markets would be even less if payments were divorced from output.

Farmers in Japan, the European Community, and the United States (at least those producing certain commodities) have been the principal winners from protectionist policies. The principal losers have been consumers and low-cost exporters of such commodities as wheat, sugar, beef, and dairy products.

Internal pressures for reform of the Common Agricultural Policy are likely to be more effective in reducing agricultural protection in the European Community than threats of retaliation by the United States. The high cost of coping with surpluses has already forced the Community to reduce the real level of support prices. It may be compelled to take further action to hold down production of commodities such as wheat, wine, and milk if support costs continue to rise.

Trade liberalization would lead to a redistribution of income among producers in the United States. Provided concessions were granted by other countries in return for lower U.S. trade barriers, farmers producing grains, soybeans and some types of livestock products would gain but at the expense of those producing milk, sugar, lambs, and wool. In theory it would be possible for the winners from trade liberalization, including consumers, to compensate losers and still come out ahead. But because compensation is seldom, if ever, paid to the losers, it is difficult to obtain the political support needed to reduce trade barriers.

Successive rounds of international trade negotiations have succeeded in reducing tariffs on a wide range of industrial products over the past two decades. Negotiators have had much less success in reducing nontariff barriers or other protectionist measures that apply to farm products. Bilateral trade negotiations and threats of retaliation have been no more effective in opening up markets for U.S. farm products in Japan and the European Community. No country wants to undercut markets for its own producers or to absorb still higher support costs. Agricultural support programs are the principal barrier to trade liberalization for farm products. Trade barriers are not likely to come down unless negotiators succeed in gaining acceptance for alternative ways of protecting farmers against losses in income.

DISCUSSION QUESTIONS

12.1. Assume Country X, a major importer of wheat, imposes a 20 percent tariff or import duty on wheat. What determines how much impact this will have on: (1) the internal price of wheat in Country X, (2) the world or import price of wheat, and (3) the volume of imports?

12.2. Assume the United States were to abandon its import quota system for sugar and instead impose a five cent per pound import duty on sugar. How would this change in policy affect U.S. sugar producers, overseas suppliers of sugar, U.S. consumers, U.S. corn producers, and government revenue?

12.3. Who or what groups would be winners and losers if the European Community were to eliminate variable levies on grains and livestock products but continue to protect European producers by making deficiency payments to producers equal to the difference between present guaranteed prices and world or import prices? How would such a change affect EC support costs and EC revenue?

12.4. Why has it proved to be more difficult to reduce international trade barriers for farm products than for industrial products?

Appendix 12-A
Hypothetical Price and Trade Effects of Imposing a Tariff on Imports

Conventional back-to-back supply and demand diagrams can be used to illustrate the price effects of imposing a tariff on imports (Figure 12.3). Assume Country A is an importer of Commodity X. The demand schedule for X in Country A (D_A) is downward sloping to the left because the quantity is measured to the left from the vertical axis. The supply schedule in Country A (S_A) intersects the demand schedule at $160 per ton, thus indicating that Country A would become self-sufficient at that price.

At any price above $60 per ton, production will exceed consumption in Country B (shown on the right hand side of Figure 12.3). The gap be-

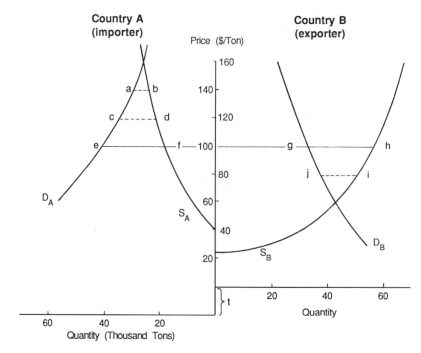

Figure 12.3   Price effects of imposing a tariff in Country A.

tween the supply and demand schedules in Country B obviously increases as the price rises.

If one assumes there are only two countries which engage in trade,
the imports of A would equal the exports of B. At an export price of $100
per ton (and no tariff), demand will exceed supply in Country A by an
amount represented by *ef*; supply will exceed demand in Country B by
the amount represented by *gh*. The horizontal difference *ef* is equal to
gh. Thus, the free-trade price is equal to $100 per ton in the exporting
country. The price in Country A will exceed this price by the cost of
transport (indicated by *t* on the vertical axis). This is shown diagram-
matically by lowering the horizontal axis for Country A by an amount
equal to the transport costs.

Assume Country A decides to impose a tax of $40 per ton on im-
ports, either to obtain revenue or to protect domestic producers. The
price in Country A, however, will not rise by $40 per ton. At a price of
$140 per ton (including the tariff), the quantity Country A would need to
import in order to bridge the gap between consumption and internal
production (*ab*) is less than Country B would be willing to export at a
price (less the tariff) of $100 per ton. New equilibrium prices and quan-
tities would be achieved at a price of $120 per ton in Country A and $80

per ton in Country B. The difference in price is just equal to the tariff or import duty of $40 per ton. The quantity imported at $120 per ton (*cd*) is equal to the quantity available for export in Country B at $80 per ton (*ij*). Demand exceeds supply in A by an amount equal to the difference between supply and demand in Country B. The effect of imposing a tariff of $40 per ton in this particular case is to raise the price in Country A by $20 per ton and to reduce the price in Country B by $20 per ton. The price effects are split evenly between the importer and exporter in this particular case, because the combined slopes of the demand and supply curves are the same over the relevant price range in the two countries. If the slopes had been different the price effects would not be equal. Only if the demand and supply schedules in Country A were vertical (that is, totally unresponsive to price between $100 and $140 per ton), would the entire cost of the tariff be borne by consumers in Country A. Under such circumstances, imports would still equal *ef* and exports would remain at *gh*. Importers in A would purchase grain at $100 per ton (plus transport costs) and sell it for $140 per ton (plus transport costs) after paying the import duty. The more inelastic the supply and demand schedules in the importing country relative to the exporting country, the greater the share of the tariff that will be borne by consumers in the importing country. Producers in exporting countries will bear a high proportion of the price effects if their demand and supply schedules are much more inelastic than those in the importing countries.

Clearly, the results are more complex when several countries are involved, but the principles remain the same. Countries A and B could, for example, be viewed as the combined demand and supply relationships for all importing and exporting nations. These relationships could then be used to construct excess demand and supply curves.

Excess demand is zero at the equilibrium price in Country A ($160 per ton). This represents the vertical intercept of the excess demand curve shown in Figure 12.4). Below this price excess demand is equal to the horizontal difference between the demand and supply curves for Country A.

The excess supply curve intercepts the vertical axis at the equilibrium price in Country B of $60 per ton. Above this price supply exceeds demand. The horizontal difference between the demand and supply curves for Country B determines the shape of the excess supply curve (shown in Figure 12.4).

In the absence of any import duties, the international price is equal to $100 per ton. This is the price at which the excess demand and supply curves intersect in Figure 12.4. Imposing a tariff of $40 per ton raises the price in importing countries to $120 per ton and reduces the price in exporting countries to $80 per ton. The effect is shown by the vertical line *ab* which is assumed to represent a tariff of $40 per ton. A higher

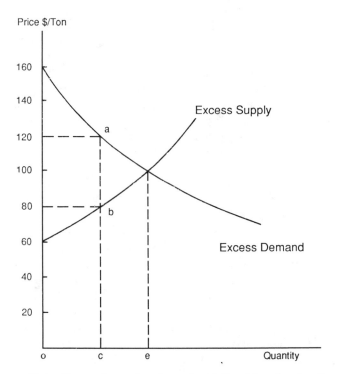

Figure 12.4   Excess demand and supply relationships showing the price and volume of trade effects resulting from the imposition of a tariff.

tariff would shift this line to the left. The distance *oc* on the horizontal axis shows the aggregate quantity of commodity X that would be exported (and imported) at these prices. The quantity traded with a tariff (*oc*) obviously is less than the free-trade equilibrium quantity *oe*. Thus, the conclusions reached earlier are reinforced, namely that protection generally raises the price in importing countries, reduces the price in exporting countries and decreases the volume of trade.

REFERENCES

ABEL, MARTIN E, "Price Discrimination in the World Trade of Agricultural Commodities," *Journal of Farm Economics,* 48 (1966), 194–208.

BERMAN, DANIEL M., and ROBERT A. HEINEMAN, "Lobbying by Foreign Governments on the Sugar Act of 1962," *Law and Contemporary Problems,* 28 (1963), 416–29.

FREEBAIRN, J. W., and GORDON C. RAUSSER, "Effects of Changes in the Level of U.S. Beef Imports," *American Journal of Agricultural Economics* 57 (1975), 676–88.

HILLMAN, JIMMYE S, "Nontariff Barriers: Major Problem in Agricultural Trade," *American Journal of Agricultural Economics* 60 (1978), 491–501.

JACKSON, GEOFFREY H., *The Impact of Eliminating the Quota on U.S. Imports of Beef,* Agricultural Economics Research 338. Ithaca, N.Y.: Department of Agricultural Economics, Cornell University, 1972.

JOHNSON, D. GALE, "The Impact of Freer Trade on North American Agriculture," *American Journal of Agricultural Economics,* 55 (1973), 294–300.

RITSON, CHRISTOPHER, *Agricultural Economics: Principles and Policy.* Boulder: Westview Press, 1982.

ROBERTS, IVAN, and GRAEME TIE, "The Emergence of the EEC as a Net Exporter of Grain," *Quarterly Review of the Rural Economy* 4 (1982), 295–304.

TOMEK, WILLIAM G., and KENNETH L. ROBINSON, *Agricultural Product Prices,* 2nd ed. Ithaca, N.Y.: Cornell University Press, 1981.

U.S. DEPARTMENT OF AGRICULTURE, *Sugar and Sweetener Situation and Outlook,* SSRV 12N2. Washington, D.C.: Economic Research Service, 1987.

U.S. DEPARTMENT OF AGRICULTURE, *World Grain Situation and Outlook,* FG 8-87. Washington, D.C.: Foreign Agricultural Service, 1987.

VERMEER, JAMES, DAVID W. CULVER, J. B. PENN, and JERRY A. SHARPLES, "Effects of Trade Liberalization on U.S. Agriculture," *Agricultural Economics Research* 27 (1975), 23–29.

13

International Commodity Agreements

The prices of internationally traded commodities such as sugar, coffee, and cocoa are notoriously unstable. Small changes in production in exporting countries or shifts in demand in importing countries can lead to large fluctuations in prices. Instability in international prices is particularly serious for countries that depend on export earnings from a few staple commodities to pay for their imports. On a number of occasions since the 1930s, exporting nations have sought to act collectively through international commodity agreements (ICAs) to reduce price instability. Attempts have also been made to use such agreements as an instrument to raise the prices of export crops. Interest in ICAs rose to a peak in the 1970s following the oil crisis. Exporters of commodities other than oil viewed with envy the initial success of the OPEC nations in raising export earnings and looked upon ICAs as an appropriate vehicle for achieving the same objective.

The arguments advanced for attempting to do something to stabilize or enhance international commodity prices correspond closely to those used to justify national support programs for agriculture. One might be described as the "terms of trade" or "fairness" argument. Producers often suffer because the prices of what they have to sell either fall or fail to rise as fast as the prices of the items they buy. Unfavorable price relationships (or terms of trade) for exporters of raw materials are often attributed to the policies of importing nations or to the exercise of superior market power by a small number of large buyers. This justifies, at least in the minds of leaders in many raw-material exporting nations, any attempt to develop "countervailing power."

The empirical evidence in support of the argument that prices are chronically depressed because of the superior market power of importers is not altogether convincing. When supplies are short, competition among buyers does lead to much higher prices. The terms of trade of farm products or export crops do not always move in one direction (Morgan). Prices for a number of export crops rose during the 1970s, although less than the price of oil. Market forces, rather than the abuse of market power, account for the declining terms of trade that occurred in the early 1980s. Macroeconomic policies that slowed economic growth, combined with rising production of internationally traded commodities such as cocoa, palm oil, and wheat, depressed economic equilibrium prices. For those suffering from low prices, however, the cause is less important than the results. Unfavorable price relationships are viewed by most exporting countries as justification for taking collective action to support or raise the prices of the products they sell.

A compelling case can be made for moderating price variability. Unstable prices can lead to stop-and-go economic policies. Nations have a tendency to inaugurate overly ambitious development plans when prices are buoyant. They may be forced to curtail development projects when earnings decline. Widely fluctuating prices also lead to cycles in output. Producers may overexpand plantings following periods of high prices. Once the new plantings come into production prices fall, thus setting the stage for a new cycle.

International commodity agreements under some conditions can be used as a mechanism to transfer income from buyers to sellers of internationally traded commodities. A strong case can be made for doing so where the recipients are relatively poor countries. Developing nations have encountered severe balance of payments problems in recent years. Raising the prices of their principal export crops is one way to help countries earn more foreign exchange. It may be less painful to compel consumers to pay moderately higher prices for such commodities as coffee, sugar, cocoa, and tea than to raise taxes to support foreign aid programs. Income transfers achieved by raising commodity prices also might help some countries to avoid defaults on international loans. Losses may have to be covered in other ways if low commodity prices persist.

Various mechanisms may be used in an attempt to stabilize or to raise international commodity prices. For this reason, the major types of ICAs are first described. A brief review of recent experience with ICAs follows. The benefits and costs of attempting to stabilize prices are then discussed.   The potential for using ICAs as an international income-transfer mechanism is assessed in the final section.

TYPES OF ICAs

International commodity agreements are of three general types: buffer stock, multilateral contract, and quota agreements. In practice, those that have been negotiated in recent years usually combine buffer stocks and quotas.

Buffer Stock Agreements

A pure buffer stock agreement is nothing more than an international storage program. The objective is to hold prices within an agreed range by purchasing commodities at a minimum price and releasing the stored commodities whenever the maximum or trigger price is reached. An international agency authorized to buy and sell commodities is usually created for this purpose. Buffer stock agreements are feasible only for storable commodities such as wheat, cotton, coffee, rubber, and cocoa. Adequate funds must be made available to the buffer-stock agency to enable it to purchase whatever quantities cannot be sold commercially at the specified minimum price. To keep prices from rising above the maximum level, adequate stocks must have been acquired earlier to bridge the gap between total demand at the maximum price and current production.

Multilateral Contracts

Multilateral contract agreements are an alternative method of protecting consumers and producers against extreme price fluctuations. Such agreements assure importers of certain minimum quantities in periods of world shortages and high prices. They protect exporters by guaranteeing a market for certain minimum quantities when supplies are excessive and prices are low. Typically, multilateral contract agreements take effect only when maximum or minimum prices are reached. If prices remain between the upper and lower boundaries, none of the signatory countries is obligated to purchase or to sell to any other country. Exporting countries are obligated to deliver certain minimum quantities to importing countries at the maximum price only when the market price rises to that level or above. In return, importers are obligated to purchase whatever amounts are specified in the agreement only if prices fall to or below the lower boundary.

Actual market prices may rise above or fall below the trigger points at which guaranteed purchases or sales take place. Multilateral contracts can help to stabilize the volume of exports and to assure a minimum price for such exports, but they cannot prevent prices from rising above or falling below the trigger points. Importing countries are free to purchase more than the minimum quantities; however, they will be compelled to pay prevailing market prices for any additional quantities purchased. Exporters, likewise, can sell more than signatory nations have agreed to purchase, but any additional sales will occur at world market prices, which are likely to be lower than those specified in the agreement.

An example may help to illustrate how a multilateral contract agreement would operate. Assume such an agreement is in effect for wheat, and that the upper trigger price is $4 per bushel and the lower trigger price is $3 per bushel. Market forces would determine how much wheat would be bought and sold as long as the price remained between $3 and $4 per bushel. If the price fell to $3 or below, each importing country participating in the agreement would be obligated to purchase a specified minimum quantity of wheat at $3 per bushel. Any country could purchase more at the prevailing market price which presumably would be less than $3 per bushel. Each exporting nation participating in the agreement would be assured of a certain volume of sales at $3 per bushel but might sell more at the prevailing world market price. If the price rose to $4 per bushel or more, exporters would be obligated to sell a specified quantity of wheat to each signatory importing country at a price of $4 per bushel.

While a multilateral contract can help to guarantee a minimum income to exporters (and to assure importers of minimum quantities in times of shortages), an agreement of this type can lead to extreme fluctuations in residual market prices. If uncommitted stocks are large, the prices for these uncommitted stocks may be severely depressed. Producers may be willing to sell such stocks at low prices because of the assurance of a guaranteed price for most of what they produce. The effect of the agreement is to maintain what amounts to a two-price system in years of excess production—a minimum price for quantities importers are obligated to purchase and a lower price for the remainder.

In years of short crops and/or strong demand, buyers may be willing to pay very high prices for additional supplies. If importers can acquire most of what they need at a guaranteed maximum price, they can afford to pay much higher prices for any additional supplies they require. The larger the quantities subject to the agreement, the smaller the residual supplies. All the impact of variations in production or demand will thus be transmitted to the residual market resulting in a high degree of price instability. The burden of adjusting to fluctuating supplies falls on the residual market. Fixing prices for part of each country's output can lead to greater price instability for residual buyers and sellers.

In contrast to a buffer-stock scheme, a pure multilateral contract agreement provides no mechanism for moderating price fluctuations by acquiring and releasing stocks. Individual exporters or importers may decide to do so, but the agreement itself does not require participants to hold stocks.

Export Quotas

A quota-type agreement relies on quantitative restrictions on sales to achieve whatever price objectives are specified in the agreement. As with a multilateral contract agreement, a quota-type agreement takes effect only when upper or lower boundary prices are reached. In an attempt to keep prices from falling below a specified level, export restrictions or sales quotas may be imposed on signatory countries. Sales quotas may then be increased or eliminated when prices rise above the upper boundary. In theory, such a scheme could be operated unilaterally by exporting countries without the acquiesence of importers. In practice, however, the latter's support is desirable to insure that exporters abide by the restrictions. As with any type of supply-control program, total revenue can be raised by restricting exports only if demand for the product is price inelastic.

In contrast to a buffer-stock scheme or a multilateral contract agreement, a quota agreement offers little or no protection for consumers other than that provided by private storers. Exporters may hold stocks for release during years of short crops, but they are under no obligation to do so. Prices will rise above the upper boundary if exporting nations do not have sufficient supplies to fulfill the higher quotas authorized when the upper trigger price is reached. Market prices can be influenced only indirectly by adjusting the size of export quotas. The allocation of such quotas among producing countries obviously becomes a critical issue when markets are limited and supplies are abundant.

COMMODITIES SUBJECT TO ICAs

At one time or another, agreements have been negotiated for wheat, coffee, tea, cocoa, sugar, and rubber. In addition, informal consultative agreements have been in effect at various times for olive oil and tea (Hillman, Peck, and Schmitz, p. 67). Attempts also have been made to stabilize the prices of a limited number of industrial raw materials, principally tin and copper. Few agreements have survived for very long.[1] An international wheat agreement, for example, was in effect for only a brief period in the late 1940s and early 1950s. It is one of the few examples of a multilateral-contract type of agreement. Attempts to revive the international wheat agreement (or an international grains agreement) that would stabilize or support world prices have not been successful.[2]

A succession of sugar agreements has been negotiated, but the most recent agreement has proved to be ineffective in keeping prices within the agreed-upon range. Similar problems have arisen in attempting to negotiate and to implement a cocoa agreement. The International Coffee Agreement has been the most successful of all the agreements negotiated over the past twenty years, but even this agreement has not prevented prices in some years from falling below the price floor. Minimum prices are difficult to enforce when supplies are abundant and demand is weak. Ironically, commodity agreements are likely to be least successful when most needed, that is, in times of declining commodity prices. Chronic oversupply and the inability to enforce quotas weakened many commodity agreements in the early 1980s, including the OPEC cartel (Sterngold).

PROBLEMS ENCOUNTERED IN NEGOTIATING AND IMPLEMENTING AGREEMENTS

International commodity agreements have proved to be extremely difficult to negotiate even when there is consensus among exporting nations that something needs to be done to stabilize or to raise prices. One of the initial problems is to persuade all the important exporters to participate. If one or more of the major suppliers are excluded or opt out for political or other reasons, there is little prospect that the agreement will be successful in holding up prices. The exclusion of North Sea oil producers obviously weakened OPEC. Attempts to stabilize the price of sugar also have been undermined by the unwillingness of several major exporters to participate, including the Soviet Union and the European Community. At various times the Ivory Coast, a major supplier of cocoa, has threatened to withdraw or has refused to participate in a cocoa

---

[1]Based on a review of fifty-one formal agreements or attempts to control international prices through cartel arrangements, Eckbo found the average duration of formal agreements was only 5.4 years (Behrman, p. 62).

[2]An existing agreement provides only for the exchange of information and a commitment on the part of signatory nations to make available certain minimum quantities of grain as food aid.

agreement. Obviously, control over a major proportion of total supplies is essential to the success of any cartel arrangement.

The cooperation of importing countries, if not their formal participation, is also desirable and, of course, essential to successful implementation of a multilateral contract-type of agreement. An importing country can undermine an agreement by purchasing from nonregulated suppliers or by taking advantage of illegal shipments from signatory countries. Quota-type agreements tend to break down in the absence of any incentive for importing countries to participate and to enforce quotas. Importers must refuse to purchase from those countries that are not signatories to the agreement and must insist on certificates of origin to insure that quotas are being adhered to by the major exporters. Importers often are reluctant to assume this obligation, partly because by doing so, they will be helping exporting nations raise prices and thereby, in effect, taxing their own consumers.

Once producing and consuming nations are brought together to negotiate an agreement, the dominant issue is usually the price band, specifically the upper and lower price boundaries that trigger changes in quotas or the release and acquisition of stocks. Importing countries almost invariably want to maintain a lower price band than exporting countries will accept. The lower price boundary is more critical to exporting nations while the upper boundary is more critical to importers. On a number of occasions, failure to agree on boundary prices has led to the breakdown of negotiations. That happened with wheat in 1971 and again in 1979 and with cocoa in 1981.

The width and level of the price band influences the need for funds to finance buffer stocks. As emphasized in Chapter 6, the wider the price band, the greater the incentive for private storage and, therefore, the less need for intervention by a buffer-stock agency. If the level of prices is established well above market-clearing levels, more funds will be required to purchase the surplus commodities. If a buffer-stock type of agreement is planned, delegates must obtain some estimate of the size of the stocks they are likely to acquire and then to decide how purchases are to be financed. If a quota-type agreement is proposed, they will need to decide when to institute quotas and how these should be allocated among suppliers. Given the complexity and divisiveness of the issues that must be addressed, it is not surprising that negotiations tend to be protracted and often end in failure.

In theory, the price band should be centered around the long-run equilibrium price, thereby making it possible to avoid accumulating excess stocks. In practice, the equilibrium price is extremely difficult to forecast, particularly when underlying demand and supply schedules are shifting. This may occur because of the development of substitutes, such as corn sweeteners or synthetic substitutes for cocoa. Unforeseen insect or disease damage or adverse weather may cause actual production to deviate from projected production. New producers also may come into the market. As a result, the price band established at the time the agreement is negotiated may turn out to be either too high or too low. For example, the cocoa price band became irrelevant in the 1970s because market forces combined with world-wide inflation led to prices which consistently exceeded the upper boundary.

An automatic correction mechanism would help to prevent the price band from getting too far out of line with long-run equilibrium prices. This could be done by adjusting the band on the basis of predetermined rules. For example, the price band might be lowered by a certain percentage if stocks exceed an upper limit (Ritson, p. 342). In periods of rapid inflation, it could be automatically adjusted by indexing the upper and lower price boundaries, that is, raising the boundary prices by an amount corresponding to the percentage increase in an index of world commodity prices.

Funding for a buffer-stock type of agreement can become a major issue. In a number of instances, agreements have collapsed because the agency charged with supporting prices ran out of money. Exporting countries generally have borne the cost of acquiring and holding stocks. Quite understandably, they would like importing countries to share the cost of maintaining reserves. Exporters point out that importing countries are the ones who benefit most from carrying larger stocks. The United States has used this argument in efforts to persuade food-deficit countries to purchase and store additional grain when prices are low.

Asking importing countries to maintain larger reserves is only one way of sharing the cost of buffer stocks. An alternative is to create a buffer-stock fund by taxing exports of raw commodities. At least part of an export tax probably would be shifted forward to importers, thus placing the burden on consumers.[3]

Another alternative is to create a common fund financed by international borrowing and contributions of capital from major importing as well as exporting nations. Such a proposal was put forward at the United Nations Conference on Trade, Aid and Development (UNCTAD) held in Nairobi in 1976. International commodity agreements were proposed for a "core" group of commodities including coffee, cocoa, tea, sugar, cotton, rubber, jute, hard fibers (such as sisal), copper and tin.

---

[3]Who bears the burden of an export tax, as with any levy, depends on the elasticity of demand and supply. If demand and supply are equally elastic or inelastic, the burden of the assessment will be shared equally by consumers and producers. If elasticities differ, those with the fewer alternatives, that is, producers or consumers with the more inelastic schedule, will bear the largest share of the burden. For a more complete explanation of the impact of changes in marketing costs, including taxes, see Tomek and Robinson, pp. 127–33.

Each agreement would then be eligible to draw on a common fund to finance the acquisition and storage of surplus commodities. Initially, a fund of $6 billion was suggested, with half the amount borrowed from the international money market and the other half provided by contributions from both exporting and importing nations. If such a fund were created, the United States, along with other relatively affluent nations, would be asked to contribute. Despite support for the concept from developing nations, the proposal has never been implemented.

Joint funding of several commodity agreements would have some advantages. Presumably, the total amount of money required would be less if a common fund were established than if separate funds were maintained for each commodity, because all commodity prices do not follow the same pattern. For example, if coffee prices were rising, it would be possible to sell stocks and, thereby, obtain revenue that could be used to finance the acquisition of other commodities, such as cocoa or sugar. By pooling risks, lenders would be less exposed and, consequently, it might be possible to borrow at a lower rate than if separate funds were maintained for each commodity.

Recent agreements either proposed or adopted for sugar and coffee have made use of export quotas in an attempt to support prices. The allocation of quotas is a sensitive issue that can lead to the collapse of negotiations. Conflicts often arise between new and old producers; the former object to basing quotas on historical patterns of shipments while the latter want to protect their market share by doing so. In general, established producers are more willing to accept quotas than those who are expanding. Negotiations are likely to break down unless the established producers are willing to accommodate the interests of new producers.

The key role of large suppliers in making a quota scheme effective is illustrated by both the coffee agreement and the OPEC oil cartel. During the 1960s, African coffee producers threatened to withdraw from the proposed coffee agreement unless they were given larger quotas. Brazil, the largest single exporter, ultimately agreed to reduce its quota, thus allowing other countries to sell more. The willingness of Brazil to bear a major share of the adjustment helped to save the agreement and to maintain the price floor. Saudi Arabia performed this function for the oil cartel in the 1970s. OPEC was successful in maintaining prices as long as Saudi Arabia was willing to cut production by enough to offset increases in sales by other suppliers; the price deteriorated when the Saudis elected to regain their market share.

Quotas must not only be agreed upon but also enforced. It is difficult to prevent countries from attempting to circumvent restrictions on sales when supplies are abundant. Smuggling coffee through third countries not party to an international agreement has been a recurring problem. In the 1960s, for example, Aruba, an island in the Caribbean that produces no coffee, became an exporter of coffee. It obviously had become a transshipment port for coffee smuggled out of one or more of the Central and South American nations whose coffee exports were restricted by quotas.

Converting products into a form not covered by the agreement is another way of circumventing quotas. Brazil did this in the 1960s by converting surplus unprocessed coffee into soluble coffee which was not subject to export quotas. The soluble coffee was then exported. Manufacturers of soluble coffee in the United States strongly objected to such sales. As a result, the United States threatened to withdraw from the agreement. African countries also were irritated with Brazil because sales of soluble coffee cut into their markets.

One of the unsolved problems with quota-type agreements is what to do with surpluses if participating countries are successful in maintaining prices above market-clearing levels. In most cases, it has been left up to individual countries to store the surplus or to attempt to dispose of excess production by selling it to nations not party to the agreement (such as the Soviet Union or Eastern Bloc countries). Few exporters of tropical products can afford to store surpluses indefinitely or to pay farmers to reduce production. In one of the coffee agreements, however, an attempt was made to assist members in reducing the area planted to coffee. Funds derived from an assessment on exports were used to pay for destroying coffee trees and diverting the acreage to other crops. The program was not very successful, and in subsequent agreements was abandoned. Chronic surpluses are a threat to any agreement; however, no mechanism has been incorporated in recent agreements to deal with this problem.

THE ECONOMIC EFFECTS OF STABILIZATION AGREEMENTS

In theory, it is possible to reduce price variability by making use of buffer stocks and export quotas, but in practice the record of ICAs as a price-stabilization mechanism has been unimpressive. They have had more success in holding up prices, at least in the short run, than in reducing the amplitude of price fluctuations (Behrman, p. 67). For some commodities, including coffee and sugar, average annual price fluctuations were greater after agreements were adopted than before (Eckbo). Wheat is an exception. Prices varied less during the period when the wheat agreement was in effect (in the 1950s) than they did before it was introduced or after it ended. But this was due as much to decisions taken by the United States and Canada as to the agreement itself. Canada and the United States tacitly agreed not to engage in a price war. The

U.S. price-support program provided a floor under international prices; the presence of excess stocks in the United States kept wheat prices from rising very far above the floor.

Reducing the amplitude of price fluctuations, as pointed out in Chapter 6, may help to preserve markets and to minimize cyclical changes in production, but storing commodities for release later may not benefit producers. Whether exporting nations gain or lose from operating a buffer-stock scheme depends on a number of factors, including the shape of the demand curve, the source of price instability and the response of producers to more stable prices (Chaplin, p. 145). Gains and losses also depend on the cost of storing commodities, the magnitude of storage losses and the length of time stocks must be held before being sold.[4]

If production fluctuates substantially from year to year while demand remains stable, it is relatively easy to even out price fluctuations by storing commodities in years of high production and then by releasing stocks in years of low production. Storage costs will be relatively low if the cycle in production is reasonably short. But that is not typically the case with internationally traded commodities. Major changes in prices usually are associated with shifts in demand or long-run cycles in production, often induced by past changes in prices. A period of low prices may persist for several years, thus necessitating the accumulation of large stocks. It may not be possible to resell the accumulated stocks for five years or more, that is, until the cycle in production turns down or a major drought or freeze reduces output. In the case of coffee, occasional freeze damage in Brazil has enabled other exporting nations to dispose of accumulated stocks. Events such as these occur infrequently, however, and cannot be accurately forecast. Consequently, it is difficult to decide how much should be stored.

When and how much of a given commodity is stored, and for how long, depends not only on subsequent changes in production but also on the price range agreed upon by those participating in the negotiations. As emphasized earlier, large stocks will be acquired if the middle of the price band is above the long-run equilibrium price. Gains in the short run will be offset in the longer run by the cost of storing commodities and by losses resulting from dumping surpluses when stocks become excessive.

As pointed out in Chapter 6, the elasticity of demand at the time commodities are sold relative to the elasticity of demand at the time stocks are acquired also influences the profitability of price stabilization. A buffer-stock scheme benefits exporters as a group only when demand

---

[4]For a more complete analysis of the theory of price stabilization and the potential effect on producers and consumers, see Newbery and Stiglitz.

is more elastic at high prices than at low prices.[5] That condition is not necessarily fulfilled for commodities which enter into world trade. The demand for wheat, for example, may be equally inelastic at high and low prices or perhaps even slightly more elastic at low prices. This condition could prevail if the price falls to a level at which wheat becomes competitive with corn or other grains used to feed livestock.

The source of price instability, that is, whether price fluctuations result from shifts in demand or changes in production, likewise can influence returns from attempts to stabilize prices. In general, exporting nations will not gain from attempts to stabilize prices by storing and releasing commodities if shifts in demand rather than fluctuations in production are the cause of price instability. The loss in revenue from limiting price increases in periods of high demand will exceed the gain in revenue from raising prices in periods of weak demand. Empirical studies indicate that demand shifts have been a major source of price instability for a majority of internationally traded commodities, including wheat, corn, tea, wool, sisal, and rubber (Brook and Grilli, p. 11). International price stabilization, according to Brook and Grilli, would benefit consumers of commodities like wheat, sisal, and rubber rather than the exporters of these commodities.

Price stabilization is likely to result in more total revenue for producers of only a small number of internationally traded commodities. The list of potential winners includes rice, sugar, coffee, cocoa, cotton, and jute. Price instability in the past, at least for these commodities, has been due more to variations in production than shifts in demand (Brook and Grilli).

The long-run effects of price stabilization are even more difficult to predict than the short-run effects. If price stabilization encourages use of the product or minimizes the threat of substitutes, producers obviously will gain. If, however, it leads to greater output because of reduced risks or a higher level of prices, short-run gains to producers will gradually be eroded.

Individual countries may fail to gain from international price stabilization, even if the scheme is successful, because variations in their production may not coincide with fluctuations in total output. Higher prices in years of short crops help to compensate for reduced output. This is less likely to occur under a price-stabilization scheme. Country A, for example, may harvest a small crop in a year in which the international stabilization agency is unloading stocks. As a result, the price

[5] The effect of acquiring and releasing stocks can be determined by constructing total revenue functions (price x quantity). If the shape of the total revenue function is convex from above, it will pay producers to even out supply; conversely, it will not pay if the total revenue curve is concave (Tomek and Robinson, pp. 278–79).

may not rise by enough to offset the effects of the smaller volume of exports. Price stability will not necessarily lead to stable export earnings.

INTERNATIONAL COMMODITY AGREEMENTS AS AN
INTERNATIONAL INCOME TRANSFER MECHANISM

Quota-type agreements may be used in an attempt to increase gross revenue from export sales, not simply to stabilize prices within a limited range. Many developing countries would like to use ICAs as an instrument to redistribute income internationally. Their goal is to duplicate for other commodities what OPEC did for oil producers in the 1970s. But not all commodities possess the characteristics that would make this possible. For a quota-type agreement to succeed in transferring income to low-income countries the following conditions must prevail:

1. Demand for the commodity must be price inelastic (that is, less than unity).
2. Producers must be able to control supplies.
3. Commodities must be produced mainly by low-income countries and imported mainly by high-income countries.

Only a few internationally traded agricultural commodities possess all three of the requisites for success. A list of potential candidates is shown in Table 13.1. Included in this list are the principal commodities exported by the less developed countries (LDCs). The major exporters of each commodity are identified in the second column. Those countries would be the principal winners if demand were inelastic and quotas were enforced. The third column indicates whether or not the elasticity condition required for success is met. A "yes" indicates the demand is inelastic; a "no" indicates the demand is probably elastic. In the last column the general direction of trade is indicated. A "yes" indicates that the commodity is exported mainly by low-income countries and imported by high-income countries. Two commodities have a "no" in this column, thus indicating that raising the international price would result in a net income transfer from low-income to high-income countries.

Bananas, cotton, hard fibers, jute, and vegetable oils fail to meet at least one (and in some cases two) of the requirements for success in transferring income to LDCs. The availability of substitutes including synthetic fibers, plastics, and paper products has made the demand for cotton, sisal, jute, and other natural fibers more sensitive to price changes. In the short run, the demand for these natural products may be price inelastic, but not in the longer run. Tropical vegetable oils such as palm oil and coconut oil face competition from vegetable oils produced

TABLE 13.1 Internationally Traded Agricultural Commodities Proposed for Commodity Agreements[a]

Commodity	Principal Exporting Countries	Conditions Necessary for Successful Income Transfers to LDCs	
		Inelastic demand	Exports mainly to developed countries
Bananas	Ecuador, Costa Rica, Honduras Panama, Philippines	No	Yes
Cocoa[b]	Ivory Coast, Brazil, Ghana, Nigeria, Cameroon	Yes	Yes
Coffee[b]	Brazil, Colombia, Ivory Coast, Guatemala, Ethiopia, Kenya	Yes	Yes
Cotton	USA, Egypt, Mexico, Turkey, Sudan, USSR	No	No
Hard Fibers (Sisal)	Brazil, Tanzania, Mexico, Angola	No	Yes
Jute and Products	Bangladesh, India, Thailand, Burma	No	Yes
Natural Rubber	Malaysia, Indonesia, Thailand, Sri Lanka	No(?)	Yes
Sugar[b]	Cuba, Brazil, Philippines, Dominican Republic, Australia, India, the European Community	Yes	Yes
Tea[b]	India, Sri Lanka, Kenya, China	Yes	Yes
Vegetable Oils	USA, Brazil, Malaysia, Zaire	No	No

[a]A sub-group of the eighteen internationally traded commodities specified in the UNCTAD Resolution of May 1976 calling for conferences and negotiations between exporting and importing countries.
[b]Commodities which satisfy both the elasticity and income-transfer criteria.

primarily in the temperate zone including soybean, cottonseed, rapeseed, and sunflower oils. The scope for raising prices of all these commodities is severely restricted by competition from closely related products. Even if it were possible to increase total revenue by restricting exports of cotton and vegetable oils, a large share of the gains would go to producers in the United States rather than to those in low-income countries, simply because the United States is a major supplier of these commodities.

The four commodities which meet at least two of the requirements for success in raising the incomes of LDCs are cocoa, coffee, sugar, and tea, precisely the ones for which ICAs have most often been proposed or implemented in the past. Even for these commodities, effective control over supply (the other requirement for success) has not been achieved. Thus, it would appear that the scope for transferring income to LDCs through international commodity agreements is limited to only a handful of commodities.

Any gains in total revenue from raising prices will not necessarily accrue to the most impoverished nations. As with any support program linked to particular commodities, benefits will be distributed in proportion to sales. Because Brazil is a large exporter of both coffee and cocoa, it would be a major beneficiary of successful ICAs for those two commodities. Two of the more prosperous countries in Africa, Kenya and Ivory Coast, would receive a high proportion of the total benefits flowing to the African continent from higher prices for coffee, tea, and cocoa. The poorest nations in Africa and Asia such as Chad, Niger, Pakistan, and Bangladesh would receive few if any benefits, because they do not export commodities that meet the requirements for successful income transfers.

Within countries, gains from higher prices for export commodities may even widen income disparities. Cocoa producers in Africa, for example, are already better off than many of their compatriots. The proceeds from higher sugar or tea prices may go to plantation owners rather than to cane cutters or those who work on tea plantations. If higher prices can be sustained only by reducing output, total employment may fall, thus imposing an additional hardship on those at the bottom of the income scale. In some countries, the government or a monopoly marketing board may succeed in siphoning off most of the additional revenue either by taxing exports or simply by neglecting to raise the price paid to producers.

Clearly, one cannot predict the ultimate beneficiaries of a successful ICA without knowing who produces the crop, how it is marketed, and whether or not it is taxed by the government. In any event, the foregoing analysis suggests that ICAs are not a very promising instrument for redistributing income in an equitable manner. Proponents of ICAs would argue, however, that some redistribution of income between rich and poor nations is better than none at all, even if the benefits are distributed unequally among nations.

CONCLUSIONS

The historical record does not offer a great deal of encouragement to those who would like to use ICAs as a means of reducing fluctuations in international commodity prices or to increase the export earnings of less developed countries. Most of the commodity agreements negotiated in the past have broken down as a result of disagreements over the range of prices, the unwillingness of one or more major exporters to participate, or the inability to enforce export quotas. Success for the most part has been temporary and made possible by the willingness of individual countries to hold stocks or by a decrease in production caused by unfavorable weather. Because of their inability to control production, ICAs have not proved to be an effective instrument for supporting prices significantly above equilibrium levels.

Only a few countries can expect to gain from quota-type agreements even if they succeed in raising prices. The demand conditions that must be met for such agreements to enhance export earnings are difficult to fulfill. Relatively few of the internationally traded commodities possess the required characteristics. Gains, if realized, are likely to be highly concentrated. As with any income transfer program tied to commodity prices, the benefits of a successful ICA will be distributed among producers in proportion to sales. Any benefits to producers, of course, will be paid for by consumers.

The most compelling arguments for adopting price-stabilization agreements are to minimize the risk of shifting to substitutes and to damp down cycles in production. Importing countries may benefit as much or more than exporting nations from buffer-stock schemes that augment private storage and thereby reduce the amplitude of price fluctuations.

DISCUSSION QUESTIONS

13.1. Why have relatively few ICAs been negotiated despite widespread pressure from producers in agricultural exporting nations to do something to raise and/or stabilize the prices of internationally traded commodities?

13.2. What type or types of international commodity agreements are most likely to be acceptable to importing nations?

13.3. International commodity agreements (most notably those for sugar and cocoa) have not succeeded in keeping prices within the boundaries spelled out in the agreement. Why?

13.4. What are the principal limitations or criticisms of using ICAs as a means of transferring income to poor countries?

REFERENCES

BEHRMAN, JERE R., *Development, The International Economic Order, and Commodity Agreements.* Reading, MA: Addison-Wesley, 1978.

BROOK, EZRIEL M., and ENZO R. GRILLI, "Commodity Price Stabilization and the Developing World," *Finance and Development* 14, no. 1 (1977), 8–11.

CHAPLIN, ANDREW, "Stabilization Theory and Policy: A Brief Review of Recent Contributions," *Oxford Agrarian Studies* 10 (1981), 143–52.

ECKBO, P. L., "OPEC and the Experience of Previous International Commodity Cartels." Cambridge, MA: M.I.T. Energy Laboratory Working Paper, 1975.

HILLMAN, JIMMYE S., ANNE E. PECK, and ANDREW SCHMITZ, "International Trade Arrangements," *Speaking of Trade: Its Effect on Agriculture,* Special Report No. 72. St. Paul: Agricultural Extension Service, University of Minnesota, 1978.

MORGAN, THEODORE, "Trends in Terms of Trade and Their Repercussions on Primary Producers," *International Trade Theory in a Developing World,* edited by R. Harrod. London: Macmillan, 1963.

NEWBERY, DAVID M. G., and JOSEPH E. STIGLITZ, *The Theory of Commodity Price Stabilization: A Study in the Economics of Risk.* Oxford: Clarendon Press, 1981.

RITSON, CHRISTOPHER, *Agricultural Economics: Principles and Policy.* Boulder: Westview, 1982.

STERNGOLD, JAMES, "A Time of Crisis for Cartels," *The New York Times,* Dec. 3, 1985.

TOMEK, WILLIAM G., and KENNETH L. ROBINSON, *Agricultural Product Prices,* 2nd ed. Ithaca, N.Y.: Cornell University, 1981.

14

International
Food Aid

International food aid is among the least controversial of all U.S. programs related to food and agriculture. Donating food or selling surplus commodities under generous long-term credit arrangements is widely supported in Congress and by farm organizations; however, U.S. food aid programs have not escaped criticism. Producers in other countries object to what they consider to be overly generous food donations, because such donations detract from their markets. Food aid also is blamed for undermining incentives to develop agriculture in food-deficit countries and creating a new form of dependency. Still others complain about the conditions attached to U.S. food aid, and argue that surplus commodities should be used to help those most in need, not as an instrument of foreign policy. Some think too little money is appropriated for food aid. These and other issues related to international food aid are addressed in this chapter.

LEGISLATION AUTHORIZING FOOD AID

Two pieces of legislation provide the authority for making food available on concessional terms to foreign governments, international agencies, and private voluntary organizations (PVOs).[1] The first of these is Section 416 of the Agricultural Act of 1949, which authorizes overseas donation of surplus commodities acquired as a result of price-support operations. The second is Public Law 480, which authorizes sales of surplus commodities under generous credit arrangements and donations to international organizations and PVOs. P.L. 480, as it is commonly referred to, was enacted in 1954, and was viewed at that time mainly as an instrument to get rid of farm surpluses and build commercial markets. The original law has been amended many times since then. Most of the changes made in the original act have been authorized in legislation relating to support programs which Congress has enacted every four or five years. While the quantity of food aid made available under Section 416 has increased in recent years, by far the greatest part of such aid has been offered under provisions of P.L. 480.

Prior to 1985, Section 416 donations were confined to dairy products, wheat, and rice. The Food Security Act of 1985 broadened the list of commodities that could be donated to include any other food product acquired by the Commodity Credit Corporation. The Act also mandated for the first time that certain minimum quantities of uncommitted stocks of grains, oilseeds, and dairy products be distributed as long as surpluses persist (Glaser, p. 40). These amendments clearly give priority to surplus disposal rather than to what might be needed by food-deficit countries.

P.L. 480 has retained a broad basis of support because it serves a multiplicity of interests. The agricultural committees of Congress like the program because it helps to dispose of surpluses; church groups and those with humanitarian concerns support the program because it helps to alleviate hunger and malnutrition; and railroads, grain handlers, and labor unions lobby for the program because it adds to the total volume of grain exported and the amount that must be transported in U.S. ships.[2] Others predisposed toward international programs support food aid although they might prefer increased appropriations for other forms of economic assistance. They recognize that it is easier to obtain funds

---

[1]Foreign aid funds also may be used in some instances to pay for food imported on concessional terms.

[2]For many years, (even before enactment of P.L. 480), Congress has mandated that certain minimum percentages of commodities donated or sold under concessional arrangements be transported in U.S. flag vessels. Prior to 1985, so-called "cargo preference" requirements compelled recipients to transport 50 percent of Title I food aid in U.S.-operated vessels. The Food Security Act of 1985 mandated a gradual increase in the proportion that must be transported in U.S. ships from 50 percent in 1985 to a maximum of 75 percent in 1988. The Act also requires that a specified amount of donated commodities be shipped from Great Lakes ports (Glaser, p. 44).

from Congress for feeding the hungry than for balance of payments support or military assistance. To a certain extent, food aid can substitute for general economic aid. This is particularly true of countries such as Egypt which must import food.

Throughout the life of P.L. 480, Congress has given priority to selling rather than to donating surplus commodities. From two-thirds to three-quarters of the food aid made available under provisions of P.L. 480 has been sold to recipient governments either for foreign currencies or under generous long-term credit arrangements (referred to as Title I sales). Recipient governments pay prevailing world market prices for the commodities acquired. Thus, the transfer of commodities is similar to a commercial sale. Those receiving Title I aid are obligated to repay the U.S. government for the market value of commodities made available to them. Title I sales become donations only if the loan is not repaid. Usually there is a grace period before repayment must begin. Repayment schedules at low rates of interest may extend for as long as forty years. Thus, there is a disguised subsidy to recipients even if loans are repaid. Congress has insisted on preserving the appearance of selling rather than giving away agricultural surpluses. This was done initially on the assumption that the primary objective of distributing commodities under Title I was to build future markets. Concessional sales were looked upon as a kind of entering wedge that ultimately would convert recipients into commercial buyers of U.S. farm products.

During the early years of the P.L. 480 program, recipients paid for Title I commodities with their own currencies. These currencies could not, by law, be converted into U.S. dollars. Consequently, they had to be spent in the country that received the food aid. Typically, Title I funds were used to pay for embassy expenses, trade fairs, and demonstration projects to promote U.S. farm products. By the late 1960s, the U.S. government had accumulated several billion dollars in unspent foreign currencies. A large proportion of these surplus foreign currencies were held as deposits in India, Pakistan, Egypt, and Israel, all countries that had been early recipients of large quantities of food aid. The excess foreign currency balances ultimately became a political liability, both for the United States and for the countries where the funds were being held. Foreign governments feared the United States might add to inflation by spending the money or might use the funds in ways that were inconsistent with the country's own development plans. Eventually, the United States decided to donate or loan the surplus currency deposits back to the recipient governments.

Congress mandated a shift from foreign currency to credit sales (with repayment ultimately in dollars) beginning in the 1960s; however, the amendments adopted in 1985 authorize a partial return to foreign currency sales. At least 10 percent of the amount repaid is to be made available for loans to support private enterprise within the recipient country. These foreign-currency loans, however, must eventually be repaid in a "manner that will permit conversion of the local currencies to dollars" (Glaser, p. 39). Foreign government repayments from credit sales under Title I also may be used for market development activities.

Title II of P.L. 480 authorizes donations to foreign governments, international agencies such as UNICEF, and to PVOs such as CARE or church-related groups. These donations may be used to meet emergency food needs or to provide continuing support for school feeding programs, food-for-work projects, and maternal and child health centers. Recent legislation allows PVOs to sell a small fraction of the food donated to them to raise cash in the country where they are providing nonemergency food aid. These sales are designed to help PVOs pay for the local transportation and distribution costs. The U.S. government provides the commodities free of charge, but the PVOs must pay local handling costs, which can be substantial.

In 1977 a new title was added. Title III authorizes the conversion of receipts from Title I credit sales into grants or loans to recipient governments provided the funds are used for approved development projects. In this way the concept of "selling" commodities is preserved, but the effect is to convert Title I commodities into a form of development aid.

Food-aid agreements are negotiated individually with recipient governments. Each agreement spells out precisely how much of specified commodities will be provided under various titles, the prices that are to be paid for Title I commodities, shipping arrangements, the amount of subsidy to compensate for higher U.S. shipping costs, repayment terms, etc. Every agreement also must specify what the recipient government will do to encourage food production and limit population growth. These so-called "self-help" provisions were included in the 1966 extension of the act at the insistence of President Johnson, who believed food aid should be used as leverage to change internal policies in food-deficit countries. Congress also has tried to insure that food aid does not displace normal commercial imports by inserting the "additionality" clause. Title I agreements specify that "normal imports" must be maintained. It is not easy, however, to define normal imports or to insure that this requirement is being fulfilled.

In the early 1970s, critics charged that the administration was attempting to use P.L. 480 as leverage to achieve foreign policy or military objectives, and that too much of the aid was being given to relatively high-income countries such as Taiwan and Israel. At that time, substantial quantities of P.L. 480 commodities were going to Vietnam and to countries such as Korea that were providing military assistance to Vietnam. In response to these criticisms, Congress included a provision in the 1973 revision of P.L. 480 legislation mandating that a minimum percentage of sales made under Title I go to low-income countries (as defined by the World Bank). In the early 1980s, the mandated minimum percentage was 75 percent. This requirement has forced the U.S. government to maintain a high volume of P.L. 480 sales to low-income countries such as Bangladesh, Pakistan, and Egypt.

MAGNITUDE AND COMPOSITION OF INTERNATIONAL FOOD AID

The United States has been by far the largest single contributor to international food aid, but it is by no means the only country offering such assistance. In recent years, the United States has provided between 60 and 70 percent of international food aid in cereals, the principal component of such aid (Figure 14.1). At one time the United States provided over 90 percent of international food aid. Other major contributors include the European Community (EC), Canada, and Australia. Japan has

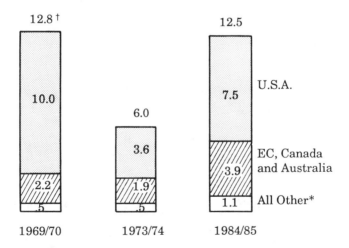

† Figures do not add to total due to rounding

* Includes contributions from Argentina, Finland, Japan, Norway, Sweden and Switzerland

Figure 14.1 International food aid in cereals from all sources, 1969/1970, 1973/1974, and 1984/1985 (figures in million tons). (Source: FAO, 1977; U.S. Department of Agriculture, 1981; and Clay, 1987.)

been an intermittent supplier of food aid, mainly rice. Minor suppliers include Argentina, Norway, Sweden, Switzerland, and even India and China in some years (Clay, p. 189).

While the U.S. has continued to be the largest provider of food aid, its contributions have been the most variable. Total U.S. aid in cereals declined from ten million tons in 1969/1970 to only 3.6 million tons in 1973/1974. As surpluses reemerged and prices declined in the early 1980s, U.S. contributions rose although the total amount of grain provided in the mid 1980s still was less than that made available in the late 1960s.

Cereals (wheat, rice, corn, and sorghum), and products derived from grains such as flour and bulgur (a wheat product), account for a high proportion of total food aid. Most of the remainder consists of skim-milk powder, vegetable oils, mainly soybean oil, and blended foods (mixtures of corn or wheat and a protein supplement such as skim-milk powder or soybean meal). The commodity composition of food aid obviously has been dictated in large measure by the availability of surpluses in temperate-zone countries. The generosity of industrialized countries in providing food aid is partly a function of their having acquired surpluses as a result of overpricing such commodities as wheat, rice, and milk.

There are sound economic reasons for providing the bulk of food aid as whole grain. Wheat, rice, corn, and sorghum are widely accepted by consumers in food-deficit regions and already supply a high proportion of the caloric intake of low-income families in most developing countries. Furthermore, grains are low-cost sources of energy and protein and are relatively easy to transport and to store. Livestock products, fruits, and vegetables, while desirable from a nutritional point of view, are much more expensive to acquire, process, and distribute. They also require more costly and sophisticated storage facilities, including refrigeration, which may not be available in areas short of food. A further disadvantage of higher-valued commodities is that they are less likely to get to those most in need. Dairy products and cooking oils, for example, are much more likely than bulk grain to be stolen or diverted to black markets.

Food aid contributions in recent years have been small in relation to the quantity of grain that is imported on commercial terms. In the mid-1980s, such aid amounted to less than 5 percent of total world trade in cereals (Clay, p. 188). U.S. P.L. 480 shipments in the early 1980s accounted for an even smaller percentage of the total value of U.S. agricultural exports. The situation was much different in the 1960s. In some years during that decade, government-assisted exports (mainly in the form of food aid) accounted for as much as a quarter of the total value of U.S. farm exports.

COSTS AND BENEFITS TO THE UNITED STATES

The cost of food aid to the U.S. taxpayer has been modest in comparison with expenditures on price-support programs and on domestic food subsidies. In the mid-1980s, P.L. 480 allocations (including repayments from previous sales) averaged between $1.5 and $2 billion annually. At that time, expenditures on domestic food-subsidy programs were running at the rate of nearly $20 billion per year, while price-support expenditures and payments to farmers, at least in some years, were even higher.

The principal effect of the P.L. 480 program has been to reduce surpluses of wheat, rice and, to a lesser extent, skim-milk powder and soybean oil. Food-aid shipments of corn and grain sorghum have been quite small in relation to total U.S. production or the quantities acquired by the government as a result of price-support operations.

Food aid at times has provided a convenient outlet for surpluses, but it probably has been a higher-cost alternative than paying farmers to retire cropland. Grain production can be reduced by idling land at less than half the cost of acquiring and storing commodities. When one takes into account the cost of transporting P.L. 480 commodities in U.S. ships and in-country distribution costs, food aid turns out to rank relatively low as a cost-effective method of solving a farm surplus problem.

The net effect of the P.L. 480 program on U.S. exports of farm products is difficult to assess. Supporters of the program argue that it has succeeded in helping to build commercial markets, especially in Taiwan, Korea, and the Middle East. Critics point out that at least some of the commodities distributed under P.L. 480 displace what otherwise might have been commercial sales. To the degree that food aid substitutes for commercial exports, there will be no net gain for U.S. agriculture. In fact, there will be a net decline in export earnings if loans are not repaid.

COSTS AND BENEFITS TO RECIPIENT COUNTRIES

Recipients of Title I commodities must pay for transporting the commodities to their own ports and for internal distribution. U.S. subsidies cover the additional costs incurred in shipping commodities in U.S. flag vessels, but not other costs. Recipient governments also incur a liability, in the form of a loan which they are obligated to repay in dollars if they import Title I commodities. Title II commodities are donated, but the internal transportation and distribution expenses must be paid for by the recipient government, the international agency or the PVO that handles such donations.

The major benefits of food aid to recipient countries are in the form of increased availability of food, a lower rate of inflation, savings in foreign exchange, and a source of revenue to the government if Title I commodities are resold. Food aid provided by the United States was particularly effective in reducing potential deaths from hunger and malnutrition in India during the mid-1960s (Aykroyd, pp. 137–40) and in East Africa during the 1980s. There have been significant failures, however, owing in part to delays in recognizing the seriousness of the problem, as with the Sahelian drought in the 1970s. Conflicts or political constraints have also made it difficult at times to deliver food when and where needed. International food distribution programs have been much more successful in meeting emergency needs than in reducing chronic hunger and malnutrition.

Government-to-government grants of food aid or purchases of Title I commodities under long-term credit arrangements have enabled recipient governments to conserve foreign exchange and to augment local food supplies. Commodities imported under concessional arrangements add to the total resources available to the government. The money that might have been spent by the recipient government for commercial food imports or purchases from indigenous suppliers is released for other purposes. Eventually, the recipient government may have to earn additional foreign exchange or obtain new international loans if the repayment obligations under Title I are to be honored, but the short-run effect is to help hold down inflation and to provide the government in power with an additional source of revenue if it chooses to sell the commodities made available by the United States under Title I. The recipient government has complete control over the distribution or use of Title I commodities: they can be sold, used to support public works projects, offered to the military, or donated to low-income families.

Title I commodities are useful to whatever group is in power because they provide a potential source of revenue. It is much easier for the government to obtain revenue by selling P.L. 480 commodities than by raising taxes. In some countries, such as Egypt, food aid sales have become a significant source of revenue to the government. Increasing the supply of food, even if commodities are sold rather than given away, also helps to hold down inflation which may be politically important. Rising food prices are a threat to insecure leaders. Civil servants, trade union leaders, and military commanders may demand cheap food in return for supporting the party or group in power.

Food aid is almost as good as general economic aid to a country which is chronically deficient in food. The money (and foreign exchange) that might otherwise have been spent on food is released for other uses. Donor nations have no control over what the government does with the money no longer needed to buy food—it may be used to finance development projects or to import military equipment. Thus, the ultimate beneficiaries of Title I food aid are difficult to predict. Whether the importing country gains, and by how much, depends on the amount of interest subsidy, whether the loans are eventually repaid, and what use is made of funds that are loaned or donated back to the recipient government.

Title II commodities (those donated to governments, international relief agencies, and private charitable organizations) are more likely than Title I commodities to be distributed to families in refugee camps or made available to school children, mothers attending maternal and child health centers, and those participating in food-for-work projects. But clearly not all of the hungry are being served by such organizations. No matter how well-intentioned, PVOs and international relief agencies often find it difficult to reach those most in need of food. No organization can distribute food without the consent of the recipient government. In some cases, the government in power has discouraged or prevented PVOs and international relief agencies from delivering food in certain areas or to certain ethnic groups. Such restrictions inhibited relief efforts in Chad during the 1970s and in Ethiopia and Sudan in the 1980s. In some countries, civil wars or unrest have made it impossible to mount an effective relief program. Dissident groups have disrupted transportation and made it dangerous to deliver food in such countries as Uganda, Angola, and Mozambique.[3] Even where there is no opposition from the government or rebel forces, logistic problems may prevent relief organizations from getting food to remote areas or to members of nomadic tribes.

ADMINISTRATIVE AND LOGISTIC PROBLEMS ASSOCIATED WITH FOOD AID

Anticipating food-aid requirements and delivering the quantities needed at the right place and the right time has proved to be a formidable task. Countries threatened with food shortages often lack the information needed to assess the magnitude of the current food deficit or may be reluctant for political reasons to acknowledge the failure of their efforts to achieve self-sufficiency. As a result, requests for food aid may be delayed, sometimes until well after the situation has become critical.

Donor countries also are responsible for delays in delivering food aid. When a request for aid arrives, the U.S. embassy or an international agency will be asked to verify the need and to estimate the quantity of

[3]Much of the aid provided to Mozambique in the mid-1980s, according to Peter Godwin, a correspondent for the London Times, was "disrupted, looted or destroyed" (Godwin).

food that is required or can be effectively utilized. The latter may be less than the former because of limited port or handling facilities. Additional time will be required to obtain the food and to arrange for transportation. Six months or more may elapse between the time a food shortage is first reported and relief shipments arrive. Sometimes the imported food will remain on the dock where it is unloaded or in a warehouse because it cannot be moved inland. There have been documented instances in which food was being distributed after the emergency had passed (Jackson, p. 11; Cathie, pp. 65–66).

The United States has tried to improve its capacity to respond more promptly to requests for food aid. Research has been conducted in a number of potential food deficit countries in an attempt to develop an "early warning system" of impending food shortages. An amendment to Public Law 480 now mandates an annual assessment of global food production and needs (U.S. Department of Agriculture, 1986, p. iii). The objective is to identify countries or regions that might be short of food and to estimate the magnitude of the food gap.

Transportation bottlenecks have proved to be a major factor limiting the capacity of donor countries to deliver food aid, particularly in sub-Saharan Africa. Port facilities in that region are already overburdened and, consequently, delays in unloading ships are common. Few countries have enough trucks or rail cars to move large quantities of food to remote areas. Africa is not served by an extensive railroad network. For this reason, most food aid must be delivered by truck. Surface transportation is costly and often slow because of the poor quality of the roads. Rural roads are unsurfaced and, therefore, become almost impassible during the rainy season. Delivery of food by air is even more expensive. Furthermore, runways capable of handling large cargo planes are nonexistent or inadequate.

PVOs and international relief agencies find they must devote a high proportion of their resources to solving the transportation problem. In some cases, they have had to import trucks, drivers, spare parts, and even the fuel needed to keep the trucks moving. One of the PVOs that contracted to deliver food in Somalia had to set up its own maintenance and repair shop because local facilities were inadequate.[4]

CRITICISMS OF FOOD AID

Few object to providing food aid when crops have been devastated by floods or drought. But not all food aid is used to feed people suffering

---

[4]Based on personal communication with Ronald Burkard, Assistant Executive Director of CARE.

from natural disasters. A substantial part is provided as a supplement (or substitute) for general economic aid (under Title I of P.L. 480) or as project food aid (under Title II). The latter category includes feeding programs for mothers and children and food-for-work projects. In addition, donated food may be used to supply refugee camps. Critics charge that food aid used for these purposes may end up doing more harm than good. Overly generous food aid can lead to:

• lower farm prices in food deficit countries and neglect of reform measures needed to increase agricultural production
• greater dependence on imported commodities and a preference for foreign rather than indigenous foods
• a more or less permanent refugee problem
• reduced markets for other exporting nations.

Food aid can be counterproductive if it allows governments to neglect agriculture or delay needed reforms. This point of view was succinctly expressed in the 1967 report of the President's Science Advisory Committee on the World Food Problem. A part of their report reads as follows:

> Expansion of concessional sales over an indefinite period is not in the interest of either donor or recipient nations nor is it physically possible... Recipient nations may use such imports as a crutch to avoid the consequences of unchecked population growth, an unproductive agriculture and irresponsibility in accelerating domestic economic growth (President's Science Advisory Committee, Vol. II, p. 141).

Some of the most strident criticism of project food aid has come from individuals who have had first-hand experience with food distribution programs in low-income countries. Tony Jackson, a consultant to OXFAM (the Oxford Committee on Famine Relief) argues strongly in his book, *Against the Grain,* that the use of donated food should be severely curtailed except in emergency situations. He is especially critical of distributing skim-milk powder and blended foods in infant feeding programs because these foods tend to undermine efforts to promote breast feeding and the consumption of locally produced foods (Jackson, p. 50). Roland Bunch, who is associated with World Neighbors, also objects to food aid based on imported commodities because it leads mothers to believe that their children can be healthy only if they consume the foods that are donated. Often these foods are not available locally or would be prohibitively expensive if families tried to purchase them (Bunch, and others).

Institutions involved in refugee feeding programs report that some inhabitants come to view free food as a right rather than a temporary expedient. Workers encounter resentment when food is withdrawn. Some long-term residents lose their initiative and, consequently, are unwilling to return to their previous home after the emergency has passed.

Competing exporters have charged that P.L. 480 commodities have, in some cases, displaced food that otherwise would have been imported on commercial terms. This criticism may be less justified now than earlier when more of U.S. food aid was going to countries like Taiwan, Korea, Brazil, and Colombia. Wheat offered to Brazil under Title I, for example, probably displaced some potential imports from Canada and Argentina. Thailand also may have been adversely affected by overly generous donations of rice to various countries in Asia and Africa.

POLICY ISSUES RELATED TO P.L. 480

Based on the foregoing criticisms, one might conclude that the United States should be somewhat less generous in providing food aid or at least more selective in offering such aid. On the other side are those who argue that because there are still millions of hungry people in the world, appropriations for food aid should be increased and a higher proportion of such aid should be donated rather than sold under Title I. Shortages of commodities are not likely to limit the quantity of food aid the United States can provide, at least not over the next five to ten years. The critical policy issues are whether funding for food aid should be increased and, if so, by how much. A related question is whether food aid should be used as leverage to achieve other objectives or distributed solely on the basis of need.

Appropriations

Doubling the availability of U.S. food aid from the level prevailing in the mid-1980s would require an increase in annual appropriations of between $1.5 and $2.0 billion (assuming prices remain constant). This would add less than one-fifth of one percent to the total federal budget. An increase in funding of this magnitude would enable the United States to provide another five to seven million tons of grain as food aid (or smaller quantities of higher-valued commodities such as soybean oil or skim-milk powder).[5]

---

[5]The estimate of the quantity of grain that could be provided for an additional $1.5 to $2.0 billion is based on the assumption that the total cost of grain delivered to recipients will average somewhere between $200 and $300 per ton.

An additional five million tons of food aid would make a substantial contribution toward reducing the total world caloric deficit, assuming the additional grain could be delivered to the right people at the right time. Five million tons of additional food aid would provide a 20 percent increase in calories for a minimum of 125 million people.[6] The number of individuals critically short of calories may be much larger than 125 million, but the average caloric deficit may be somewhat smaller (Poleman, pp.67–71). In any event, it is doubtful if an increment in total food aid of more than this amount could be distributed effectively, given the political and logistic constraints that are likely to prevail in food deficit countries.

An increase in annual food aid of 5 to 7 million tons would require little or no increase in U.S. grain production. Annual grain surpluses during the mid-1980s greatly exceeded this amount. For example, in four of the five years between 1981 and 1986, total U.S. production of all grains combined (wheat, corn, rice, etc.) exceeded use (including exports) by 20 million tons or more (U.S. Department of Agriculture, 1987, p. 22). Nor would increasing food aid by 5 to 7 million tons per year make a large dent in carryover stocks. In 1987, U.S. grain carryover stocks exceeded 200 million tons.[7] More grain could be made available within a year or two simply by releasing land idled under government programs or by reducing set-aside requirements. Unless production declines drastically because of a series of poor crop years, grain supplies are likely to be more than adequate to fulfill P.L. 480 commitments.

A convincing case can be made for increasing the flexibility of funding. Food aid requirements, particularly requirements for emergency aid, are not the same every year. Tying the amount of food aid to a fixed appropriation also means that availability will decline in years of high prices. If widespread drought occurs in Africa or Asia, for example, in a year in which grain supplies are short and prices are high, the United States may be unable to provide the quantities needed to avoid severe distress or starvation unless appropriations are increased. The impact of a relatively fixed appropriation on the availability of food aid was demonstrated during the 1970s. Grain prices tripled between 1971 and 1974, but appropriations for P.L. 480 remained about the same. This reduced the amount of grain the United States was able to provide from

[6]A metric ton of grain will provide two-thirds to three-quarters of the total caloric needs for five adults per year. Thus, five million tons of grain could feed approximately 25 million people for a year or could be used to provide a 20 percent supplement for five times that number.

[7]Much of the grain surplus at that time consisted of corn rather than wheat or rice, but for many uses one type of grain can be substituted for another.

nine to ten million tons in the early 1970s, to less than four million tons in the mid-1970s (Clay, p. 194).

Appropriations may need to be increased in a particular year, not only because of higher grain prices but also because of higher transportation costs. Distributing food in remote areas, particularly where there is a weak transportation system, can be extremely expensive. For example, it cost as much as $800 per ton to deliver food to areas in Southern Sudan in 1986 and 1987. The price the U.S. farmer received for the grain delivered to Southern Sudan averaged little more than $100 per ton. Distribution costs can greatly exceed the cost of the raw product. Admittedly, the Sudan example is extreme, but it illustrates the importance of providing some mechanism for authorizing additional expenditures in years when distribution costs are exceptionally high.

Title I vs. Title II Allocations

The allocation of funds between Title I (sales) and Title II (donations) is another issue that policymakers must address. As pointed out at the beginning of this chapter, Congress has favored Title I sales over donations. But the allocation in recent years has shifted slightly toward donations to international relief agencies and PVOs. Recipient governments like Title I sales because the commodities they receive can be used to generate revenue and also can be distributed in ways consistent with their own priorities (at least within limits established by the P.L. 480 agreement). Congress likes Title I because selling commodities preserves the image of a commercial transaction and may at some future date generate revenue if the loans are repaid. Repayments now do, in fact, augment P.L. 480 appropriations. But at the same time, lobbyists for internationally oriented and humanitarian organizations have succeeded in convincing Congress to make more food available to PVOs, because they are viewed as being less inhibited by political constraints and are more likely to reach the hungry and malnourished.

Conditions Attached to Food Aid

Much of the controversy surrounding P.L. 480 has been associated with amendments designed to use food aid as an instrument to achieve objectives other than alleviating hunger and malnutrition. An amendment adopted in 1985 requires that a certain proportion of repayments from Title I sales be used to support private enterprise in recipient countries. Another amendment mandated an increase in the proportion of Title I commodities that must be transported in U.S. ships. In response to lobbying from the food processing industry, Congress accepted an amendment requiring the Department of Agriculture to provide minimum percentages of non-emergency food aid in the form of processed, fortified and/or bagged commodities rather than bulk grain (Glaser, p.39). These amendments illustrate the difficulty of insulating food aid policy decisions from domestic political considerations.

Past efforts to use food aid as an instrument of foreign policy have not been very successful. President Johnson, for example, adopted what became known as a "short-tether" policy with respect to food aid shipments to India. He delayed authorizing aid in an attempt to influence India's internal food and agricultural policy decisions and also to soften their criticism of U.S. policies in Vietnam (Paarlberg, pp. 151– 69). His actions, according to Paarlberg, helped persuade the Indian government to accelerate internal agricultural policy reforms, but also created resentment and produced little or no lasting benefits to the United States.

The record of using food aid as an instrument of foreign policy in the Middle East is mixed, although it probably has helped to preserve peace between Egypt and Israel. Egypt has been a major recipient of U.S. food aid in recent years. Title I commodities are part of the foreign aid package that was offered to Egypt in return for its willingness to enter into a peace agreement with Israel.

An earlier attempt to influence Egyptian policies was less successful. Aid was withdrawn at one time because the U.S. government thought the aid was being misused. Cotton growers objected to food aid which made it possible for Egyptian farmers to divert land from food crops to cotton. Some of the additional cotton was exported, thus adding to competition with U.S.-grown fibers. Another reason for cutting off food aid was to make it more difficult for Egypt to purchase arms for possible use against Israel. The availability of food aid freed foreign exchange which may have been used to buy armaments.

In recent years, the U.S. government has been more willing than in the past to grant food aid to Marxist-oriented governments. Substantial quantities of P.L. 480 commodities, for example, were shipped to both Ethiopia and Mozambique in the mid-1980s. Legislative restrictions still prohibit shipments to former enemies such as Cuba, North Korea, and Vietnam. The issue of whether or not food should be donated to Communist-dominated governments becomes critical when a country suffering from acute food shortages such as Cambodia is overrun by a former enemy (Vietnam). Obviously there are difficult moral choices to be made, as well as strategic issues involved in deciding where and to whom food aid should be offered.

CONCLUSIONS

Budgetary, logistic, and administrative constraints are more likely to limit the quantity of food aid provided by the United States and other donor countries over the next decade than shortages of commodities. Inadequate port and inland transportation facilities will impose an upper limit on how much food aid can be effectively utilized, particularly in Africa.

Food aid needs are likely to fluctuate from year to year, thus suggesting the need for flexibility in funding and in allocating money between Title I and Title II. An increase in appropriations in years of good crops abroad could be counterproductive if the additional food aid displaces commercial exports and/or reduces incentives to maintain or increase production in food-deficit countries.

Food aid is not a very cost effective method of coping with the problem of excess capacity in agriculture, because surplus commodities are so expensive to transport and to distribute in food deficit countries. Grain surpluses could be eliminated at less cost by idling additional acreage.

In some cases, the commodities required for emergency food assistance or food-for-work projects could be obtained more cheaply by purchasing from local sources or neighboring countries. Measures to stimulate local production are likely to be more cost-effective in the long run than importing food. Diets might be improved at less cost by donating fertilizer to food deficit countries rather than surplus commodities.

Hunger persists mainly because of low incomes, not a shortage of food. Imported food on concessional terms can help to alleviate a temporary shortage, but food aid can do little to solve the underlying income problem unless it is used in such a way as to stimulate economic development and/or increase employment opportunities for the disadvantaged.

DISCUSSION QUESTIONS

14.1. Why does the P.L. 480 program command broad support in Congress?

14.2. Who or what groups benefit most from Title I sales: (1) in the United States and (2) in recipient countries? Who or what groups are likely to be adversely affected by an increase in Title I sales?

14.3. What might be done to ensure that more of the food aid provided by the United States and other donor nations actually gets to those most in need of additional food?

14.4. What are likely to be the principal constraints or limitations to expanding international food aid over the next three to five years?

14.5. What conditions or obligations on the part of recipient governments (if any) should be attached to food aid?

REFERENCES

AYKROYD, W.R., *The Conquest of Famine.* New York: Readers Digest Press, 1975.

BUNCH, ROLAND, MARY MCKAY, and PAUL MCKAY, *Problems with Food Distribution Programs: A Case in Point.* Oklahoma City: World Neighbors, no date.

CATHIE, JOHN, *The Political Economy of Food Aid.* New York: St. Martin's, 1982.

CLAY, EDWARD J., "Food Assistance: Implications for Development and Trade," *U.S. Agriculture and Third World Development—the Critical Linkage,* edited by Randall B. Purcell and Elizabeth Morrison. Boulder: Lynee Rienner Publishers, 1987.

GLASER, LEWRENE K., *Provisions of the Food Security Act of 1985,* Agriculture Information Bulletin No. 498. Washington, D.C.: Economic Research Service, 1986.

GODWIN, PETER, "Mozambican Misconceptions," *Wall Street Journal,* May 21, 1987, p.28.

JACKSON, TONY with DEBORAH EADE, *Against the Grain.* Oxford: Oxfam, 1982.

PAARLBERG, ROBERT L., *Food Trade and Foreign Policy.* Ithaca, N.Y.: Cornell University Press, 1985.

POLEMAN, THOMAS T., "World Hunger: Extent, Causes and Cures," *The Role of Markets in the World Food Economy,* edited by D. Gale Johnson and G. Edward Schuh. Boulder: Westview Press, 1983.

PRESIDENT'S SCIENCE ADVISORY COMMITTEE, *The World Food Problem,* vol. II. Report of the Panel on the World Food Supply. Washington, D.C.: The White House, 1967.

U.S. DEPARTMENT OF AGRICULTURE, *World Food Needs and Availabilities,* 1986/87. Washington, D.C.: Economic Research Service, 1986.

U.S. DEPARTMENT OF AGRICULTURE, *World Grain Situation and Outlook,* FG-8-87. Washington, D.C.: Foreign Agricultural Service, 1987.

15

The Politics of Food and Agriculture

An understanding of how the political process works is essential to anyone seeking to change policies or to forecast what direction future policies are likely to take. Traditionally, those concerned with food and agricultural policies have focused on legislative initiatives. But enacting new legislation is only one way in which policies can be altered. Cutting appropriations or attaching conditions to money bills is another way. Policies also can be altered by administrators. For this reason, individuals and organizations that want to influence policies must be familiar with the appropriations process and maintain lines of access to key technical personnel or administrators as well as to the agricultural committees of Congress.

The purpose of this chapter is to provide a guide to the politics of food and agriculture. The factors that influence or shape major farm bills are described in the first section. This is followed by a review of the appropriations process and what influences the decisions of the appropriations committees or subcommittees. Interest groups and their role in shaping farm and food policies are described in the final section.

THE LEGISLATIVE PROCESS

Since 1970, Congress has considered major revisions in price-support legislation every four or five years. Omnibus farm bills covering commodity programs, international food aid, domestic food subsidy programs, and other activities were approved by Congress in 1973, 1977, 1981, and 1985. Each of these acts was written in the first year of a new administration or the year following the reelection of a president. Congress decided in 1985 to alter the traditional procedure. Provisions of the Food Security Act of 1985 extend through 1990, a five-year period rather than the traditional four years. The change was made to allow the administration elected in 1988 more time to prepare its recommendations and submit them to Congress.

Farm bills have become exceedingly complex in recent years. Those enacted in 1981 and 1985 require more than 100 pages to spell out the details and to describe what Congress intended in reconciling House and Senate versions of the proposed legislation.

Getting a farm bill approved by both houses of Congress and signed by the president is a formidable undertaking. Most bills never get out of the committee to which they are assigned. Even then, proposed legislation faces an uphill battle, because it must be approved by a majority vote in both the Senate and the House. Thus, it is not surprising that of over 12,000 bills introduced in Congress in 1983-84, only 623 survived and eventually became law (U.S. News and World Report, 1985). The attrition rate on farm bills is not unlike that of other proposed legislation. Typically, no more than one out of ten bills relating to food and agriculture emerges from the House or Senate agricultural committee and is sent to the floor for a vote. Of these, less than a third are likely to be approved. The system of checks and balances built into the U.S. political system makes it much easier to defeat a bill than to enact new legislation.

Drafting Proposed Legislation

Proposals for major new farm legislation or modifications of existing policies can originate anywhere in Congress, but both the Senate and House agricultural committees traditionally wait for the president and his advisers to send up their recommendations before holding hearings. Whatever the administration proposes usually has the inside track, particularly when Congress is controlled by the same party as the president. Legislative proposals that originate outside the Office of the President, the Secretary of Agriculture or the agricultural committees of Congress have little chance of being seriously considered. In order to influence the substance of legislation, one must have access to those in policy-making positions within the executive branch and/or the agricultural committees of Congress.

The president and his advisers do not start with a clean slate in making policy recommendations. Among other things, they are constrained by past commitments and inherited party positions. For example, it is unlikely that a Republican president would seek to impose compulsory marketing quotas on farmers or that a Democratic president would propose to abandon all support programs. In drafting proposed legislation, the administration must also keep in mind budgetary constraints and what will be acceptable to party leaders in Congress.

Farm and food policies generally rank relatively low on the president's policy agenda, because the farm vote no longer swings elections. For the nation as a whole, farmers account for less than 3 percent of the total population and an even smaller proportion of the voting population in such key presidential states as California, Texas, New York, Illinois, Michigan and Pennsylvania. Many senators and representatives from rural areas, most notably in the Great Plains and the South, still consider the farm vote important, but the states where this is true do not have many electoral votes.

Multiple centers of power and conflicts among personalities within the executive branch of the government complicate the decision-making process. In recent years, the task of developing a set of policy recommendations has become much more complex (Hathaway, p. 783–84). At one time, the administration's farm and food policy recommendations were formulated by the Secretary of Agriculture in consultation with representatives of farm groups, commodity organizations, and key members of the Senate and House agricultural committees. But consultation with these groups is now only a first step. Whatever the secretary proposes must be cleared with a great many other individuals within the Executive branch, including the Office of Management and Budget (OMB), the Council of Economic Advisers (CEA), and even the State Department and the Treasury. Farm policy decisions are important to members of the White House staff and heads of departments outside of agriculture because of the impact such decisions can have on the budget, foreign exchange earnings, and relations with other countries. Broadening the policy agenda to include domestic food subsidy programs also has made it necessary to consult with groups not traditionally part of the agricultural bloc. Much of the work of drafting proposed legislation falls on staff members within the Department of Agriculture, the Council of Economic Advisers, and the Senate and House agricultural committees.

In some cases, the administration may let Congress take the lead in drafting proposed legislation. Individual members of Congress also may seek to amend existing legislation that originally was enacted to cover a period of four or five years. Members of Congress, particularly those holding key positions on the Senate or House agricultural committees, are more likely to respond to the requests for legislative changes made by farm organizations or commodity groups than is the President. The economic effects of changes in support policies, for example, are much more critical to those representing rural constituencies than to the President. The budgetary and trade effects of new or amended legislation are of greater concern to the White House, the OMB, and the Council of Economic Advisers.

Committee Action

The old adage that the "President proposes, but Congress disposes" still holds true for agricultural legislation. The fate of proposed farm bills is determined largely by the agricultural committees or subcommittees of Congress. The power and prestige of these committees have declined in recent decades, but they are still the principal arbiters of food and agricultural policy. A bill has almost no chance of becoming law if it is not supported by senior members of the Senate and House agricultural committees. These key individuals can no longer insure passage of farm legislation, but they can effectively block any proposal they do not favor.

The two principal functions of the congressional committees are to hold hearings and to draft or "mark-up" the bill, which ultimately will go to the floor for a vote. Hearings are scheduled for only a small minority of the bills referred to the committee. The hearing process gives the committee members an opportunity to identify sources of support or opposition to particular provisions of a proposed bill. Much of the testimony of the general farm organizations and commodity groups is predictable because their views are already well known by the more senior members of the agricultural committees. The Secretary of Agriculture or members of his staff are invariably invited to present their case. In some instances, particularly when Congress is controlled by the opposing party, the committee may use the hearings as a vehicle to attack or embarrass the Secretary. Thus, the function of committee hearings is not only to obtain information, but also to build a case for or against the administration's proposal.

The drafting (or redrafting) of bills is done by subcommittees in what are called "mark-up" sessions. This process may take weeks if there is a great deal of controversy surrounding a bill. In an attempt to work out acceptable compromises, committee members commonly confer with representatives of commodity groups and staff members in the secretary's office and the White House. Once the draft of a bill is completed and the proposed bill has been approved by the subcommittee, it goes to the full committee for its consideration. The full committee then has the option of tabling the bill (in effect killing it) or reporting it out of committee with either a favorable or an unfavorable recommendation. Only occasionally will a bill be forwarded to the floor without a recommendation (Knutson, Penn, and Boehm, p.40).

It is important to be aware of the biases of committee members if one wants to influence legislation or predict what kinds of compromises are likely to be adopted by the committee. For the past fifty years, the majority of Senate and House agricultural committee members have been elected from states in the Great Plains, the Corn Belt, and the South. The original Agricultural Adjustment Act of 1933, with its selective support system, reflects this regional coalition. Senior members of the agricultural committees almost invariably come from areas where a substantial proportion of farm income is derived from wheat, corn, cotton, rice, tobacco, and dairy products. Typically, representatives of districts or states located in the Midwest (including the Great Plains) and the South account for 75 to 80 percent of the total membership of the agricultural committees. Those representing urban areas have shown little interest in serving on the agricultural committees, despite the broadening of the food and agricultural policy agenda that has occurred over the past two decades. Members of Congress who are elected from areas which benefit from existing programs are more likely to seek membership on the committee and to remain there; those who might be more critical of farm programs prefer to serve on other committees. As a result, the agricultural committees are biased toward preserving existing support programs.

Members of the Senate and House agricultural committees are keenly aware of the need to form coalitions with other groups if they are to preserve support programs for agriculture. For this reason, they have made efforts to broaden legislation in recent years to incorporate activities of interest to representatives of urban areas and environmentalists. Titles pertaining to domestic food subsidy programs, international food aid, and conservation are now routinely included in the omnibus farm bills that are considered every four or five years.

The views of subcommittee chairmen and staff members are extremely influential in determining the outcome of proposed legislation. Senior members no longer have as much power as they had when seniority dictated who would be chairman. But subcommittee chairmen still have a great deal of influence in drafting the specific details of commodity programs. This is particularly true in the House. The legislative reform act passed in 1973, which was designed to curb the power of Congressional committee chairpersons, ended up by strengthening the role of subcommittees and their chairmen. Clifford M. Hardin, former Secretary of Agriculture, summarizes the effect of these changes as follows:

> The consequence[of the 1973 legislation]... is that each subcommittee has a nearly complete jurisdictional monopoly over some set of policies and programs. More important, subcommittee members possess veto power

over changes in legislation within their policy area. This ensures that no policy change can take place unless it first obtains the blessing of the appropriate subcommittee. Since this involves precisely those congressmen whose constituents and supporters gain from current policies, it is hardly surprising that subcommittee members are not disposed to alter them (Hardin, Shepsle, and Weingast).

The House livestock, dairy, and poultry subcommittee, for example, now writes the dairy section of any new farm bill, while the wheat, soybeans, and feed grains subcommittee drafts whatever provisions relate to wheat and corn. Commodity organizations seek to build lines of access to subcommittee chairmen and their staff because of the critical importance of subcommittee action.

Floor Votes

Once a bill is reported out of committee, it goes to the Rules Committee to determine its place on the legislative agenda. Bills which are opposed by party leaders may be deferred or held up indefinitely although that seldom happens with farm bills. A floor manager is selected by supporters to guide the bill through Congress. Among other things, the floor manager must decide which amendments to accept or reject. Votes on key amendments often determine the final outcome. For example, an amendment to eliminate tobacco or sugar supports, if carried, may split the coalition of commodity interests and, thus, lead to rejection of the final bill. On the other hand, a favorable vote on an amendment to lower or raise the support price for a particular commodity may swing just enough votes to insure final passage. Voting patterns on amendments are frequently confusing, because they reflect the results of vote trading and political maneuvering designed, in some cases, to make a bill so unacceptable that it will be defeated.

Senate approval of farm bills generally is easier to obtain than House approval. It is not difficult to put together a majority based on a coalition of senators from states with an interest in cotton, corn, wheat, dairy products, tobacco, and peanuts. Votes usually cut across party lines. Regional or commodity interests outweigh party positions in determining the votes of most senators from the Great Plains and the South. Those elected from North Dakota and Kansas, for example, whether Republicans or Democrats, will usually vote to continue support programs for wheat.

Floor votes in the House frequently are very close. The Agriculture and Food Act of 1981, for example, was finally approved by a margin of only two votes. There are too few districts in which agriculture holds the balance of power to pass a farm bill, even if commodity groups are united in support of the proposed legislation. Representatives of urban areas clearly can outvote those representing rural districts; consequently, it is necessary to avoid antagonizing urban voters. The marginal votes needed to insure passage of an omnibus farm bill can be obtained by incorporating something of interest to urban voters such as more generous food stamp benefits or by trading votes. The backing of party leaders also is important. Because urban constituents know or care little about farm policies, representatives of urban districts have considerable freedom in voting on omnibus farm bills. In many cases, they can be persuaded to vote in favor of a farm bill if, in return, they can obtain the support of those representing farm districts or the party leadership for bills of more immediate interest to their constituents.

The majority of House members have neither the time nor the inclination to become fully informed on agricultural issues. They usually rely on the judgment of a colleague or one of their staff members in deciding how to vote, especially on complex amendments. More and more policy decisions are being made by congressional aides, not only on farm legislation but on other issues as well. Elected representatives find they must devote an increasing proportion of their time to responding to constituent requests, traveling to and from their home district, raising money, and campaigning for the next election. As a result, they are compelled to turn to their assistants for advice on complex issues not addressed in the legislative committee to which they are assigned. Senators and representatives are knowledgeable about labor legislation or defense issues, for example, if they are a member of the committee that deals with those issues, but are often poorly informed about other issues.

Action by the Conference Committee

The bills that are finally approved on the floor of the Senate and the House are seldom identical. Whenever the two versions differ, they are sent to a Conference Committee for reconciliation. The Conference Committee is made up of a select group of senior members of the Senate and House agricultural committees. Thus, the final compromise is worked out by those who played a major role in drafting the bills which were originally reported out of their respective committees. Usually some parts of each chamber's bill will be accepted, although the final bill may differ substantially from either the House or Senate version. Items that were left out of the House or Senate bill may be reinserted to satisfy particular interests. Conferees must continually keep in mind what their respective chambers and the president are likely to accept. They also must consider the budgetary cost or "treasury exposure" in the jargon of Washington. The process of reaching agreement on a compromise farm bill may take several weeks. In 1981, for example, more than a month elapsed between the time farm bills were approved by the Senate and House and a compromise bill emerged from the Conference Committee.

Lobbyists and the Conference Committee staff often play a critical role in drafting the final bill. Commodity organizations follow the proceedings closely and may even help to work out acceptable compromises. It is not uncommon for committee members to confer with lobbyists in deciding what to accept or reject. Representative Harkin from Iowa (now Senator Harkin) conceded in 1981 that he often checked strategy with lobbyists for the dairy industry as a kind of insurance policy to protect against making errors that would cause serious problems later (Roberts).

The final product is a Conference Report that explains what parts of each bill were accepted or rejected and provides a rationale for the decisions that were made. This document is important to administrators who must implement provisions of the act because it indicates the intent of Congress.

Once the final bill and the Conference Report have been submitted to the House and Senate, each chamber can only accept or reject the compromise bill; it cannot be amended. Most conference reports are accepted even though many members of Congress may be dissatisfied with the report and some of its provisions. Pressure to accept the Conference Committee bill rises as the time for adjournment approaches. By the time the Conference Committee has submitted its report, there often is insufficient time to consider alternatives.

A fixed termination date, which Congress has incorporated in recent farm legislation, adds to the pressure to accept the Conference report. Failure to adopt a new bill means that programs in subsequent years will be governed by so-called "permanent legislation." Provisions of the 1949 act go into effect if Congress does not amend the law. Some of these provisions are regarded as unacceptable, particularly those relating to acreage allotments. Thus, the threat of reverting to earlier legislation in the case of agriculture is a spur to passing a new farm bill when the authority to continue existing programs is about to expire.

Presidential Veto

Few farm bills in recent years have been vetoed by the president, and none has been enacted over a presidential veto. It is generally acknowledged that it would be very difficult to obtain the two-thirds vote necessary to over-ride a rejection of a farm bill by the president. The principal function the veto has served in recent years has been to modify the Conference Committee report. It is the threat of a veto rather than the veto itself that usually influences legislation.

The veto is likely to be most successful as a weapon when the permanent legislation is more acceptable to the administration. President Eisenhower, for example, used the veto or the threat of a veto to gain acceptance for flexible (lower) price supports in the 1950s. Congress earlier had authorized a move toward lower support prices, but tried to delay the time when these provisions would go into effect. By vetoing bills to extend the existing level of support prices, the President was able to implement the earlier legislation.

Amending Legislation

Every farm bill is the result of many compromises, but such compromises often are unsatisfactory, even to those who were responsible for negotiating the agreements. As a result, it is not uncommon for Congress in the next session to attempt to modify provisions that presumably were to guide agricultural policies for the next four years. This happened, for example, in 1978 and again in 1982.

BUDGETARY CONSTRAINTS

Budgetary procedures imposed by legislation adopted in 1974 can, at least in theory, influence legislation pertaining to farm and food policies as well as other government activities and programs. The Budget Reform Act of 1974 was passed in an attempt to bring the total budget under more effective control. Congress recognized that each committee acting independently often recommended new programs or appropriations for existing programs that, if approved, would lead to larger budget deficits or the need for additional taxes. There was no effective mechanism for reviewing the combined budgetary impact of all proposed programs or appropriations. To provide such a mechanism, Congress created the Senate and House budget committees. The principal function of these committees is to prepare a budget resolution which must be submitted to Congress by May 15 of each year. In theory, this resolution provides a blueprint for action and establishes expenditure ceilings for every major activity, including agriculture. Legislative and appropriations committees are obligated to stay within these ceilings. In the event that anticipated expenditures exceed the limits imposed by the Budget Committee, the 1974 Act provides for what is called the "budget reconciliation" process. The ultimate objective is to limit total spending to an acceptable level (Fuerbringer).

In practice, the budget committees have not succeeded in disciplining the legislative and appropriations committees. The budget ceilings are widely ignored and subject to frequent alterations during the succeeding months (Birnbaum). This has led Congress to look for other ways of bringing expenditures under control. The Gramm-Rudman-Hollings Act of 1985 represented an attempt to solve this problem by providing for automatic spending cuts to achieve deficit reduction goals.

Enforcement of the 1974 Act (or similar legislation) could have a significant impact on farm and food policies. This was demonstrated in 1981. Expenditure ceilings imposed in that year forced the Senate and House agricultural committees to consider lower-cost alternatives. In this instance, the Senate was more responsive to the budget resolution than the House. The net effect of this pressure was reflected in the Conference Committee bill which was somewhat less liberal in providing support to farmers than otherwise might have been the case (Infanger, Bailey, and Dyer).

Strict adherence to budgetary guidelines would compel the agricultural committees to engage in a zero-sum game, that is, to reduce the level of support or benefits for one commodity if more liberal benefits are to be offered to another commodity or group. The agricultural committees have often found it expedient to resolve conflicts by accepting provisions that, in effect, add to the federal deficit. Congress has found it easier to live with the consequences of a higher deficit than lower support prices or reduced payments to farmers.

Budget ceilings also can be circumvented, at least temporarily, by authorizing agencies or government-owned corporations to borrow money or engage in other "off-budget" activities. The Commodity Credit Corporation, for example, can continue to finance support programs by borrowing more money, selling commodities to generate additional revenue, or issuing PIK certificates which represent claims on stored commodities. Eventually, any impairment of CCC capital must be restored, but not necessarily in the year in which losses are incurred.

APPROPRIATIONS

Congress must authorize expenditures before appropriations can be considered. The legislative committees of Congress handle the authorizing function. Ceilings on expenditures for particular activities, such as food stamps or international food aid, are commonly incorporated in omnibus farm bills. The level of spending approved in any given year can be less than the amount authorized but cannot exceed the upper limit.

In practice, it is the subcommittees of the appropriations committees of Congress that largely determine the amount of money to be allocated to various activities. The full appropriations committee usually accepts the recommendations of the various subcommittees. By trading votes, subcommittee members avoid conflicts that might jeopardize each other's recommendations. Agricultural budget recommendations are seldom challenged on the floor of the Senate or House (Kotz, p.89).

The appropriations subcommittees have much greater control over some types of expenditures than others. Price-support commitments, for example, are open-ended. They will vary from year to year depending on market forces, the level of production, and the number of farmers who qualify for price-support loans and payments. If, for example, the government is compelled to make large deficiency payments or to purchase substantial quantities of dairy products, expenditures will rise. Congress cannot renege on its commitments and, therefore, must pick up the check for these additional expenditures. A similar situation prevails with entitlement programs that are automatically indexed, such as Social Security or food stamp benefits.

The annual appropriations process is critical for such agencies as the Soil Conservation Service, the Extension Service, the Farmers Home Administration, and the Agricultural Research Service. For this reason they must spend time and effort justifying their programs and maintaining good relations with members of the appropriations subcommittees. Most budget allocations are based on the preceding year's level of expenditures, but the OMB may at times recommend substantial cuts for particular agencies or activities. The subcommittee then must decide whether to accept or reject these proposed cuts.

Personalities and politics obviously affect budgetary decisions. Those for agriculture have been strongly influenced over the past two or three decades by Jamie L. Whitten, the congressman from Mississippi who has served as chairman of the agricultural subcommittee of the House appropriations committee. By threatening to retaliate against those who oppose him, he has been able to exert a substantial degree of control over the USDA budget. Every Secretary of Agriculture in recent years, whether a Republican or Democrat, has found it expedient to pay particular attention to the preferences or biases of Jamie Whitten. He has been called the "permanent Secretary of Agriculture" (Kotz, p. 84). Politics often determines where funds are spent. For example, the USDA's only soil sediment laboratory is located in Congressman Whitten's district (Apcar). The strategy of the House subcommittee in general, and that of Jamie Whitten in particular, has been to offer something for every state or district in doling out federal funds. Congressman Whitten has opposed targeting of conservation funds or abandoning formula funding for research and extension allocations to states, because such action might result in less money going to some of the poorer states, and also might weaken the basis of support for agricultural programs.

THE ROLE OF INTEREST GROUPS

Many more organizations now seek to influence farm and food policies than when support programs were first introduced. Only three farm organizations (The Grange, the Farm Bureau, and the Farmers Union) were directly involved in drafting the Agricultural Adjustment Act of 1933. During the 1950s and 1960s, commodity organizations began to exert more influence over farm policies, although the farm policy agenda was still dictated mainly by the traditional agricultural bloc consisting of the U.S. Department of Agriculture, the Land Grant colleges, and the agricultural committees of Congress. But this loose coalition of agricultural interest groups no longer controls the farm policy agenda. Policymakers must now deal with a much larger number of specialized commodity organizations as well as lobbyists representing consumers, environmentalists, agribusiness, and those seeking to expand international food aid and domestic food subsidy programs.

The proliferation of interest groups has complicated the task of reaching agreement on new legislation. Hearings take longer because so many organizations want to testify. With more organizations and interest groups seeking to influence farm policies, there are more conflicts to be resolved. Interest groups with strongly held positions tend to neutralize each other. The effect is to immobilize Congress, thus preserving the status quo even when there is general agreement that current programs are unsatisfactory.

Lobbyists have been compelled to alter their strategies in seeking to influence legislation because of reform efforts that have led to a reduction in the power of committee chairmen. Interest groups still must maintain lines of access to key members of Congressional committees and their staff, but these personal relationships are no longer sufficient. A successful lobbyist needs to reach a wider audience because legislation is no longer controlled by a few senior members of each committee. The current situation is described by a professional lobbyist as follows: "It used to be that if you could get the (Committee) Chairman and the leaders behind you, you were 90 percent home free. Now you have to work on each member of a committee" (*U.S. News and World Report*, 1983, p.66).

Interest groups find they must devote a substantial amount of resources to educating their members and to organizing mail campaigns. Successful lobbying organizations seek to identify individuals in each congressional district who can express the organization's views in conversations with their elected representative or members of his or her staff. Legislators are more likely to be influenced by a letter or a call from one of their constituents than by a visit from a paid lobbyist in Washington. When legislation is at a critical stage, the Washington office will frequently call a member of the organization and urge that individual to contact his or her senator or representative.

While congressional votes are no longer openly bought and sold as they were at one time, there is no doubt that financial contributions to the campaign fund of a senator or representative help to predispose the legislator to the organization supplying the funds. Political contributions made by farmer-supported interest groups generally are small relative to those made by such organizations as the National Association of Manufacturers, the Chamber of Commerce, the American Medical Association, and labor unions; however, an association of dairy cooperatives was listed in 1982 as one of the top twenty contributors to congressional campaign funds. The willingness of Congress to continue relatively expensive support programs for dairy farmers has been linked by many observers to the financial contributions made by a few large dairy cooperatives.

Interest groups representing farmers seldom have enough political clout to threaten a member of Congress with retaliation at the polls. There are not enough farm votes in most congressional districts to swing an election. Moreover, the interest group knows that it cannot deliver the votes of its members to a particular candidate, especially if the individual they are supporting is opposing a popular incumbent. Increasingly, elections are won by incumbents.[1] For this reason, most farm interest groups try to work with whoever is elected, regardless of party affiliation.

Forming coalitions is as important for success among interest groups as it is among legislators. Commodity organizations traditionally have used logrolling tactics ("I'll back your proposal if you'll go along with mine") in building support for farm bills. Consumer organizations, labor unions, and public interest groups have also formed coalitions at various times to support more liberal food subsidy and nutrition programs. Occasionally, as in 1973, commodity groups and those representing consumers or labor will work together. In that year, labor unions agreed to back more generous price supports in return for a commitment by commodity organizations to go along with legislation making striking workers eligible for food stamps (Knutson, Penn, and Boehm, p.86).

Lobbying by agricultural interest groups, of course, is not confined to legislation. An increasing number of decisions that affect farmers, agribusiness firms, and consumers are made by administrators rather than elected officials. This includes issuing regulations regarding pesticide residues, food or feed additives, farm labor, safety, and health. Discretionary authority granted by Congress to the Secretary of Agricul-

---

[1]In the 1986 election, 98.4 percent of incumbents who decided to seek reelection retained their seats in the House (Weaver).

ture also makes it more important for interest groups to have access to individuals who are in a position to make the critical decisions regarding support levels, set-aside requirements, the eligibility of land for Conservation Reserve contracts, the issuance of PIK certificates, how and at what price they will be redeemed, etc.

Traditional Farm Organizations

General farm organizations, commodity groups, and organizations representing cooperatives all vie for influence with legislators. Over the past four or five decades, the influence of general farm organizations has declined while that of commodity groups has risen. Organizations representing particular commodities (for example, wheat, corn, or cotton) find it easier to agree on policy recommendations than general farm organizations. The latter have to take account of different and often conflicting commodity and regional interests. Conflicts may arise, for example, between feed-grain producers and livestock feeders over the level of support prices for feed grains or between new and old cotton growers over a proposal to reintroduce acreage control programs. A general farm organization has to accommodate these diverse views.

Among the general farm organizations, the American Farm Bureau Federation (AFBF) is by far the largest and probably also the most influential with members of Congress, although the organization no longer occupies the dominant position it held in the 1930s. During the early days of the New Deal, Farm Bureau lobbyists worked closely with leaders of the Democratic party and influential individuals in the office of the Secretary of Agriculture in developing and building support in Congress for the Agricultural Adjustment Act of 1933 (Campbell). Shortly thereafter, conflicts began to arise between the Democratic administration and leaders of the Farm Bureau. The rift widened in the 1940s and has never completely healed. As a result, Farm Bureau leaders tend to be ignored by the Secretary of Agriculture whenever the Democrats are in power. The reverse holds true whenever the Republicans are in control of the White House.

The Farm Bureau not only has the largest membership but also the broadest geographical representation. It is particularly strong in the Corn Belt, in the old cotton South, and in California. The elected leaders tend to come from the Midwest or the South. Its broad geographical coverage, combined with greater financial resources and a larger staff, give the Farm Bureau more influence in Congress than its rivals. But geographical dispersion adds to the difficulty of presenting a united front. On some issues, such as support programs for cotton, tobacco, and peanuts, there may be serious conflicts within the organization. Not all Farm Bureau members oppose supply-control measures or think price supports should be reduced. State Farm Bureaus retain considerable autonomy and often have more influence with their local representatives and senators than the AFBF. The organization originated as a federation of state Farm Bureaus and has retained that structure. Consequently, diversity within the organization is to be expected.

The generally conservative, market-oriented views expressed by AFBF leaders and paid lobbyists reflect the opinions of those who are elected as delegates to annual meetings. Those participating in such meetings usually are the more successful, affluent farmers. Thus, it is not surprising that the positions taken by Farm Bureau leaders tend to be conservative, not only in matters pertaining to price-support programs, but also on taxes, labor legislation, and welfare programs.

Farmers who favor government intervention in agriculture and want to see support prices maintained or raised are more likely to be affiliated with the Farmers Union (FU) than with the Farm Bureau. The membership of this organization is much smaller than that of the Farm Bureau and is more concentrated geographically. A large majority of Farmers Union members come from the Great Plains and the Upper Midwest. The organization is relatively weak in the South, the Northeast, and on the West Coast. Through affiliated cooperatives, the Farmers Union provides members with grain storage and marketing facilities. In some areas, they are a major handler of wheat.

Lobbyists for the Farmers Union generally support liberal causes, including more generous food stamp and international food-aid programs. They favor higher support prices and more generous assistance for farmers. The organization has maintained close working relationships with labor unions and the Democratic party. One of their paid staff members for many years was a former Secretary of Agriculture in a Democratic administration. During the 1960s, when Kennedy and Johnson occupied the White House, individuals affiliated with the Farmers Union frequently were brought into the Department of Agriculture or appointed to advisory committees. Farmers Union members tend to be excluded from the corridors of power whenever the Republicans are in control of the White House.

The Grange occupies an intermediate position between the Farm Bureau and the Farmers Union. It frequently seeks a compromise solution to issues which divide farm organizations; however, its influence is modest. The organization is relatively weak in the South and in California and probably attracts fewer full-time commercial farmers than it did a generation ago. A substantial proportion of its members are rural residents or part-time farmers. Grange membership figures, as with other farm organizations, are inflated by those who join mainly to take advantage of services offered, especially insurance. The Grange traditionally has favored protectionist policies for agriculture, marketing orders, and multiple-price plans which would maintain higher prices at home and lower prices abroad.

The National Farmers Organization (NFO) at one time attracted substantial numbers of farmers who had become disenchanted with the traditional farm organizations. Growth in membership occurred mainly in the 1950s. The leaders persuaded farmers that it was unrealistic to expect much help from Washington. They argued that farmers should rely on their own collective efforts to enhance prices rather than government programs. Their proposed strategy was to bargain collectively and negotiate contracts with buyers. They hoped to duplicate the actions of successful labor unions by withholding produce from buyers. In a few instances, their attempts to coerce farmers into joining the organization and to withhold supplies led to violence (Knutson, Penn, and Boehm, p.69). The influence of the NFO has been strongest among dairymen and other producers of livestock products; however, the organization has failed to achieve significant gains for its members, and, consequently, membership has declined.

The American Agricultural Movement (AAM) flourished briefly as an influential general farm organization in the 1970s; however, both its membership and influence declined drastically thereafter. Unlike other major farm organizations, they lack a regular dues-paying membership and a permanent staff. The organization was founded in 1977 among farmers disenchanted with declining prices and suffering from large debts. A high proportion of its original membership consisted of young farmers. Geographically, its support came mainly from the Great Plains and the Corn Belt, although it also attracted a substantial following from disenchanted farmers in the Southeast, especially in Georgia where the effects of drought added to the problems of farmers who had expanded earlier. The organization is best remembered for sponsoring the invasion of Washington by hundreds of farmers driving tractors. They occupied parts of the mall, stalled traffic, and camped in the offices of senators and representatives. While unpopular with the public, the organization can justifiably claim major responsibility for having persuaded Congress in 1978 to liberalize support programs, especially for wheat.

Commodity Organizations

Nearly every major agricultural commodity is now represented in Washington by an organization. Commodity interest groups have become more influential than general farm organizations in working out details of price-support and supply-management programs in recent years. They also have influenced legislation relating to trade, food aid, and grain reserves. The most important commodity organizations include the National Milk Producers Federation, the National Association of Wheat Growers, the National Corn Growers Association, the American Soybean Association, the National Cotton Council, and the National Cattlemen's Association. Lobbying activities of the National Milk Producers Federation are reinforced by those of several large regional dairy cooperatives.

Consumer and Public Interest Groups

Consumer and public interest groups such as the Community Nutrition Institute, the Consumer Federation of America, and the Center for Science in the Public Interest had relatively little influence on food and agricultural policies until the 1970s. Their importance as lobbying organizations rose with the expansion of domestic food subsidy programs, food price inflation in the 1970s, and growing concern about food safety and water quality. These organizations are joined by the so-called "Hunger Lobby" (which consists mainly of church-related and welfare-oriented organizations) in seeking more liberal food subsidy programs. They are also strong supporters of nutrition labeling and more restrictions on the use of food additives and chemicals. The Community Nutrition Institute and the Consumer Federation of America have been critical of marketing orders and support programs, particularly those relating to sugar and milk.

Agribusiness Interest Groups and Clientele Organizations

Agribusiness firms including grain exporters, fertilizer companies, lime distributors, and meat packers have their own lobbying organizations. The lobbyists for such organizations frequently have close ties with the individuals who administer price-support, export-subsidy, storage, and international food-aid programs. The lobbyists themselves may at one time have served in the USDA or a related agency, thus creating what is referred to in Washington as the "revolving door syndrome," that is, the interchange that occurs between those who make policy decisions and those who seek to influence such decisions (Knutson, Penn, and Boehm, p.74). Agribusiness organizations generally support programs aimed at expanding production and exports and oppose those which keep land idle. Lime producers have been consistent backers of the Agricultural Conservation Program, which has helped to promote lime use among farmers, while meat packers have sought to liberalize (or at least not to restrict) imports of low-fat beef.

In addition to organizations seeking to promote agribusiness interests, there are those whose principal objective is to promote or to preserve certain agencies or activities. These are sometimes referred to as clientele-related interest groups. The Land Grant College Association, for example, lobbies for increased appropriations for agricultural research and extension, while the National Association of Soil Conservation Districts comes to the defense of the Soil Conservation Service whenever it is under attack or appropriations are threatened. Another organization that performs a similar function is the National Rural Electric Cooperative Association. The organization has helped to maintain a subsidized credit program for rural electric cooperatives far beyond the time when the original objective of electrifying all farms was achieved.

CONCLUSIONS

The U.S. political system is characterized by expediency, compromise, and a bias toward preserving the status quo. Congress has a propensity to adopt programs or policies that will enable members to get by the next election. They are not unaware of the longer-run effects of their decisions, but fear the short-run consequences of reducing benefits to their constituents.

Current events exert a powerful influence on policy decisions. Often the policies adopted in response to conditions prevailing at the time the legislation was passed turn out to be inappropriate because conditions have changed. Congress may then be forced to consider changes in programs that were supposed to extend for a period of three or four years. The threat of program changes adds to the uncertainty confronting farmers and agribusiness firms.

Farm programs survive partly because the agricultural and appropriations committees of Congress have a vested interest in preserving such programs. The Constitution also helps to insure the survival of farm programs, because it provides for the election of two senators from every state. Wheat, corn, cotton, and milk production are important in a sufficient number of states to assure majority support in the Senate for continuing commodity programs. Thus far, neither budgetary pressures nor opposition from those representing urban areas have been strong enough to kill price-support and farm-subsidy programs.

The proliferation of interest groups and lobbying activities has complicated the task of reaching agreement on new legislation. Many are dissatisfied with existing policies but they cannot agree on what changes should be made. This tends to preserve the status quo.

The political process can be frustrating to those who want to move decisively in one direction or another, for example, to get the government out of agriculture or to provide much more generous support to small-scale family farms. The system of checks and balances inevitably leads to compromise solutions. One should not expect more of Congress. On the big issues, Congress does tolerably well at working out acceptable compromises. The programs enacted have provided some, but not too much, protection for farmers. They have not seriously inhibited the adoption of improved methods of production, nor have they prevented successful farmers from expanding. Sufficient food aid has been made available to avoid massive starvation, and consumers in the United States have been provided with more than adequate food supplies at reasonable cost. The evolutionary process which characterizes the U.S. political system has proved to be flexible enough to avoid serious overpricing and to accommodate a broad array of interests, although the resulting mixture of policies and programs has imposed a substantial financial burden on the taxpayer.

DISCUSSION QUESTIONS

15.1. What constraints are likely to limit the President's freedom of action in proposing a new farm bill?

15.2. Assume a conservative president proposes to reduce and eventually eliminate price supports for all commodities including wheat, corn, and cotton. What is likely to be the reaction of the Senate and House agricultural committees to such a proposal? Which of the general farm organizations (if any) might be expected to support the president and which might be expected to oppose him on this issue?

15.3. Both Democratic and Republican presidents have sought on various occasions to target conservation and rural development expenditures to areas of greatest need. Why has it proved so difficult to reduce expenditures for activities or programs introduced in the 1930s or to target funds to particular areas?

15.4. Assume you are interested in a particular bill and want to insure its passage. As a lobbyist, what kinds of actions or what strategies would you suggest adopting in an attempt to achieve your objective?

15.5. What accounts for the continuation of support programs on a selected group of commodities, despite the declining political influence of the general farm organization and a marked reduction in the proportion of the population engaged in farming?

REFERENCES

APCAR, LEONARD M., "Big Spender: Rep. Whitten Pushes Money Bills Through by Baffling Opponents," *Wall Street Journal,* October 4, 1983, p.1.

BIRNBAUM, JEFFREY H., "Painful Process: Congress Pokes Again at Perennial Problem, the Budgetary System," *Wall Street Journal,* Feb. 27, 1987, p.1.

CAMPBELL, CHRISTIANA MCFADYEN, *The Farm Bureau and the New Deal: A Study of the Making of National Farm Policy, 1933-40.* Urbana, Ill.: University of Illinois Press, 1962.

FLINCHBAUGH, B.L., and MARK A. EDELMAN, "The Changing Politics of the Farm and Food System," no. 26 in *The Farm and Food System in Transition: Emerging Policy Issues.* East Lansing, MI: Michigan State University, Cooperative Extension Service, 1984.

FUERBRINGER, JONATHAN, "The Budget Process? What's That?" *New York Times,* November 25, 1983, p. 14.

HARDIN, CLIFFORD M., KENNETH A. SHEPSLE, and BARRY R. WEINGAST, "Government by Subcommittee," *Wall Street Journal,* June 24, 1983, p.22.

HATHAWAY, DALE E., "Government and Agriculture Revisited: A Review of Two Decades of Change," *American Journal of Agricultural Economics* 63 (1981), 779–87.

"How Our Government Works," *U.S. News and World Report,* Jan. 28, 1985, 37–54.

INFANGER, CRAIG L., WILLIAM C. BAILEY, and DAVID DYER, "Agricultural Policy in Austerity: The Making of the 1981 Farm Bill," *American Journal of Agricultural Economics* 65 (1983), 1–9.

KNUTSON, RONALD D., J.B. PENN, and WILLIAM T. BOEHM, *Agricultural and Food Policy.* Englewood Cliffs, N.J.: Prentice Hall, 1983.

KOTZ, NICK, *Let Them Eat Promises: The Politics of Hunger in America.* Englewood Cliffs, N.J.: Prentice Hall, 1969.

"Lobbyists: Washington's 'Hidden Persuaders,'" *U.S. News and World Report,* Sept. 19, 1983, 63–66.

ROBERTS, STEVEN V., "Congress: Conferences Are Site of Legislative Showdowns," *Wall Street Journal,* Nov. 20, 1981.

WEAVER, WARREN, "More and More, House Races Aren't Races but Runaways," *New York Times,* June 15, 1987, p.1.

Index